REVISION WORKBOOK

Conflict of Laws

SECOND EDITION

DR CHARLES WILD
BSc (Lond), LLM, PhD (Sheff), Head of the Centre
for International Law, University of Hertfordshire

OLD BAILEY PRESS

OLD BAILEY PRESS
at Holborn College, Woolwich Road,
Charlton, London, SE7 8LN

First published 1997
Second edition 2003

ISBN 1 85836 425 6

British Library Cataloguing-in-Publication.

A CIP Catalogue record for this book is available from the British Library.

Printed and bound in Great Britain.

Contents

Acknowledgement

Some questions used are taken or adapted from past University of London LLB (External) Degree examination papers and our thanks are extended to the University of London for their kind permission to use and publish the questions.

Caveat

The answers given are not approved or sanctioned by the University of London and are entirely our responsibility.

They are not intended as 'Model Answers', but rather as Suggested Solutions.

The answers have two fundamental purposes, namely:

a) to provide a detailed example of a suggested solution to an examination question, and

b) to assist students with their research into the subject and to further their understanding and appreciation of the subject.

Introduction

This Revision WorkBook has been designed specifically for those studying conflict of laws (or private international law to give the subject its other common name) to undergraduate level. Its coverage is not confined to any one syllabus, but embraces all the major conflict of laws topics to be found in university examinations.

Each chapter contains a brief introduction explaining the scope and overall content of the topic covered in that chapter. There follows, in each case, a list of key points which will assist the student in studying and memorising essential material with which the student should be familiar in order to fully understand the topic.

Additionally in each chapter there is a key cases and statutes section which lists the most relevant cases and statutory provisions applicable to the topic in question. These are intended as an aid to revision, providing the student with a concise list of materials from which to begin revision.

Each chapter ends with several typical examination questions, together with general comments, skeleton solutions and suggested solutions. Wherever possible, the questions are drawn from University of London external conflict of laws papers, with recent questions being included where possible. However, it is inevitable that, in compiling a list of questions by topic order rather than chronologically, not only do the same questions crop up over and over again in different guises, but there are gaps where questions have never been set at all.

Undoubtedly, the main feature of this Revision WorkBook is the inclusion of as many past examination questions as possible. While the use of past questions as a revision aid is certainly not new, it is hoped that the combination of actual past questions from the University of London LLB external course and specially written questions, where there are gaps in examination coverage, will be of assistance to students in achieving a thorough and systematic revision of the subject.

Careful use of the Revision WorkBook should enhance the student's understanding of conflict of laws and, hopefully, enable you to deal with as wide a range of subject matter as anyone might find in a conflict of laws examination, while at the same time allowing you to practise examination techniques while working through the book.

Studying Conflict of Laws

The conflict of laws is unlike the other legal subjects (contract, tort, criminal law, etc) which you might have studied. Indeed, it is often described as being almost like another layer of law in that it may prove relevant to all the domestic laws that you have encountered to date. The reason for this is that in the conflict of laws we are not concerned with the application of rules of law to particular facts. Rather we are concerned with the selection of the appropriate legal system to govern a dispute with an international element or elements. This is the first subject with which the conflict of laws is concerned: the choice of law issue.

However, the conflict of laws is much more than the choice of law issue. Two other areas are considered in England. First, there is the question of jurisdiction. Plainly not every dispute that might arise in the world can or should be litigated in England; and the rules of the law of jurisdiction determine which disputes (which might have very little or nothing to do with England) may be litigated before the English courts and when, even though the English courts might have power to hear the case, it is not appropriate that they do so. Second, a plaintiff may sue a defendant in a foreign court, hear judgment given in his favour, and then discover to his dismay that the defendant (with all his assets) has absconded to England. 'Can the foreign judgment be enforced in England?' Answering that question is a major element in the conflict of laws area.

From this it can be seen that the conflict of laws is concerned with the various ways in which English law interrelates with other legal systems.

However, to return to the choice of law issue, one further unique aspect of the conflict of laws is the following: the selection of the appropriate legal system to govern the dispute through the application of the choice of law rule generates those theoretical problems for which the conflict of laws is renowned, namely, renvoi, characterisation (or classification) and the incidental question. Students often find these problems daunting (and practitioners in the subject are often unaware of their existence), but they are not as difficult as is sometimes supposed. With care and a refusal to be baffled by terminology, the student will be able to master these problems without too much difficulty. Indeed, they should be mastered as these problems or difficulties may arise in a wide range of contexts. Indeed, one sign of a good student is the recognition by that student of one of these theoretical issues in a problem dealing with choice of law in a more mundane area.

The place to begin the study of the conflict of laws is by reading a good textbook. At the same time as reading the text the student should read a selection of the leading cases, as well as the more important statutes. Indeed, this points to two important and related changes over the past ten to 15 years in the conflict of laws. In recent years the conflict of laws has changed from being a subject based in the case law to that of one in which statute plays a much more important role. This change may be attributed to the fact that many of these statutes have been enacted in order to implement various European conventions. For instance, the Brussels Convention 1968 was enacted by way of the Civil Jurisdiction and Judgments Act 1982 and until recently dominated the law in regard to jurisdiction and the recognition and enforcement of foreign judgments. This has now been superseded by Council Regulation 44/2001/EC. In terms of the choice of law issue, then the Rome Convention 1980 (in force through the Contracts (Applicable Law) Act 1990) currently dominates choice of law in contract. Students must ensure that they are well acquainted with these provisions.

Good preparation is obviously important for the student who wishes to obtain a good result in this subject. There is simply no substitute for hard study of the textbook, the decided cases and the relevant statutes. However, the good student will do more than this; the good student will cultivate flexibility of mind and will always try to see a new or fresh aspect to old problems. This shows the examiner that the student is not simply a rote learner and helps to distinguish your answer to a particular question from the hundreds of others that the examiner has read. The student who does this will be rewarded. Conflict of laws, given its theoretical aspect, lends itself to this kind of flexibility and thus offers opportunities for the lively student.

Revision and Examination Technique

Revision Technique

Planning a revision timetable

In planning your revision timetable make sure you do not finish the syllabus too early. You should avoid leaving revision so late that you have to 'cram' – but constant revision of the same topic leads to stagnation.

Plan ahead, however, and try to make your plans increasingly detailed as you approach the examination date.

Allocate enough time for each topic to be studied. But note that it is better to devise a realistic timetable, to which you have a reasonable chance of keeping, rather than a wildly optimistic schedule which you will probably abandon at the first opportunity!

The syllabus and its topics

One of your first tasks when you began your course was to ensure that you thoroughly understood your syllabus. Check now to see if you can write down the topics it comprises from memory. You will see that the chapters of this WorkBook are each devoted to a syllabus topic. This will help you decide which are the key chapters relative to your revision programme. Though you should allow some time for glancing through the other chapters.

The topic and its key points

Again working from memory, analyse what you consider to be the key points of any topic that you have selected for particular revision. Seeing what you can recall, unaided, will help you to understand and firmly memorise the concepts involved.

Using the WorkBook

Relevant questions are provided for each topic in this book. Naturally, as typical examples of examination questions, they do not normally relate to one topic only. But the questions in each chapter will relate to the subject matter of the chapter to a degree. You can choose your method of consulting the questions and solutions, but here are some suggestions (strategies 1–3). Each of them pre-supposes that you have read through the author's note on key points and key cases and statutes, and any other preliminary matter, at the beginning of the chapter. Once again, you now need to practise working from memory, for that is the challenge you are preparing yourself for. As a rule of procedure constantly test yourself once revision starts, both orally and in writing.

Strategy 1

Strategy 1 is planned for the purpose of quick revision. First read your chosen question carefully and then jot down in abbreviated notes what you consider to be the main points at issue. Similarly, note the cases and statutes that occur to you as being relevant for citation purposes. Allow yourself sufficient time to cover what you feel to be relevant. Then study the author's skeleton solution and skim-read the suggested solution to see how they compare with your notes. When comparing consider carefully what the author has included (and concluded) and see whether that agrees with what you have written. Consider the points of variation also. Have you recognised the key issues? How relevant have you been? It is possible, of course, that you have referred to a recent case that is relevant, but which had not been reported when the WorkBook was prepared.

Strategy 2

Strategy 2 requires a nucleus of three hours in which to practise writing a set of examination answers in a limited time-span.

Select a number of questions (as many as are normally set in your subject in the examination you are studying for), each from a different chapter in the WorkBook, without consulting the solutions. Find a place to write where you will not be disturbed and try to arrange not to be interrupted for three hours. Write your solutions in the time allowed, noting any time needed to make up if you are interrupted.

After a rest, compare your answers with the suggested solutions in the WorkBook. There will be considerable variation in style, of course, but the bare facts should not be too dissimilar. Evaluate your answer critically. Be 'searching', but develop a positive approach to deciding how you would tackle each question on another occasion.

Strategy 3

You are unlikely to be able to do more than one three hour examination, but occasionally set yourself a single question. Vary the 'time allowed' by imagining it to be one of the questions that you must answer in three hours and allow yourself a limited preparation and writing time. Try one question that you feel to be difficult and an easier question on another occasion, for example.

Mis-use of suggested solutions

Don't try to learn by rote. In particular, don't try to reproduce the suggested solutions by heart. Learn to express the basic issues in your own words.

Keeping up-to-date

Keep up-to-date. While examiners do not require familiarity with changes in the law during the three months prior to the examination, it obviously creates a good impression if you can show you are acquainted with any recent changes. Make a habit of looking through one of the leading journals – *Modern Law Review, Law Quarterly Review* or the *New Law Journal*, for example – and cumulative indices to law reports, such as the *All England Law Reports* or *Weekly Law Reports*, or indeed the daily law reports in *The Times*. The *Law Society's Gazette* and the *Legal Executive Journal* are helpful sources, plus any specialist journal(s) for the subject you are studying.

Examination Skills

Examiners are human too!

The process of answering an examination question involves a communication between you and the person who set it. If you were speaking face to face with the person, you would choose your verbal points and arguments carefully in your reply. When writing, it is all too easy to forget the human being who is awaiting the reply and simply write out what one knows in the area of the subject! Bear in mind it is a person whose question you are responding to, throughout your essay. This will help you to avoid being irrelevant or long-winded.

The essay question

Candidates are sometimes tempted to choose to answer essay questions because they 'seem' easier. But the examiner is looking for thoughtful work and will not give good marks for superficial answers.

The essay-type of question may be either purely factual, in asking you to explain the meaning of a certain doctrine or principle, or it may ask you to discuss a certain proposition, usually derived from a quotation. In either case, the approach to the answer is the same. A clear programme must be devised to give the examiner the meaning or significance of the doctrine, principle or proposition and its origin in common law, equity or statute, and cases which illustrate its application to the branch of law concerned. Essay questions offer a good way to obtain marks if you have thought carefully about a topic, since it is up to you to impose the structure (unlike the problem questions where the problem imposes its own structure). You are then free to speculate and show imagination.

The problem question

The problem-type question requires a different approach. You may well be asked to advise a client or merely discuss the problems raised in the question. In either case, the most important factor is to take great care in reading the question. By its nature, the question will be longer than the essay-type question and you will have a number of facts to digest. Time spent in analysing the question may well save time later, when you are endeavouring to impress on the examiner the considerable extent of your basic legal knowledge. The quantity of knowledge is itself a trap and you must always keep within the boundaries of the question in hand. It is very tempting to show the examiner the extent of your knowledge of your subject, but if this is outside the question, it is time lost and no marks earned. It is inevitable that some areas which you have studied and revised will not be the subject of questions, but under no circumstances attempt to adapt a question to a stronger area of knowledge at the expense of relevance.

When you are satisfied that you have grasped the full significance of the problem-type question, set out the fundamental principles involved.

You will then go on to identify the fundamental problem (or problems) posed by the question. This should be followed by a consideration of the law which is relevant to the problem. The source of the law, together with the cases which will be of assistance in solving the problem, must then be considered in detail.

Very good problem questions are quite likely to have alternative answers, and in advising a party you should be aware that alternative arguments may be available. Each stage of your answer, in this case, will be based on the argument or arguments considered in the previous stage, forming a conditional sequence.

If, however, you only identify one fundamental problem, do not waste time worrying that you cannot think of an alternative – there may very well be only that one answer.

The examiner will then wish to see how you use your legal knowledge to formulate a case and how you apply that formula to the problem which is the subject of the question. It is this positive approach which can make answering a problem question a high mark earner for the student who has fully understood the question and clearly argued their case on the established law.

Examination checklist

a) Read the instructions at the head of the examination carefully. While last-minute changes are unlikely – such as the introduction of a compulsory question or an increase in the number of questions asked – it has been known to happen.

b) Read the questions carefully. Analyse problem questions – work out what the examiner wants.

c) Plan your answer before you start to write.

d) Check that you understand the rubric before you start to write. Do not 'discuss', for example, if you are specifically asked to 'compare and contrast'.

e) Answer the correct number of questions. If you fail to answer one out of four questions set you lose 25 per cent of your marks!

Style and structure

Try to be clear and concise. Basically this amounts to using paragraphs to denote the sections of your essay, and writing simple, straightforward sentences as much as possible. The sentence you have just read has 22 words – when a sentence reaches 50 words it becomes difficult for a reader to follow.

Do not be inhibited by the word 'structure' (traditionally defined as giving an essay a beginning, a middle and an end). A good structure will be the natural consequence of setting out your arguments and the supporting evidence in a logical order. Set the scene briefly in your opening paragraph. Provide a clear conclusion in your final paragraph.

Table of Cases

Table of Statutes and Other Materials

Chapter 1

Introduction

1.1 Introduction

Conflict of laws is one of the most difficult and complex subjects on the syllabus of many law degree courses. In order to understand how the conflict of laws rules work, it is first necessary to have a sufficient knowledge of a number of areas of law including contract, tort, family law and property law. Only once these core subjects have been grasped is it possible to consider the legal position when foreign elements are introduced to these fields.

As a prelude to the rest of this work, this chapter is intended to set the background to this area of law by placing the subject in its proper context. Since this chapter is intended as an introduction to the topic, no examination questions or suggested solutions have been included. The purpose of this chapter is merely to introduce some of the main concepts and distinctions before moving on to consider the subject in more detail.

1.2 Key points

The legal issues which are involved in conflict of laws

The subject of conflict of laws essentially concerns the rules which are applied when an English court is faced with a case involving some foreign legal element. Regardless of the subject matter of the litigation before the court, where a foreign element is involved, the court must ask itself three principal questions before proceeding to consider the merits of the case:

a) Can the court exercise jurisdiction over the subject matter of the dispute and the persons involved in the dispute?

b) Which law should be applied by the court to the facts before it – English law or the law of another country?

c) What account should the court take of foreign judgments and decisions made earlier in connection with the dispute?

Providing the answers to these three questions is the function of the body of rules known as conflict of laws.

Questions involving jurisdiction, choice of law and the enforcement of foreign judgments

The three issues involved in the subject of conflict of laws can be conveniently grouped under three headings: (1) the jurisdiction of the courts; (2) choice of law; and (3) the enforcement and application of foreign judgments.

Jurisdiction

The jurisdiction of a court is its power and authority to issue a decree or order resolving a dispute between two or more parties and which resolves the contentious issue and can be enforced in the United Kingdom or will be recognised as valid in the courts of third countries.

Jurisdiction in this context refers exclusively to civil jurisdiction and not to criminal jurisdiction. It should be borne in mind that, for the most part, criminal jurisdiction is based on a different set of principles from those established to found civil jurisdiction.

Choice of law

Once a court has decided that it can exercise jurisdiction over a particular dispute, it must then ask itself which law is applicable to the facts – English law or the law of another country. A body of rules has been established by the English courts to allow them to decide which is the most appropriate law to apply in the circumstances.

In essence, this requires the identification of the relevant connecting factors involved in the case which tend to vary according to the subject matter of the dispute, ie contract, tort, family law, etc.

Enforcement of foreign judgments

Finally, a national court must decide what effect, if any, should be given to the decisions and judgments of foreign courts. Putting this another way, the court must determine whether litigation has already been conducted in the courts of another country and evaluate the effect of any decision reached by the foreign court.

A distinction should be made at this point between the recognition and the enforcement of a foreign judgment. Recognition does not necessarily imply that a foreign decree will be enforced. For example, it may be the case that the foreign judgment is relevant only to decide an issue subsidiary to the matter being adjudicated in the English court.

Enforcement on the other hand means that the courts are willing to recognise and give effect to a foreign decision inside the jurisdiction of the English courts.

The nature of conflict of laws

While the subject of conflict of laws deals with the relationship between the English legal system and foreign legal systems, it is by its nature a part of English law. It concerns the rules of English private law which direct that, in certain circumstances, particular aspects of foreign law are applicable to a case.

These rules have largely been evolved by the courts, although in recent times many of the developments in this area have been based on statutes. Rules of conflict of laws remain creatures of the English legal system even though, on occasion, these rules are enacted by statute to give effect to international conventions on specific topics: see, for example, the Civil Jurisdiction and Judgments Act 1982 and the Contracts (Applicable Law) Act 1990. More recently, the area of jurisdiction has been amended by way of European regulation: see Chapter 5.

The distinction between countries and legal systems in conflicts of law

The term 'country' in conflict of laws has a different meaning from that usually attributed to the term. In this context, the term refers to a territory which is subject to the same legal system and not a state in the political sense.

Thus, in the United Kingdom there are three separate legal systems within the one state – the legal systems of England and Wales, Scotland and Northern Ireland. There are major and important differences among the laws of these three legal systems. Another example is the United States which, although one sovereign state in international law, is composed of numerous individual states with their own legal systems.

In conflict of laws we deal with legal systems and not countries in the normal sense of that term simply because within each state there may be more than one legal system. Resolution of the legal issues raised in conflict problems is achieved by the application of the laws of legal systems and this important point should always be borne in mind.

Introduction to the terminology used in the subject

Legal systems are assigned different Latin names when they play particular roles in conflict of laws problems. It is useful to elaborate on these names at this point before confusion arises in later chapters when the terms themselves are referred to in applying conflict rules.

The main terms are as follows:

a) Lex fori – the law of the place where a case is being adjudicated.

b) Lex causae – the law of the legal system which is applicable to the dispute.

c) Lex loci contractus – the law of the place where a contract was negotiated.

d) Lex loci delicti – the law of the place where a tortious act occurred.

e) Lex situs – the law of the place where property is situated.

f) Lex domicilii – the law of a person's domicile.

These terms are often used to denote the laws of particular legal systems when a choice between one or more legal systems is possible.

The relationship between conflict of laws and public international law

Conflict of laws should be distinguished from another form of international law – public international law. Public international law deals with the legal relationships between sovereign states and establishes a special legal order to regulate these relationships. Hence, the subjects of public international law are essentially sovereign states while those of conflict of laws are private individuals.

However, there are a number of areas where the two subjects overlap to a certain degree:

a) Sovereign immunity – as a general principle, a foreign sovereign state cannot be sued in the English courts unless it has voluntarily submitted to the jurisdiction. This principle has been developed in the State Immunity Act 1978 (which implements the European Convention on State Immunity 1972).

Section 1(1) declares that states are immune from the jurisdiction of the courts of the United Kingdom but a number of exceptions are subsequently elaborated. These include the following situations:

   i)   Where the state has voluntarily submitted to the jurisdiction of the court.

   ii) A state is not immune in regard to commercial transactions (which is defined in broad terms).

   iii) A state is not immune in regard to contracts (whether commercial transactions or not) to be performed wholly or partially in the United Kingdom.

   iv) No state is immune from proceedings in respect of death or personal injury or damage or loss of tangible property caused by an act or omission within the United Kingdom.

A number of additional exceptions are elaborated in the statute, but the principal exception remains that concerning commercial transactions.

b) Diplomatic immunity – diplomats also enjoy similar immunities from civil proceedings and the present law is contained in the Diplomatic Privileges Act 1961 (which implements the Vienna Convention on Diplomatic Relations 1961).

c) The rights of international organisations – special rules are created in English law under the International Organisations Act 1968 to accord immunity from suit to international organisations and their officials. See, for example, the International Tin Council Immunities and Privileges Order 1972.

d) The laws of unrecognised states and governments – unrecognised states cannot sue or be sued in English courts: *City of Berne* v *Bank of England* (1804) 9 Ves 347. Hence, the principles of law applied by the UK courts to the recognition of foreign states and governments – as far as these comply with the rules of public international law – are relevant in determining the standing of unrecognised entities: see *Republic of Somalia* v *Woodhouse Drake and Carey (Suisse) SA* [1992] 3 WLR 744.

Chapter 2

Preliminary Topics

2.1   Introduction

2.2   Key points

2.3   Key cases and statutes

2.4   Questions and suggested solutions

2.1 Introduction

Although the preliminary topics chapters of most textbooks deals with a range of different topics – the exclusion of foreign law, the relationship between substance and procedure, the time factor, as well as the special conceptual topics of renvoi, characterisation and the incidental question – most questions on preliminary topics deal only with the special conceptual topics. This is not to say that the other topics are not covered; it is just that they are more likely to be tested as an aspect of a question dealing primarily with another topic.

2.2 Key points

The issue of jurisdiction – preliminary points

The jurisdiction of a court operates in two dimensions:

a) jurisdiction over persons (known as jurisdiction in personam); and

b) jurisdiction over subject matters.

In every case, a court must have jurisdiction over both the defendant and the cause of action before it may hear the case and resolve any dispute.In practice, the jurisdiction of the court over the defendant is the most important issue. If a court cannot exercise effective jurisdiction over a defendant, it may be unable to order the enforcement of any decree issued as a consequence of the action. Similarly, any decree pronounced by an English courts on a tenuous ground of jurisdiction may be considered by a foreign court to amount to an exorbitant exercise of power and the foreign court may refuse to recognise any decree pronounced.

Even though there are clearly occasions when the exercise of jurisdiction by English courts is wholly inappropriate to the circumstances of a case, the courts have traditionally taken an excessive view of their own powers in this respect: see *Re*

Paramount Airways Ltd (In Administration) [1992] 3 WLR 690. As we shall see later, the English courts are even willing, in certain circumstances, to exert jurisdiction over persons who are not physically located or resident in England.

Establishing the jurisdiction of a court is a critical preliminary step in any action. Without jurisdiction, a court cannot rule on the dispute and the related issues of choice of law and recognition and enforcement of foreign decrees become irrelevant.

Choice of law – preliminary points

Characterisation

As a preliminary step to selecting the law of the legal system which is applicable to a dispute, the courts must classify a dispute into a particular legal category, ie contract, delict, succession, etc. This process is known as characterisation and is critical in selecting the applicable law to resolve the questions of law before a court.

A court must decide, for example, whether a dispute concerns the law relating to succession, property law or family law. The importance of deciding this issue at the outset is simply that different conflict rules are applicable depending on the legal category or class into which the issue falls.

In the above example, the courts may decide that matters of succession and family law are for the laws of a foreign country, while matters concerning property within the United Kingdom are to be resolved under English law. So, if a dispute is characterised as a matter of succession or family law, the rules of a foreign legal system will apply, but if it is a matter of property law, English law will apply. Hence, the characterisation of the dispute will, to a large extent, determine the applicable law.

Often, characterisation is not a clear-cut issue. Thus, it is necessary to determine the issue of characterisation as a preliminary point to the selection of the choice of law and a number of legal principles have been developed by the courts to assist in this process. For cases in this area see: *Ogden v Ogden* [1908] P 46; *Re Maldonado* [1954] P 223; *Re Cohn* [1945] Ch 5; and *Re Bonacina* [1912] 2 Ch 394.

The Private International Law (Miscellaneous Provisions) Act 1995 also recognises this problem and specifies rules for the process of characterisation in delictual questions. Section 9(2) states that, for the purposes of private international law, the characterisation of issues relating to tort is a matter for the courts of the forum seized of a dispute.

Selection of the lex causae

Once the court has decided that it may exercise jurisdiction and the appropriate characterisation has been made, it is necessary to select the law which is applicable to the facts of the dispute. The legal system which prevails in this selection is known as the lex causae.

Application of the lex causae

English judges are not deemed to be familiar with the laws of all the other countries and legal systems of the world. Therefore, there has to be some mechanism to enable them to apply rules of foreign law when the occasion arises.

In general terms, foreign law is treated by the courts as a question of fact. Expert evidence is therefore required to support the application of the lex causae when this is a foreign legal order.

The exclusion of the applicability of certain types of foreign law

If the lex causae selected is that of a foreign legal system, in the normal course of events the rules of that legal system will be applied by the court to the matter.

But there are certain circumstances when an English court will decline to apply certain types of foreign laws. This will occur when the application of a foreign lex causae will lead to a result which is inconsistent with a fundamental principle of public policy of English law. There are six main instances when this will occur.

a) The application of criminal laws – English courts will not enforce foreign penal laws. As Lord Watson pointed out in *Huntingdon* v *Atrill* [1893] AC 150:

> 'This rule has its foundation in the well recognised principle that crimes ... are local in the sense that they are only recognisable and punishable in the country where they were committed.'

b) The enforcement of foreign revenue laws – the collection of tax is considered by the courts not to be a matter of contract but rather of authority and administration between the state and those within its jurisdiction: *Government of India* v *Taylor* [1955] AC 491. Hence, foreign revenue laws will not be applied by English courts.

c) Expropriatory laws – the property of foreign nationals may sometimes be requisitioned or seized by the governments of the states in which the property is located. This process is known as expropriation and the English courts have manifested a reluctance to enforce rules of expropriation in relation to property that has come within the jurisdiction of the court.

d) Public policy considerations – just as certain contractual terms will not be enforced in normal contractual relations on the grounds of public policy, the same considerations apply where foreign laws infringe the accepted principles of public policy.

For example, the courts will not enforce contracts involving trade with countries at war with the UK: see *Dynamit AG* v *Rio Tinto Zinc* [1918] AC 260. Similarly, contracts which are incompatible with resolutions of the Security Council of the United Nations will not be enforced by the courts: see *Wahda Bank* v *Arab Bank* (1992) The Times 23 December.

e) Foreign public laws – this classification includes all laws which amount to an exercise of sovereign power within the territory of that sovereign: see *United States* v *Inkley* [1988] 3 WLR 304.

f) The doctrine of the evasion of the law – foreign laws will not be applied by the English courts where the parties have contrived that their legal relationship be regulated by a foreign legal system solely for the purpose of avoiding their obligations under English law.

This principle has often been adopted into statute: see, for example, the Unfair Contract Terms Act 1977, s27(2) which provides that the restrictions imposed by the statute will not be circumvented by a choice of law 'imposed wholly or mainly for the purpose of enabling the party imposing (the choice of law) to evade the operation of the Act'.

The distinction between laws of substance and laws of procedure

A distinction is made between the procedural and substantive laws of a foreign legal system when applying foreign law as the lex causae. As a general principle, only the substantive laws of the lex causae will be applied by an English court and the English law of procedure will regulate proceedings in a case where a foreign lex causae has been selected. This is primarily a matter of convenience; it would be impractical for an English court to apply foreign procedural laws.

However, the ambit of procedural law, as defined by the English courts, is wider than normal in cases of conflict. In the past, the following legal matters have been considered issues of procedure: statutes of limitation (prior to the Foreign Limitation Periods Act 1984), evidence, certain remedies and the quantification of damages.

Recognition and enforcement of foreign judgments – preliminary points

If a plaintiff sues a defendant in a foreign country, and finds that the decree of that court is ineffective because the defendant is not physically present in that state or has no assets located within the jurisdiction, he or she may seek to enforce the judgment in England. In order to be successful, the plaintiff must abide by the relevant rules of English law regulating the recognition and enforcement of foreign judgments.

This area of the law was then largely regulated by statute, the Civil Jurisdiction and Judgments Act (CJJA) 1982, until Council Regulation 44/2001/EC came into force in 2002. (The CJJA 1982 implemented the Brussels Convention 1968, the 1971 Protocol and the 1978 Convention on Accession which preceded the Regulation.) Refer to Chapter 11 for further discussion of this point. The CJJA 1982 also corrected a number of the flaws and irregularities in the English common law on this matter.

The Brussels Convention was designed to simplify the enforcement of judgments within the jurisdictions of the European Union countries. The Regulation replicates a significant amount of the Convention, though students should be warned that the numbering has changed. Article 38 of the Regulation (art 31 of the Convention), provides that:

> 'A judgment given in a member state and enforceable in that state shall be enforceable in another member state when, on the application of any interested party, it has been declared enforceable there.'

Unfortunately, as we shall see, the implementation of this general principle is not so simple.

Where the statute 'is inapplicable, the common law continues to apply subject to the alterations made by the 1982 Act to remedy the flaws in the common law principles.

The problem of renvoi

The problem of renvoi arises when a court has characterised the matter and the connecting factor points to a particular lex causae but the conflict of laws rules of the lex causae indicate that the law of the lex fori are applicable. Thus, the issue of the applicable law bounces back and forth between the two respective legal systems.

The situations in which this problem arise are best illustrated by an example. Suppose that according to English conflict of laws, the marital status of a person is to be decided by reference to his or her domicile. However, under French law, this status is to be decided by reference to nationality. If an English person is divorced after acquiring a domicile of choice in France, and proceedings are raised in England, the English courts would refer to French law as the law of the domicile of that person. But, under French law, the matter would be regulated by the law of the nationality of the person, ie English law. The result is a legal impasse incapable of producing a conclusive answer.

A number of solutions have been proposed to resolve this problem:

a) To apply the internal law of the lex causae without reference to the conflict of laws provisions of that legal system: see *Re Annesley* [1926] Ch 692.

b) The single or partial renvoi theory – once the original reference under the conflict of laws rules of the lex causae has referred the matter back to the lex fori, then the courts of the lex fori should accept the return referral and apply their own internal rules: see *Collier v Rivaz* (1841) 2 Curt 855.

c) The foreign court theory or the 'double renvoi' approach – according to this theory, the English court puts itself in the place of the foreign court and decides whether, as a matter of practice, the foreign court would refer the case back to the English courts. If the answer is negative, the matter is decided in accordance with that legal system; whereas if the answer is affirmative, English law applies.

The problem of renvoi mainly arises when different legal systems adopt different connecting factors for the regulation of particular legal subject matters, ie nationality as opposed to domicile.

Where areas of law have been regulated by international conventions, the problem is least likely to arise: see, for example, the Rome Convention on the Law Applicable to Contractual Obligations 1980.

The incidental question

An additional problem which, like renvoi, arises from the different conflict rules among different countries is that of the incidental question. This issue arises when a dispute involves a principal matter and a subsidiary question. Again the problem is best illustrated by an example.

Frequently in matters of intestate succession, the question of the formal validity of marriage (or divorce) arises. The rules of characterisation of the lex fori may require these two questions to be resolved under the rules of separate legal systems. However, the resolution of the first question is integrally linked to the resolution of the second question even though the second question is incidental to the primary issue.

The incidental question therefore concerns the issue of which rules of law should apply in these circumstances bearing in mind the relative significance of each of the issues. Again a number of proposals have been made to resolve this issue, mostly by academics, and none of which is particularly convincing. See *Lawrence* v *Lawrence* [1985] Fam 106 and *Schwebel* v *Ungar* (1963) 42 DLR (2d) 622.

The proof of foreign law

The law of a foreign legal system is treated as a question of fact in English law. As such, it is normally established by expert evidence and the evidence required to prove the foreign law 'must be that of qualified experts in the foreign law': *Lazard Brothers & Co* v *Midland Bank* [1933] AC 289. Under the terms of s4(l) of the Civil Evidence Act 1972, it is not an essential prerequisite that such an expert has practical experience in the application of the foreign law.

The burden of proof of foreign law lies on the party who seeks to rely on its terms to substantiate a claim or to support a defence. If that party fails to adduce any evidence of the foreign law, or adduces insufficient evidence of that law to enable the judge to form an opinion of the relevant question, then the court will apply English law.

The nature and extent of the remedy

Remedy not known to the lex fori

Where the plaintiff seeks a remedy unknown to the lex fori he will be unsuccessful: see *Phrantzes* v *Argenti* [1960] 2 QB 19.

Damages

In terms of damages, a distinction should be made between remoteness of damage and the quantum (amount) of damages in question. The question of remoteness of damage is a substantive issue and as such governed by the lex causae: see *Boys* v *Chaplin* [1971] AC 356.

By contrast, the question of quantification is a matter for the lex fori: see *D'Almeida Araujo Lda* v *Sir Frederick Becker & Co Ltd* [1953] 2 All ER 288.

2.3 Key cases and statutes

* *Amin Rasheed Shipping Corp* v *Kuwait Insurance Co* [1983] 2 All ER 884
  Renvoi has no place in the law of contract

* *Annesley, Re* [1926] Ch 692
  Orthodox view of renvoi – English courts will take account of foreign choice of law rules

* *Attorney-General of New Zealand* v *Ortiz* [1982] 3 All ER 432
  English courts will not enforce foreign public laws

* *Cohn, Re* [1945] Ch 5
  Lex fori – characterisation

* *Collier* v *Rivaz* (1841) 2 Curt 855
  Application of renvoi – validity of will and codicils

* *D'Almeida Araujo Lda* v *Sir Frederick Becker & Co Ltd* [1953] 2 All ER 288
  Remoteness of damage is question of substance – measure of damages is a question of procedure

* *Dynamit AG* v *Rio Tinto Zinc* [1918] AC 260
  Contracts to trade with enemy will not be enforced

* *Lazard Brothers & Co* v *Midland Bank Ltd* [1933] AC 289
  Foreign law is a question of fact to be proved by expert evidence

* *Ross, Re* [1930] 1 Ch 377
  Orthodox view – English law will adopt approach of foreign court

* Foreign Corporations Act 1991 – regulates the law to be applied to ascertain the status of a corporation under a foreign legal system

* Private International Law (Miscellaneous Provisions) Act 1995, s9 – where a claim is brought in the English courts, it is those courts that determine whether the claim involves an 'issue relating to tort'.

2.4 Questions and suggested solutions

QUESTION ONE

'An English court should solve problems of characterisation by applying the only concepts with which it is familiar, namely those of the forum.'

Do you agree? Discuss this proposition critically with reference to decided cases.

University of London LLB Examination
(for External Students) Conflict of Laws June 1990 Q1

General Comment

The temptation with this type of question is to provide a very basic yes/no answer. The key to providing a good answer is in the final line to the question, namely 'with reference to decided cases'. The student must display a wide appreciation of the area – including cases and academic opinion – and to support this with their own interpretation.

Skeleton Solution

Description of the problem – fundamental nature of the problem – approaches to the problem by English judges – drawbacks of the lex fori – drawbacks of the lex causae – the enlightened lex fori: the approach that should be adopted by English judges and which to a degree they do adopt.

Suggested Solution

Although considerable support can be found in the decided cases for classification by the lex fori, it will be submitted in this essay that this is a mistaken view and that what the courts should do is to classify by either the late Professor Kahn-Freund's 'enlightened lex fori' or by Falconbridge's via media. The statement given above, although largely supported by the decided cases, is, as we shall see, superficial and uncritical.

But first the problem of classification or characterisation as it is often called should be explained. The problem arises when, although all the relevant legal systems have the same choice of law rules, it is unclear whether a particular claim of one of the parties is covered by one choice of law rule or another.

Consider the celebrated Maltese Marriage Case (a nineteenth-century French case) in which the problem first came to the fore. A husband and wife had married while they were domiciled in Malta. The husband thereafter acquired a domicile in France where he bought some land. On his death his widow claimed a usufruct (a form of right similar to the life tenancy of English law) over the land. She was entitled to this under French law but not under Maltese law. Now, French law and Maltese law had the same choice of law rules; succession to land was governed by the lex situs (France) and the proprietary consequences of marriage were governed by the law of the husband's domicile at the time of the marriage (Malta). But what was not clear was whether the widow's claim related to succession or to the proprietary consequences of marriage; and answering that question is the problem of characterisation.

Characterisation is one of the fundamental problems of the conflict of laws, and numerous academics have written about it and developed various theories as to how it should be solved. It is a serious problem for it shows that even if one was successful in unifying all the choice of law rules in every legal system in the world, there would still be disharmony of decision for there could still be differences over the characterisation of particular claims.

For us the problem is made worse because, in England at any rate, the judges have been rather silent about what the correct approach to adopt to the question of characterisation is. The general view is that, by and large, English judges have characterised by the lex fori. Certainly, *Ogden* v *Ogden* [1908] P 46 and *Huber* v *Steiner* (1835) 2 Bing NC 202 can be read in that way. The more recent case of *G & H Montage* v *Irvani* [1990] 1 WLR 667 suggests that this is the correct approach. Not too much should be made of this. There is no English case in which the problem of characterisation has been fully and thoughtfully discussed. Generally, the judges characterise without realising that is what they are doing.

In any event, there are profound difficulties with characterisation by the lex fori: the most obvious one is revealed by asking what it is that is characterised. It is being widely accepted by legal writers that that which is characterised is a rule of law or a group of rules of law rather than a fact or group of facts. After all, in the Maltese Marriage Case it is plain that the dispute was over whether the rule of law that granted the widow a usufruct fell within the category of succession or whether it fell within the category of the proprietary consequences of marriage. (And all the other well-known cases can be analysed in this way.)

Now, of course, English law, the lex fori, does not contain within it categories in which the rules of foreign law fit snugly. Thus what has to happen if the lex fori is to be applied is that the nearest analogue in English law of the foreign rule has to be used to indicate the category into which that foreign rule falls. As Kahn-Freund remarks, this means either cutting the foreign rule down to size or elongating it 'but in any case depriving it of life'. Moreover, characterisation by the lex fori breaks down entirely when a concept that has no analogue in English law has to be characterised, as was the case in *Irvani* where the concept of an aval (a form of surety for the obligations on a bill of exchange) – something quite unknown to English law but commonplace in civilian legal systems – had to be characterised.

In response to these difficulties, it is sometimes suggested that the lex causae should be used for this task. Although there are some dicta in the Court of Appeal in *Re Maldonado* [1954] P 223 which can be seen as supporting this approach (Spanish law was used to determine whether the claim of the Spanish state to the movable property of a Spanish domiciliary who had died without next of kin was a matter of succession (and so governed by Spanish law) or a ius regale – a claim of the Crown – in which case the English Crown not the Spanish state would take) there remain difficulties with using the lex causae.

The most obvious such difficulty is that at the stage that one is called upon to classify a rule one simply does not know what the lex causae is. The object of the exercise is to determine the lex causae, and so it is circular to seek to use the lex causae for that task. Although sometimes this difficulty may be able to be overcome by characterising by all the potentially applicable leges causae, this will simply not work in many cases. One can easily be left with more than one lex causae seeking to be applied. This is called the problem of 'cumulation'. Associated with it is the problem of 'gap' where the characterisation process leads one to the conclusion that no law at all is applicable to the problem. There can be little doubt that characterisation by the lex causae lends itself to the creation of such problems.

Recognising these difficulties various writers have sought a path between these two extremes. Falconbridge suggested his via media in which a two-stage process would be adopted: first, there would be a provisional classification in which the lex causae would be dominant followed by a final stage in which the lex fori would predominate. This approach is non-mechanical for the judge is not supposed to follow the rule of either the lex fori or the lex causae blindly in making the appropriate selection. A fair measure of support for this approach is found by Morris (as well as other writers) in *Re Cohn* [1945] Ch 5.

However, Kahn-Freund's 'enlightened lex fori' shares many of the advantages of Falconbridge's via media, but is more closely tied to the English judicial process. Kahn-Freund argues that there is nothing to stop the lex fori from developing special principles and categories for use in conflicts cases. Such principles of characterisation would be enlightened for they would take into account the different approaches of the various leges causae, as well as the importance of striving wherever possible for uniformity of decision. Indeed, Kahn-Freund argues that this is exactly what is already happening in English law, whether the judges realise this or not. Three examples from the decided cases can be given.

First, Kahn-Freund points to the fact that for the purposes of the conflict of laws English law abandons the division of property into realty and personalty and adopts (as do all other legal systems) the division into movables and immovables: this is the enlightened lex fori at work.

Second, for the purposes of the conflict of laws, English law regards as a contract an agreement unsupported by consideration: *Re Bonacina* [1912] 2 Ch 394. Once more this is the enlightened lex fori at work.

Finally, in *Irvani*'s case, referred to above, Purchas LJ in the Court of Appeal interpreted the concept of 'indorsement' of a bill of exchange widely so as to include the concept of an aval. This too is the enlightened lex fori at work.

Although one could not support every decision on characterisation (*Ogden* as well as *Huber* v *Steiner* are unfair and awkward) it appears from this that English judges, although unaware of the theoretical issues, are in their pragmatic fashion stumbling towards the enlightened lex fori. And this approach promises to be the most useful of all those on offer; it is non-mechanical so that the judge can shape his decision according to the wider considerations of the case, the various leges causae are taken into account, but it is recognised that the lex fori has the final say.

QUESTION TWO

a) Explain the significance of the distinction between movable and immovable property.

b) Last year, whilst on a hiking holiday in Remotia, Jim, a domiciled Englishman who lives in Birmingham, uncovered an ancient statue. He removed it and on the way back to England when he was in Antiqua he sold the statue to Henry, an Antiquan dealer. Henry paid Jim partly in cash and partly by assigning to Jim a percentage of his royalties on a new book of his on ancient statues. Henry has now put the statue up for auction at a dealers in London. The Remotian government claims that the statue is state property. There is a Remotian law which prohibits the export of ancient statues without permission from the Ministry of Antiquities (which Jim did not obtain). By the law of Antiqua the assignment of future royalties is not permitted.

Advise the Remotian government whether it can recover the statue from the auction house and Jim whether he can sue Henry for the outstanding royalties. Henry is visiting England next week to attend an annual trade fair.

University of London LLB Examination
(for External Students) Conflict of Laws June 1993 Q7

General Comment

The question immediately poses two problems for students: first, time management, namely how much time should be devoted to each section?; and, second, how much material is expected for each section? This is difficult to assess at the best of times. If there is no indication to the contrary then equal amounts of time should be devoted to (a) and (b). As such a simple description will satisfy part (a).

Skeleton Solution

a) Why classification of property in private international law differs from that in domestic law – characterisation of interests.

b) Significance of lex situs – non-enforcement of foreign public laws – significance of establishing applicable law under the Rome Convention – provisions of art 12.

Suggested Solution

a) The principal categories of proprietary interests in things in English domestic law are those of realty and personalty. However, this is a division not recognised by many other legal systems. Accordingly, for the purposes of the conflict of laws, 'in order to arrive at a common basis on which to determine questions between the inhabitants of two countries living under different systems of jurisprudence, our courts recognise and act on a division otherwise unknown to our law into movable and immovable': per Farwell LJ in *Re Hoyles* [1911] 1 Ch 179. Indeed, this division of property into movable and immovable was recognised in *Freke* v *Carbery* (1873) LR 16 Eq 461.

However, this near-universal agreement on the categorisation of divisions of property for the purposes of the conflict of laws does not necessarily extend to the characterisation by different countries of a particular proprietary interest. For example, whereas a mortgagee's interest in land has been regarded as an immovable in English law (*Re Hoyles*), it has been described as a movable both by the New Zealand courts in *Re O'Neill (dec'd)* [1922] NZLR 468 and by the Australian courts in *Haque* v *Haque* (1965) 114 CLR 98. Furthermore, the characterisation of a proprietary interest for the purpose of the English conflict of laws does not necessarily correspond with its counterpart in English domestic law; for example, leasehold interests in land in England for the purpose of the conflict of laws have been characterised as immovable in *Freke* v *Carbery*, whereas domestic law regards them as personal estate.

Perhaps the most significant feature of the characterisation of property into immovables and movables is to be found in matters relating to intestate succession. Whereas the general rule is that intestate succession is governed by the law of the deceased's domicile in the case of movables, it is governed by the lex situs in the case of immovables. Whether an interest in land held on trust for sale would convert an immovable into a movable via the doctrine of conversion was considered in a case which focused on intestate succession: *Re Berchtold* [1923] 1 Ch 192. Here a domiciled Hungarian died in Hungary leaving freehold land in England which was subject to a trust for sale. However, before the land was sold, his beneficiary, N, died. By Hungarian law, N's next-of-kin claimed this interest in the land on the basis that it had been converted into personalty (ie equity regards as done that which ought to be done: the doctrine of conversion). However, Russell J decided that an interest in land held on trust for sale was an immovable. He reasoned that:

> ' ... the equitable doctrine of conversion only arises and comes into play where the question for consideration arises as between real estate and personal estate. It has no relation to the question whether property is movable or immovable. The doctrine of conversion is that real estate is treated as personal estate, or personal estate is treated as real estate; not that immovables are turned into movables, or movables into immovables.'

This judge-made doctrine of conversion contrasts with the statutory doctrine of conversion as contained in s75(5) of the Settled Land Act 1925. This provision states that capital moneys 'arising under this Act ... shall for all purposes ... be considered as land'. Thus, in *Re Cutcliffe* [1940] Ch 565 an intestate's interests in investments which resulted from the reinvestment of the proceeds of sale of English freehold settled land were held to be immovables.

The distinction between the two cases was noted by Dr Morris and repeated by Professor McClean (author of the fifth edition of Morris: *The Conflict of Laws*). They say that

> '... in the *Berchtold* case the judge-made doctrine of conversion which had to be considered said that realty was to be treated as personalty, and was therefore inapplicable on the conflicts plane; whereas in the *Cutcliffe* case the statute which had to be considered said that money was to be treated as land, and was, therefore, applicable on the conflicts plane.'

b) The advice to the Remotian government on the prospect of recovering the statue from the auction will focus, initially, on whether the statue was within or outside their territory at the time of the decree prohibiting removal of the statue from Remotia unless particular formalities were complied with. If the decree was effective when Jim took the statue from Remotia and sold it in Antiqua, then it would be for the Antiquan law (the lex situs) to determine whether this sale conferred good title on Henry. A transfer of title regarded as valid by the lex situs would be recognised in England: *Cammell v Sewell* (1860) 5 H & N 728. Thus, if Henry has a good title to the statue the Remotian government will be unable to recover it from the auction house.

Even if the Antiquan law agreed with Remotian law that Henry had not acquired good title it still would not necessarily mean that the Remotian government could succeed in an action to recover the statue. The basis for this is that English law does not enforce a foreign penal law or a foreign public law: *Attorney-General of New Zealand v Ortiz* [1982] 3 WLR 570. In essence, this means that laws will not be enforced if they involve an exercise by a government of its sovereign authority over property beyond its territory. In the case of *Attorney-General of New Zealand v Ortiz*, a Maori carved door which had been removed from New Zealand without permission of the appropriate authorities came to be auctioned in London. The plaintiff (the Attorney-General of New Zealand) claimed that the New Zealand state was the owner of the door, and he sought an injunction restraining the sale and an order for delivery up of the door. The claim was based on the provisions of a New Zealand statute which provided for the forfeiture, without compensation, of historic articles. The *Attorney-General of New Zealand*'s case did not succeed, however. In the Court of Appeal, reasons for finding in favour of the defendant included that the statute only provided for the forfeiture of historic articles when the goods had been seized by the appropriate New Zealand authorities, and this had not happened in the present case; regarding the statute as a penal law which would not be enforced in England; and, per Lord Denning, regarding the statute as some other public law (along with penal laws and revenue laws) which would not be enforced in England. The House of Lords upheld the decision of the Court of Appeal but only on the point of interpreting the statutory provision. It did not express an opinion on whether the statute was a public or a penal law.

In the present case the Remotian statute may be applicable only in relation to ancient statues still within its territory and be judged not to have extra-territorial effect. Furthermore, in *Williams & Humbert* v *W & H Trade Marks (Jersey) Ltd* [1986] 1 All ER 129, foreign laws which purport to confiscate property situated in this country were held to be a class of laws to which recognition could be given but which would not be enforced.

If the decree had been made only when the statue had already left Remotian territory then it is virtually certain that the Remotian government would not succeed in an action to recover the statue. First, if the statute was not intended to have extra-territorial effect then their claim would be baseless: *Lecouturier* v *Rey* [1910] AC 262. Second, if it was intended to have such effect, the fact that they are not in possession or control of the statue means that Henry's title to it will not be affected: *Bank voor Handel en Scheepvaart NV* v *Slatford* [1953] 1 QB 248.

Royalties are a form of intangible movable, assignment of which is governed by art 12 of the Rome Convention on Contractual Obligations 1980. The Rome Convention has been given the force of law in England via s2(1) Contracts (Applicable Law) Act 1990. Article 12 provides that 'the mutual obligations of assignor and assignee under a voluntary assignment … shall be governed by the law which under this Convention applies to the contract between the assignor and assignee.'

In the absence of an express choice of law under art 3(1), or, indeed, an inferred choice which can be demonstrated with reasonable certainty, resort may be had to art 4(1) which provides: 'The contract shall be governed by the law of the country with which it is most closely connected.' The presumption in art 4(2) is that the contract is most closely connected with the country where the party who is to effect the performance which is characteristic of the contract has, at the time of the conclusion of the contract, his habitual residence. Now if delivery of the statute to Henry is regarded as the performance characteristic of the contract, then England will be the country most closely associated with the contract since that is the country where Jim is habitually resident. Certainly the *Giuliano-Lagarde Report* provided that the characteristic performance is usually the one for which the payment is due. Nothing in the facts of the problem and in the application of art 4(2) indicates that England would not be the country most closely connected with the contract between Jim and Henry.

Accordingly, it is English law which governs the material validity of the contract whereas the form may be validated by the applicable law or Antiquan law (as the parties were in the same country when the contract was concluded). Thus, the prohibition on assigning future royalties under Antiquan law is ineffective.

During Henry's voluntary visit to England next week, he may be served with a writ and 'whoever is served with the [Queen's] writ … is a person over which the courts have jurisdiction': *John Russell & Co Ltd* v *Cayzer, Irvine & Co Ltd* [1916] 2 AC 298. That Henry may be present in England for a short time is immaterial. In *Maharanee of Baroda* v *Wildenstein* [1972] 2 QB 283 the defendant was paying only a fleeting visit to England to attend the Ascot races. Nevertheless, this fleeting visit on British soil was held to be sufficient for the taking out and serving of the writ.

In summary, it is submitted that the Remotian government would not succeed in an action for recovery of the statue but Jim would have a good case on which to serve a writ on Henry.

QUESTION THREE

Does the foreign court doctrine of renvoi achieve justice?

University of London LLB Examination
(for External Students) Conflict of Laws June 1993 Q9

General Comment

This type of question is relatively straightforward to pass. However, for the better student to attain an excellent mark, then organisation is essential (ie content, structure, argument). This demands the student to demonstrate a thorough knowledge of case law. In addition, the student must discuss the various doctrines of renvoi (single, double/total renvoi) and their scope of application, as well as comment upon the rationale for the exclusion of renvoi from the areas of tort and contract law.

Skeleton Solution

Explanation of how renvoi arises – introduction of renvoi into English law – conclusions drawn from case law.

Suggested Solution

The basis of choice of law rules, which is common to all systems of private international law, is that the law to apply to the situation in question is ascertained from the relationship of a juridical category being governed by a connecting factor. So, for example, intestate succession to movables (the category) is governed by the law of the domicile of the propositus at the time of his death (the connecting factor).

However, the connecting factor employed by the choice of law rules of the forum might differ from the one employed by the courts of a foreign country. Consequently, if the choice of law rules of the lex fori, country X, refer an issue to the courts of another country, Y, which, under its rules of choice of law, refers the issue back to the law of the forum or, perhaps, on to the law of a third country, Z, the forum has to decide whether it should apply the domestic (or municipal) law of Y as the country selected by its own choice of law rules, or the choice of law rules of that country (Y). The problem in selecting the applicable law, which arises from the employment of different connecting factors or from giving different interpretations to the same connecting factor, is that of renvoi.

To ignore the choice of law rules of the foreign system first indicated and apply its domestic law appeared to be a 'simple and rational solution' to Russel J in *Re Annesley* [1926] Ch 692, even though he went on to apply what has become known as double or total renvoi or the foreign court doctrine of renvoi: in essence, the focus of this essay.

If the choice of law rules of the foreign system first indicated by the forum would refer a matter back to the forum and the forum would 'accept the renvoi', this would be a case of 'single' or 'partial renvoi'. Renvoi was introduced into English law via partial renvoi in *Collier v Rivaz* (1841) 2 Curt 855, although, it is conceded, the ambiguous dicta in this case could be interpreted as supporting double renvoi or the foreign court doctrine. At the time that this case was decided, only the law of the testator's last domicile (the lex ultimae domicilii) could be applied to determine the formal validity of a will. In this case, T, an Englishman, died domiciled in Belgium according to the English conflict of laws, but in England according to the Belgian rule. T left a will and six codicils, two of which were made in the acceptable Belgian form; these were admitted to probate in England without any challenge to their validity. However, the other four codicils were opposed because they did not comply with the Belgian formalities, although they did conform to the English form. Prima facie, the codicils were invalid because T had died domiciled in Belgium and only Belgian law could be used to test formal validity. Nevertheless, Sir Herbert Jenner admitted each of the codicils to probate. He did so on the basis that Belgian law in such a case would have referred the validity of the codicils to the law of the foreigner's own country. Accordingly, he accepted the renvoi from Belgium and applied English law to test the validity of the codicils. He held that the codicils were valid. Thus, the legitimate expectations of T were upheld.

Whereas credit could be given for upholding the clearly expressed intention of the testator, it is a decision that attracts severe criticism on at least two grounds. First, Sir Herbert aimed to achieve 'justice' with regard to the testator's intentions by holding that the formal validity of a will was not to be denied if it satisfied *either* the internal law *or* the private international law of the selected legal system. This is a remarkable conclusion, bearing in mind that the function of the English choice of law rule is to determine whether it is the internal law *or* the private international law of the selected system which is to prevail, ie selection of one system of law excludes application of the other. Second, the manipulation of the law in order to achieve 'justice' in a particular case is questionable – especially when the principles employed are not extended to another case having similar facts. This is highlighted by the Privy Council decision in *Bremer v Freeman* (1857) 10 Moo PC 306 where the testator's will was declared to be formally invalid.

Nevertheless, until 1926 decisions in cases recognising renvoi were consistent with the single or partial theory of renvoi. In 1926, however, Russel J in *Re Annesley* gave full recognition to the double or total or foreign court doctrine of renvoi. In this case, concerning the essential validity of a will, T was domiciled in France according to the English choice of law rules and in England according to the French choice of law rules. She (T) left a will which purported to dispose of all her property without making provision for her two surviving children. Whereas this was valid by English domestic law it was invalid by French domestic law as her children would each be entitled to one-third of the property, leaving T only the remaining one-third to dispose of. Russel J decided that the correct approach would be to 'don the mantle' of a judge hearing the case in France who would reason that he (the French judge) was bound to refer to English law as T's national law but would then accept the renvoi back to French (domestic) law. Accordingly, French law applied, and T's will was only effective to dispose of one-third of her property, the other two-thirds having to go to her children. In contrast, but still applying the foreign court doctrine, the testator, T, in *Re Ross* [1930] 1 Ch 377 was able to dispose of her property exactly as she wished, to the exclusion of an interest claimed by her son. Although T was domiciled in Italy in both the English and the Italian sense, it was accepted that Italian choice of law rules would refer to the law of the nationality of T and would not accept the renvoi. Accordingly, English law applied, the claim of the son failed, and 'Mrs Ross was allowed to evade one of the cardinal rules of the legal system the protection of which she had enjoyed for the last 51 years of her life' (Cheshire & North, *Private International Law*).

The foreign court doctrine of renvoi was extended to encompass a case relating to legitimacy in *Re Askew* [1930] 2 Ch 259. Here, X, an Englishman domiciled in Germany, had a child by Z when he was still married to (although separated from) his first wife, Y. During the substance of his first marriage he provided that if he should remarry he would partially revoke a settled trust and make a new appointment to the children of such subsequent marriage. When the case was litigated before the English court, no consideration was given to the fact that the child was not a child of the 'subsequent marriage'. Maugham J decided that, by English choice of law rules, the child's legitimacy was to be decided by the law of the domicile of her father, German law. Evidence was accepted that German choice of law rules would first refer to the nationality of X and then accept the renvoi back to German domestic law where the daughter would be regarded as legitimate. Accordingly, the appointment in favour of the daughter was declared to be valid.

Conclusions drawn from these cases would neither confirm nor deny the ability of the foreign court doctrine of renvoi to achieve justice. Whereas that would appear to be a selective and subjective judgment, that, of itself, is probably sufficient to suggest that the balance is against the consistently objective achievement of justice. Reasons for this may be attributable to the following points. First, it would appear that renvoi was introduced into English law in a case of doubtful authority: *Collier v Rivaz*. Second, whereas the application of renvoi appeared to achieve 'justice' in *Collier v Rivaz*, it did so by acting as an 'escape mechanism'; it was employed to avoid the rigidities of the then prevailing English law. While it may appear unobjectionable to determine the formal validity of a will by employing renvoi, it is impossible to extend this application to the essential validity of a will. Thirdly, it may be claimed that Mrs Annesley was denied the benefit of justice that Mrs Ross was able to benefit from, or that the children in *Re Annesley* had the benefit of justice that was denied to Mr Ross. Fourthly, it could be claimed that no reference to foreign law – domestic or private international – was necessary to interpret the meaning of legitimacy in *Re Askew*, and that in such a case a reference could only defeat a 'common sense' interpretation of justice.

Even if the purpose of renvoi is the apparently laudable one of the avoidance of defeating the reasonable expectations of individuals in the light of other systems of law, it is difficult to see how it has consistent application in the cases noted above. Indeed, the foreign court doctrine of renvoi only applies if it is recognised in one of the countries concerned and rejected in the other. Consequently, it is difficult 'to approve a doctrine which is workable only if the other country rejects it' (per Lorenzen). Cheshire has condemned the doctrine as 'nothing less than a substitution of the foreign for the English choice-of-law rules.' He notes that as 'a rule for the choice of the applicable law is essentially selective in nature [then] it should have no other effect than to select another and contradictory rule of selection savours of incompatibility and paradox'.

Furthermore, it is difficult to accord justice as an attribute of the foreign court theory of renvoi in the light of both the potential difficulty of its application (*Re Duke of Wellington* [1948] Ch 118), and when it does apply, the potentially absurd decisions which may flow from its application: *Re O'Keefe* [1940] Ch 124.

In *Re Duke of Wellington* Wynn-Parry J was faced with declaring what view then prevailed in Spain in relation to single renvoi. The difficulty was that he had to 'expound for the first time either to this country or to Spain the relevant law of Spain as it would be expounded by the Supreme Court of Spain, which up to the present time has made no pronouncement on the subject, and having to base that exposition on evidence which satisfies me that on this subject there exists a profound cleavage of legal opinion in Spain and two conflicting decisions of courts of inferior jurisdiction'. It is difficult, if not impossible, to deduce from this how it could be claimed that 'justice' could be achieved in this or any other case in the absence of such authority.

Finally, in *Re O'Keefe* the English court had to decide on the distribution of the movables of a spinster who died intestate. Although she had an Irish domicile of origin, she had only entered the country on a short visit when she was seven years of age (some 60 years before her death), and it had only become a separate political unit when she had reached the age of 62. She was born in India where she lived for the first seven years of her life. For the next 13 years she lived in three different European countries, including England, before finally settling in Italy where she lived for the remaining 47 years of her life. Whereas English choice of law rules selected Italian law as the law of her domicile of choice, Italian choice of law rules referred to her nationality. When evidence was being adduced as to what was her nationality – it could have been Irish, English or Indian – the expert witness stated that it would be the law of the country to which she 'belonged' at the time of her death. In fact, all of these were rejected by Crossman J. Instead, he held that she belonged to Ireland because that was the country where her father was domiciled at the time of her birth. Thus a country which she had only once fleetingly visited and of which it was impossible in the circumstances for her to claim citizenship was the country the law of which governed the succession to her property.

In conclusion, then, it is submitted that any role the foreign court doctrine of renvoi has to play in giving effect to a status, or to rights arising from a status, is either balanced by, or weighed in favour of, legal argument rejecting it. It cannot be stated unequivocally that it achieves justice.

QUESTION FOUR

i) Explain the 'incidental question' and its significance.

ii) John and Mary are brother and sister and are aged 21 and 23 respectively. They are domiciled in Utopia.

   Whilst holidaying in England they are involved in a motor accident and killed. It is uncertain which of them died first. John died intestate. He owned a large number of shares in an English company. His sole next of kin are Mary and another sister, Elizabeth, who is still living. Mary left a will in which she gave all her property to a friend, George.

   By Utopian law, the male is deemed to die first. This is a rule of procedure, not substance.

   By English law, the elder is deemed to die first, and this is a rule of substance, not of procedure.

   Who is entitled to John's shares?

University of London LLB Examination
(for External Students) Conflict of Laws June 1987 Q7

General Comment

At first glance this appears very straightforward, and if the student has a thorough knowledge of the area, it is. However, it is easy to 'dry up' with this type of question. Ensure that you are familiar with appropriate amounts of case law/academic opinion.

Skeleton Solution

i) Example of the incidental question – approaches to the solution of the problem – difficulties with the lex causae approach – uniformity of decision – which is the incidental question?

ii) The boundaries of form and substance: a characterisation problem – what is it that is characterised? – 'gap' and 'cumulation'.

Suggested Solution

i) Of the unique conceptual problems that arise from the application of choice of law rules, the incidental question is the most recently discovered. Like renvoi, but unlike characterisation, the incidental question arises from the differences between the choice of law rules of different legal systems, ie the fact that different legal systems resolve different choice of law issues in different ways.

Let us make this clear with an example. Suppose that H, a national of Utopia, dies intestate leaving securities deposited in a bank in London. At the time of his death, H is domiciled in Hades. In terms of English choice of law rules, the securities would be distributed according to the law of H's last domicile. However, one of the claimants for a share of the securities is W who claims to be H's wife. But how do we decide whether W is H's wife? This is the incidental question for it arises incidentally to the major question: how are H's securities to be distributed?

The real problem is that English law might use different choice of law rules to determine the validity of the marriage of H and W to the choice of law rules that may be used by the law of Hades. We know that English law will test formal validity by the lex loci celebrationis and essential validity by the law of the parties' ante-nuptial domiciles, but the law of Hades may test the validity of marriage by the lex patriae; and the law of Utopia may impose some requirement quite inconsistent with English law.

The academic writers are divided about how the question should be resolved. On the one hand, if the incidental question is determined by the lex causae (in our example the law of Hades (note that the law of Hades would apply the law of Utopia as the lex patriae, so applying the lex causae to the issue requires the recognition of a kind of renvoi) then uniformity of decision will be advanced. Whether the matter is litigated in Hades or in England the same result will be reached. We know that the uniformity of decision is one of the major purposes of the conflict of laws, so this is a weighty consideration in favour of the lex causae.

On the other hand, applying the lex causae is not beyond criticism. First, it will often be difficult to determine in a case with complicated facts which is the primary question and which is the incidental question; and different results would be reached depending upon the answer to that question. So following the lex causae would not always lead to uniformity of decision for there might be disagreement over which was the lex causae. Second, suppose that before his death H had approached the English courts seeking a declaration that his marriage to W was valid. Plainly in these circumstances the English courts, being unaware that they were deciding the incidental question, would apply the ordinary English rules. Should then H die intestate, the English courts could hardly go back on their prior ruling and hold that the law of Hades should be applied to determine that the marriage was valid.

In these circumstances, it is not surprising that there is little academic consensus.

The most thoughtful writers (Kahn-Freund, Morris and Gottlieb) generally advocate a non-mechanical approach to the issue.

Although a trifle recondite there are cases which pose the problem of the incidental question, although no English judge has ever approached the issue in a principled way. In England the clearest incidental question type case is *Lawrence* v *Lawrence* [1985] Fam 106. Here where the recognition of a divorce decree (made in Nevada and governed by the then applicable rules of English law) arose incidentally to the question of capacity to marry (probably governed in *Lawrence* by the law of Brazil) the English court recognised the divorce (although it would not have been recognised in Brazil) in order to uphold as valid the subsequent marriage of the parties. This was not the application of the lex causae, for that would have required the application of the law of Brazil. On the other hand, in the Canadian case of *Schwebel* v *Ungar* (1963) 42 DLR (2d) 622 the court applied the lex causae in an incidental question case. But the effect of applying the lex causae was to uphold the validity of a subsequent marriage entered into in the belief that an earlier marriage was validly dissolved by an extra-judicial ghett. The ghett was recognised under the law of Israel (the lex causae) but was not recognised under the ordinary Canadian rules in regard to the recognition of divorces. These two cases, alas, tell us more about the policy of the judiciary towards upholding marriages believed to be valid, and little about the proper approach to adopt to the incidental question.

ii) This is an interesting problem raising a particular aspect of characterisation about the boundary between form and substance. From the facts given it is likely that in a dispute between George and Elizabeth for the shares that: (a) the matter will be litigated in England for that is where the shares are, so English law is the lex fori; and (b) since the issue raised is intestate succession to movables which is governed by the law of the last domicile, ie the law of Utopia (where John and Mary are domiciled) will be the lex causae.

Now in the normal course when it is unclear whether the Utopian law (in terms of which John is deemed to die first, so Mary inherits from him before dying; thus her heir George gets the shares) applies, or whether the English law (in terms of which Mary, as the elder, is deemed to die first so she never owns the shares; so they go to Elizabeth not George), the question that arises is the characterisation of these rules relating to the time of death. And one could then discuss the various ways in which these rules could be characterised. Should they be categorised by the lex fori (and the difficulties that arise therefrom) or by the lex causae (and the difficulties that arise therefrom). So should Kahn-Freund's enlightened lex fori or Falconbridge's via media be applied?

However, in this case we are told how the rules are to be characterised: the English rule relates to substance (we are told) and this has the plain consequence that the English rule does not govern since English law, as the lex fori, governs only issues of procedure. On the other hand, the Utopian rule relates to procedure and thus does not apply, for Utopian law is the lex causae and only governs issues of substance.

The conclusion reached is that neither rule applies. This is the problem of 'gap' and there is the related problem of 'cumulation' where the conclusion of the characterisation process is that two or more conflicting rules are applicable. Such cases do occur, though rarely. There is, for instance, a German case in which a bill of exchange which had long gone stale under both the lex fori (German law) and the lex causae (Tennessee) was nonetheless enforced because of the problem of 'gap'. And 'gap' was narrowly avoided in the South African case of *Laconian Maritime Enterprises* v *Agromar Lines* (1986) also in the context of statutes of limitation. It is more difficult to know quite how the matter is to be resolved.

The English cases are of little use. *Re Cohn* [1945] Ch 5 had rather similar facts (it concerned the death of a mother and daughter both domiciled in Germany who were killed by the same bomb during a German air raid on London and the question arose of who died first). But the conclusion there reached by Uthwatt J was that the German rule (which deemed them to have died at the same time) was substantive (so did apply) but that the English rule (which deemed the elder to have died first) was also substantive, so it did not apply. Neither 'gap' nor 'cumulation' arose.

So how does one get out of the difficulty? Some suggestions may be made. First, one may apply the lex fori. The lex fori is always there as a law of last resort and, like a lifebelt, can be grabbed in an emergency. In *Laconian Maritime Enterprises* the lex fori was used to avoid 'gap'. If this were done then Mary would be held to have died before John, and Elizabeth would take the share. This would probably be the approach of the English judges were the case ever to arise before them in this form.

Alternatively, one could follow the suggestion of Kahn-Freund and Professor Steindorff and develop special rules to deal with these problems. Unfortunately, at present, these special principles do not exist in English law, so this will probably not be an easy solution.

QUESTION FIVE

Why does *renvoi* have no place in the law of contract or tort? Should it have a place in any other part of private international law? If so, what view of *renvoi* should be held?

University of London LLB Examination
(for External Students) Conflict of Laws June 1996 Q9

General Comment

At first sight, students may think that critical analysis of a very controversial area of the conflicts of law is not required for this question. Certainly this is the impression that many pe;ople would get when asking questions which begin with: 'Why ...'; 'Should it ...'; and 'If so, what ...'. In essence, whereas this is meant to be a fair, thought-provoking question, it is one in which many students may not impress or influence the examiner to the extent they would wish unless they take the trouble to construct and present the structured response that, prima facie, the question appears not to require.

Skeleton Solution

How renvoi arises – theories of renvoi where renvoi applies – where renvoi might have applied and reasons why it doesn't apply in contract and tort; principal advantage of applying renvoi might be outweighed by the disadvantages of applying renvoi – double or total theory is the better theory.

Suggested Solution

When the choice of law rules of a forum, England, for example, point to the application of a foreign law, Utopia, say, three logical possibilities arise as to what is meant by 'Utopian law'. First, the internal or domestic law applicable to the citizens of that state could be applied. This approach disregards the possibility that the foreign forum might decide the issue in accordance with English internal law because it does not require any knowledge of Utopia's conflict rules and whether Utopian law would refer the issue to English law. In *Re Annesley* [1926] Ch 692, Russell J said: 'This appears ... to be a simple and rational solution'. However, he then went on to reject this 'internal law' theory and decided the case under the third possible approach to be outlined here – the approach which has now become the orthodox approach in English law – as noted below.

The second and third logical possibilities have in common the requirement of some knowledge of the Utopian conflicts rules. It is when the conflicts rules of a foreign forum remits the issue back to the referring country, or transmits the reference to some third country, that the renvoi theories emerge. What has to be decided under such circumstances is the extent to which the foreign law is then taken into account.

The second logical possibility – and the first of the renvoi theories – is that reference to Utopian law would be a reference to its conflicts rules which might remit the issue back to English domestic law or transmit the reference to some third country, Ruritania, say, discounting the possibility that England or Ruritanian conflicts rules would again refer to Utopian law. This single reference from the law of the country chosen by the conflicts rules of the first forum is known as single or partial renvoi and is adopted for most issues by Belgian, French and German conflicts rules. Selective application of this type of renvoi gave formal validity to the testator's wishes in *Collier* v *Rivaz* (1841) 2 Curt 855.

The third logical possibility gives rise to the second theory of renvoi, known as double or total renvoi or foreign court theory. When this applies, the English courts refer, ultimately, to the internal law – Utopian or English – of the country that would be chosen by the Utopian courts (so far as the English courts can deduce, anyway). So, if the Utopian courts would apply the internal law theory, then English domestic law would determine the issue. Conversely, if the Utopian courts would apply partial renvoi, ie, they would accept the renvoi from the English courts, then Utopian domestic law would determine the issue.

It is the second theory of renvoi, the double or total renvoi or foreign court theory, that has become the orthodox theory in the English conflicts of laws since its introduction by Russel J in *Re Annesley* (above). Here, according to the English conflict of laws, Mrs A died domiciled in France. Evidence was adduced that whilst, according to the French conflict of laws, Mrs A died domiciled in England, a French court would accept the renvoi and apply French domestic law. Russel J held that French law applied and Mrs A's property was disposed of accordingly. Thus, application of total renvoi requires a knowledge of Utopian conflicts of law rules and its rules relating to renvoi, if it has any. Moreover, the total renvoi theory applies in a forum only if other countries reject it! Had the French courts applied it in *Re Annesley* a state of impasse would arise: the English courts would refer the issue to the French courts who would remit the issue to the English courts, and so on ad infinitum – the circulus inextricabilis.

In English law, the general rule is that renvoi does not apply to contracts: simple contractual relationships are decided on the internal law theory since most contractual issues are governed by the applicable law (or the proper law) of the contract. To import renvoi would be to undermine the concept of party autonomy and the expectations of each property to the contract. That renvoi was specifically excluded from the common law rules governing the choice of law in contract was stated by Lord Diplock in *Amin Rasheed Shipping Corporation* v *Kuwait Insurance Co* [1984] AC 50, where his Lordship expressed the proper law of a contract as being 'the substantive law of the country which the parties have chosen as that by which their mutually legally enforceable rights are to be ascertained, but excluding any renvoi, whether of remission or transmission'. This position has been retained by the Rome Convention on the Law Applicable to Contractual Obligations which provides in art 15 that: 'The application of the law of any country specified by this Convention means the application of the rules of law in force in that country other than its rules of private international law.'

Prior to the enactment of Part III of the Private International Law (Miscellaneous Provisions) Act 1995, the leading case on the choice of law in tort in respect of a tort committed abroad but litigated in England, was *Boys* v *Chaplin* [1971] AC 356. In *Boys*, Lord Wilberforce noted the attraction of the internal law theory before going on to qualify it. His approach is reminiscent of Russell J's in *Re Annesley*. Lord Wilberforce said: 'A tort takes place in France: if action is not brought before the courts in France, let other courts decide as the French courts would. This has obvious attraction. But there are ... disadvantages.'

The fundamental objections to the application of the lex locus delicti commissi (law of the place where the tort occurred) include the lex fori regarding as tortious an act not regarded as such in the locus delicti; and as between the tortfeasor and the victim, the tortious act may have a much closer connection with another law district – as in *Boys* v

Chaplin, for example. Indeed, *Boys* had affirmed, albeit with some modification, the 'double actionability' rule propounded in *Phillips* v *Eyre* (1870) LR 6 QB 1. That is, to be actionable as a tort in England, the general rule is that a defendant's conduct must be 'actionable as a tort according to English law, subject to the condition that civil liability in respect of the relevant claim exists as between the actual parties under the law of the foreign country was done'. With regard to each system of law, the reference is to the internal or domestic law of that country (or law district).

However, s10 Private International Law (Miscellaneous Provisions) Act 1995 expressly abolishes, inter alia, the double actionability rule, and the general rule is now contained in s11 which provides that 'the applicable law is the law of the country in which the events constituting the tort ... in question occur'. Of course, the general rule can be displaced by the law of another country if, in all the circumstances of the case, it is substantially 'more appropriate' for the law of that country to apply. Section 9(5) expressly provides that: 'The applicable law to be used for determining the issues arising in a claim shall exclude any choice of law rules forming part of the law of the country or countries concerned.' Accordingly, renvoi does not apply to tort. However, and notwithstanding the enactment of these statutory provisions, a further comment advocating the potential role of renvoi in tort will be noted near the end of this essay.

Whereas renvoi does not have a role to play in the law of obligations – contract and tort – it does have a role to play in other parts of private international law. For example, case law has determined that renvoi is applicable in matters of: intestate succession to movables (*Re Johnson* [1903] 1 Ch 821; *Re O'Keefe* [1940] Ch 124); to the intrinsic or essential validity of wills, whether in respect of movables (*Re Annesley*) or immovables (*Re Ross* [1930] 1 Ch 377); and the determination of a person's capacity to marry: *R* v *Brentwood Superintendent Registrar of Marriages, ex parte Arias* [1968] 2 QB 956.

Whether renvoi should have a role to play is another matter and is dependent on whether one believes its advantages outweigh the disadvantages of its application. The principal advantage of renvoi relates to it being a technique which tends to aid uniformity in decision-making. In particular, there appears to be universal agreement that where a choice of law rule requires application of the lex situs, renvoi should be employed. This may be outweighed by the disadvantages associated with the application of renvoi, however. First, for example, some legal systems, such as Italy, use nationality as a connecting factor and ascribe to a deceased person a 'national law' having no meaningful relationship with where that person lived or was domiciled: *Re O'Keefe*. Second, the process of renvoi is arbitrary. Why, for example, a maximum of two references in partial renvoi – A to B then back to A; or A to B to C? Why not more onward references – C to D, for example – or why not just settle for a single reference, ie, reject the whole idea of renvoi? Third, total renvoi only operates because other countries reject it! How, then, does one approve a doctrine which is workable only if the courts of the other country reject it? Finally, it may be impossible to state with conviction the 'law' of another country when, at the time of making a decision, there had been no pronouncement by the Supreme Court of that country of the law on that particular issue and what opinions had been expressed suggested a profound cleavage of legal opinion: *Re Duke of Wellington* [1948] Ch 118.

If renvoi is to be advocated and applied, notwithstanding the aforementioned disadvantages, it would appear that the most favourably received type is that of total renvoi or foreign court theory, especially with reference to the lex situs and the law of a deceased's last domicile governing most aspects of movable succession.

That total renvoi might have been appropriate in tort, perhaps dispensing with the perceived need for legislation, is merely a matter of conjecture and academic interest. Lord Wilberforce had said in *Boys* v *Chaplin* that:

> '... no purely mechanical rule can properly do justice to the great variety of cases where persons come together in a foreign jurisdiction for different purposes with different pre-existing relationships, from the background of different legal systems.'

However, as noted (above), s10 Private International Law (Miscellaneous Provisions) Act 1995 now expressly abolishes the double actionability rule, and ss11 and 12 provide the new statutory provisions relating to the choice of applicable law.

What prompts the academic discussion is not only the reservation of Lord Wilberforce but also the contention of Stone (P Stone, *The Conflict of Laws* (1995), at p395) that:

> 'It is ... arguable that total renvoi is appropriate where the main purpose of the English conflict rule is to respect the interest of the country considered to have the greatest concern with the issue in question; for example ... in tort, where departure from the lex loci delicti depends on its lacking any substantial interest in the application of its rules in the connectional circumstances of the case.'

Given that 'There are no issues for which English law appears to adopt a partial renvoi theory' (P Stone, ibid, at p394), it would seem that total renvoi will remain the orthodox theory in the English conflict of laws until such time as it might be dispensed with.

Chapter 3
Domicile

3.1   Introduction

3.2   Key points

3.3   Key cases and statutes

3.4   Questions and suggested solutions

3.1 Introduction

Domicile is a connecting factor and as such provides a link between an individual and the legal system of a state to which that individual 'belongs'. The law of that state is then held to be applicable to that individual and governs his/her personal relationships. Generally speaking a person is domiciled in that place which the law considers to be his permanent home. However, it is quite possible for the law to consider a person domiciled in a place to which he has never been or with which he has but a slight connection.

The rules that operate in this area are often criticised as being antiquated and having little real connection to the modern world (particularly in the area of the domicile of children). As such, other linking factors such as habitual residence and nationality have been forwarded as possible replacements. Nevertheless, despite such criticism, domicile still remains the favoured tool of the English courts to determine an individual's personal law.

3.2 Key points

The significance of domicile as a connecting factor

As noted above, the principal function of the concept of domicile is to provide a link between individuals and legal systems. In many areas of the conflict of laws, the choice of law is determined by reference to domicile. It is used to determine the applicable law, inter alia, in the following areas:

a) the law of succession;

b) questions of contractual capacity;

c) the law of marriage and divorce; and

d) family law.

The concept is also applicable in other areas but these are the most significant.

The definition of domicile

Domicile signifies a special link between an individual and a particular legal system. As Sir Jocelyn Simon observed in *Henderson* v *Henderson* [1967] P 77, domicile denotes:

> '... the legal relationship between a person ... and a territory subject to a distinctive legal system which invokes [that] system as [his] personal law'.

While domicile is a legal term, it is synonymous with a person's permanent home at least in the eyes of the law.

Three forms of domicile

Conflict of laws distinguishes between three separate types of domicile:

a) Domicile of origin – the law imputes a domicile of origin to each child at birth and is the domicile of the father if the child is legitimate and the domicile of the mother if illegitimate. It should be noted that the domicile of origin is unique in the fact that it will revive whenever an individual casts off a domicile of choice (or dependence) and does not replace it with another one.

b) Domicile of dependence – a domicile may be imputed to a person. For example, the domicile of a child is imputed by reference to one or other of its parents depending on whether or not it is legitimate. (See below for further discussion.)

c) Domicile of choice – once a person reaches the age of 16 he may acquire his own domicile by choice if certain conditions are satisfied. Broadly speaking, two conditions must be satisfied – physical presence and intention to reside there permanently – in order to acquire a domicile of choice.

General principles relating to domicile

At a general level, there are four important principles relating to the law of domicile. These are as follows:

a) No person can be without a domicile. As Lord Westbury observed in *Udny* v *Udny* (1869) LR 1 Sc & Div 441, 'it is a settled principle that no man shall be without a domicile'.

b) No person can have more than one domicile. Thus, a domicile of choice extinguishes a previous domicile of dependency, origin or even choice.

c) The burden of establishing a change of domicile rests on the party asserting that there has been a change. However, the problem would appear to be that the burden seems to vary with the type of domicile that is in question.

d) For the purposes of conflict of laws, domicile means domicile in the English sense of the term. Thus, a court may find that a person is domiciled in France even although a French court applying principles of French conflict of laws might decide that he or she is domiciled elsewhere.

Domicile of origin

The central rule of domicile of origin is that a legitimate child acquires the domicile of his father at the time of birth and an illegitimate child takes that of his mother. Adopted children are treated as legitimate children after adoption and take the domicile of origin of the adoptive father by virtue of s8 of the Children Act 1975.

It is important to understand that, while each individual has a domicile of origin, frequently this domicile is inoperative (dormant) as a connecting factor because the same person may have a domicile of dependence or a domicile of choice, both of which prevail over a domicile of origin.

At the same time, the character of a domicile of origin is formidable. As Lord MacNaugten declared, 'the character [of the domicile of origin] is more enduring, its hold stronger, and less easily shaken off': *Winans* v *Attorney-General* [1904] AC 287. See also *Ramsey* v *Royal Liverpool Infirmary* [1930] AC 588.

A domicile of origin cannot be abandoned and can only be displaced through the acquisition of a domicile of choice. Consequently, if a domicile of choice is lost by an individual, then his domicile of origin is revived until another domicile of choice is acquired: *Udny* v *Udny* (above). This rule has been strongly condemned as unrealistic and frequently forms one of the main arguments for the reform of this area due to the sometimes inappropriate results that the rule generates. However, this is inevitable, given the fact that the courts are attempting to fill a gap, often retrospectively.

Domicile of dependence

Children

The common law rule is that a child acquires the domicile of his father at birth if legitimate and the domicile of his mother if illegitimate as a domicile of dependence: see *Henderson* v *Henderson* [1967] P 77 and *Potinger* v *Wrightman* (1817) 3 Mer 67.

This domicile will coincide with the child's domicile of origin at birth but whereas the domicile of origin is fixed at birth, the domicile of dependence will change as the domicile of the person on whom it depends changes. For example, a legitimate child born in England to a father domiciled in England will acquire a domicile of origin in England and a domicile of dependence in England. But, if the father acquires a domicile of choice in New York the child will acquire a domicile of dependence in New York, although its domicile of origin will remain England.

There are other rules for special cases. These are as follows:

a) Legitimated children – these children take the domicile of their mother until legitimation and the domicile of their father once the legitimation takes effect.

b) Fatherless children – where a legitimate child's father has died, they are treated as illegitimate and follow the domicile of their mother: see *Re Beaumont* [1893] 3 Ch 490.

c) Orphans and illegitimate children whose mothers have died – the domicile of these unfortunate children remains the same as it was when the parent on whom they depended for domicile died.

d) Adopted children – these children are treated as the legitimate children of their adoptive parents: s8 Children Act 1975.

The common law rules have been altered slightly by the Domicile and Matrimonial Proceedings Act 1973. Section 4 of this Act creates special rules for the determination of the domicile of dependent children whose parents are separated. The scheme of this section is to make the domicile of such a child dependant upon the parent with whom the child has its home.

Thus the central provision is that a child whose parents are living apart has the same domicile as his mother if 'he then has a home with her and has no home with his father.' This maternal domicile persists even if the child ceases to have a home with its mother, provided that it does not subsequently have a home with its father.

Where s4 is inapplicable – for example, because the parents are not living apart or because the child has never lived at home with either parent – the common law rules continue to apply.

Section 4 is not retroactive. The domicile of a child prior to 1 January 1974 is determined in accordance with the common law rules.

Married women

At common law a married woman took the domicile of her husband as a domicile of dependence. As her husband's domicile changed so too did her domicile irrespective of her wishes or intentions: see *Lord Advocate* v *Jaffey* [1921] 1 AC 147.

This rule was abolished by s1(1) of the Domicile and Matrimonial Proceedings Act 1973. This statute expressly provides that:

'The domicile of a married woman as at any time after the coming into force of this section [1 January 1974] shall, instead of being the same as her husband's by virtue only of marriage, be ascertained by reference to the same factors as in the case of any individual capable of having an independent domicile.'

As a transitional provision, s1(2) of the Act provides that if immediately before the Act came into effect a woman was married and had a domicile of dependence, she is to retain this domicile unless and until she acquires a domicile of choice. In this situation, a women retains her husband's domicile as a domicile of choice pending the acquisition of a new domicile: see *IRC* v *Duchess of Portland* [1982] Ch 314.

Domicile of choice

General rule

Every independent person over the age of 16 may acquire a new domicile, called a domicile of choice, through their own actions. To acquire such a domicile, a person must take up residence in a new country with the intention of remaining there permanently and indefinitely. Hence there are two separate elements involved – an actual period of residence and an intention to acquire a new domicile.

Requirement of residence

There is no specific period of residence required to acquire a domicile of choice, but the residence must be accompanied by an intention to settle permanently. As Lord Chelmsford stated:

> 'If the intention of permanently residing in a place exists, residence in pursuance of that intention, however short, will establish domicile': *Bell* v *Kennedy* (1868) LR 1 Sc & Div 307.

Thus, in *White* v *Tennant* (1888) 8 SE 596, residence for a single afternoon was considered sufficient when accompanied by an intention to reside permanently.

However, residence must be lawful and an illegal immigrant cannot acquire a domicile of choice in the country to which he or she unlawfully emigrates: see *Puttick* v *Attorney-General* [1980] Fam 1.

Requirement of intention

The strongest indicator in establishing a domicile of choice is the intention to reside permanently in another country. (Note that the person does not actually have to reside there for the rest of his life in order to satisfy this element. The courts are simply looking at a snapshot in time and posing the question as to whether the individual, at that time, had the intention to reside in this new country permanently.)

Therefore, such an intention will not be held to exist where a person resides in a territory for a definite period and then leaves or, alternatively, resides in a country until a specific purpose is achieved, eg completion of an employment contract.

However, a person who enters a country with the intention of residing there regardless of what may happen in the future has sufficient intention to establish a domicile of choice.

If a person enters a country with the intention of residing for an indefinite period, pending the occurrence of an uncertain event, that intention may not be sufficient to satisfy this element. For instance, in *IRC* v *Bullock* [1976] 1 WLR 1178 a Canadian pilot who had resided in England for 40 years did not acquire a domicile of choice in England because he had always intended to return to Canada in the event that his wife predeceased him, which in fact occurred. For a rather extreme example of this see *Ramsey* v *Royal Liverpool Infirmary* [1930] AC 588.

In the final analysis, the critical issue is whether the particular contingency on which residence depends is sufficiently clear to prevent the acquisition of a domicile of choice: see *Re Fuld* [1968] P 675, where Scarman J stated that what was required was 'a clearly foreseen and reasonably anticipated contingency'.

Proof of intention

The factors which may be taken into account when establishing the intention of a person in determining a domicile of choice are virtually unlimited. As Kindersley V-C stated in *Drevon v Drevon* (1834) 34 LJ Ch 129:

> 'There is no act, no circumstance in a man's life, however trivial it may be in itself, which ought to be left out of consideration in trying the question whether there was an intention to change domicile. A trivial act might possibly be of more weight with regard to determining this question than an act which was of more importance to a man in his lifetime.'

A period of long residence will not, of itself, provide sufficient evidence of the necessary degree of intention. It is necessary to investigate a person's frame of mind and aspirations in order to prove his or her intentions.

Abandonment of a domicile of choice

A domicile of choice is abandoned when a person ceases to reside in the country and revokes the intention to reside permanently or indefinitely in that country: see *IRC v Duchess of Portland* [1982] Ch 314.

Of course, if a person leaves the country which has been adopted as his or her domicile of choice, but only for a temporary period, and intends to return, he or she does not lose that domicile of choice.

Two alternative domiciles may come into operation when a domicile of choice is abandoned. Either a new domicile of choice is acquired or the domicile of origin is revived. In other words, until a new domicile of choice is adopted, the domicile of origin revives and provides the individual with a personal law.

Special cases

The adoption of a domicile of choice is dependent on the ability to freely select a particular place as a permanent home. In the event that this freedom is constrained by certain circumstances, special rules are applied.

Four special cases merit further consideration:

a) Prisoners retain the domicile which they held prior to their imprisonment and do not acquire the domicile of their place of imprisonment: see *Re the late Emperor Napoleon Bonaparte* (1853) 2 Rob Eccl 606.

b) Refugees may acquire a domicile of choice in their country of refuge but only if they abandon their hope of returning to their country of origin: see *Re Lloyd Evans* [1947] Ch 695.

c) Fugitives from justice who are forced to live in another country retain their previous domicile unless they decline to return to their previous country and adopt the intention to remain in the adopted domicile: *Re Martin* [1900] P 211.

d) Employees, diplomats and soldiers are subject to the same rule. Such persons retain the domicile of their country of origin unless they manifest an intention to reside permanently in the country of their posting: *Donaldson v Donaldson* [1949] P 363.

Domicile of companies

The rule for corporations is simple. Corporations are domiciled in their place of incorporation: *Gasque v IRC* [1940] 2 KB 80.

The domicile of a corporation cannot be altered, even if the company conducts business within the jurisdiction of another legal system.

Reform of the law of domicile

The rules relating to domicile are often described as being complex and cumbersome. The application of the rules has also been criticised by both the courts themselves and academics. Many of the concepts employed to determine domicile have an artificial character (though this could be levelled at many rules) and the process of examining a person's life to decide the question of domicile is often arduous.

In 1985, the Law Commission published a Working Paper on the proposed reform of the law of domicile (Working Paper No 88 (1985)). The Commission's paper made four primary recommendations:

a) The doctrine of domicile of origin should be abolished, (and with it the doctrine of revival).

b) The domicile of any person under 16 should be that of his or her mother. If the child has its home with only one parent, then the domicile of the child should be the same as that of the parent.

c) A domicile should persist until a new domicile is acquired. (This proposal would replace the current doctrine of the revival of the domicile of origin in the event that a domicile of choice is abandoned.) In addition, the intention necessary to acquire a new domicile should be that of indefinite residence and that intention should be presumed after continual residence for seven years (after reaching the age of 16).

d) The insane and others incapax should be domiciled in the country with which they have the closest connection.

Statutory modifications of the concept of domicile

The traditional notion of domicile is a creation of the common law. Where a court is searching for a connecting factor in the context of the personal law of an individual – ie in relation to marriage, divorce, succession, etc – it is the common law concept which is employed.

Unfortunately, the position has been confused somewhat by the introduction of an alternative concept of domicile in the Civil Jurisdiction and Judgments Act 1982. This statute uses the concept of a looser form of domicile to establish connecting factors for the purposes of establishing jurisdiction over defendants in civil and commercial matters. Domicile in this context is synonymous with a period of residence.

However, the statutory concept of domicile applies only in relation to the rules for establishing jurisdiction under the Act. This should be considered a concept divorced from the common law doctrine of domicile although admittedly the use of the same term to denote two different notions is confusing to say the least.

The statutory definition of domicile is considered in Chapter 5. Where the term is used in this book other than in Chapter 5, it is the common law definition which is being referred to.

3.3 Key cases and statutes

- *Beaumont, Re* [1893] 3 Ch 490
  Change of domicile of fatherless child

- *Bell* v *Kennedy* (1868) LR 1 Sc & Div 307
  Domicile of origin persists until replaced by acquisition of new domicile

- *Drevon* v *Drevon* (1834) 34 LJ Ch 129
  Proof of intention

- *Furse, Re* [1980] 3 All ER 838
  Effect of a vague and indefinite contingency on acquisition of domicile

- *IRC* v *Duchess of Portland* [1982] Ch 314
  Married women – change of domicile

- *Plummer* v *IRC* [1988] 1 WLR 292
  Where there is more than one residence

- *Ramsay* v *Liverpool Royal Infirmary* [1930] AC 588
  Acquisition of a domicile of choice – intention as well as residence

- *Udny* v *Udny* (1869) LR 1 Sc & Div 441
  Domicile of origin revives whenever there is no other domicile

- *White* v *Tennant* (1888) 31 Wva 790
  Acquisition of new domicile – physical presence – time spent

- Children Act 1975, s8 – adopted children treated as if born to adoptive parents in wedlock

- Domicile and Matrimonial Proceedings Act 1973, s1 – rules governing domicile of married women

- Domicile and Matrimonial Proceedings Act 1973, s3 – individual ceases to be a child and becomes capable of having an independent domicile at the age of 16

- Domicile and Matrimonial Proceedings Act 1973, s4 – rules governing domicile of children whose parents live apart

- Law Commission Working Paper No 88 (1985) – recommendations for the reform of the rules of domicile

3.4 Questions and suggested solutions

QUESTION ONE

i) 'Habitual residence should replace domicile as the connecting factor in relation to matters of personal status.

   Do you agree?

ii) Fatima and Yasser, both domiciliaries and nationals of Iran and supporters of the Shah, married in 1973. A daughter, Bibi, was born to them in 1975. In 1979, Yasser sent Fatima, who was pregnant, and Bibi to New York because he was frightened for their safety under the regime of Ayatollah Khomeini. He intended to follow as soon as he sold the family business. However, shortly after their departure, Yasser was arrested and executed.

   Mohammed was born to Fatima in New York in 1979. Fatima intended to return to Iran as soon as the Ayatollah was overthrown. In 1988, Fatima married Hussein and went with the two children to live with him in France. Bibi did not like France and in 1989 returned to live with her aunt in New York. In 1993, she came to study in London.

   a) Trace Bibi's domicile from her birth.

   b) What is Mohammed's domicile of origin?

University of London LLB Examination
(for External Students) Conflict of Laws June 1994 Q5

General Comment

This is a straightforward question to do with the domicile subject and is ideal as a first question to steady the candidate's nerves. The essay section of the question gives the opportunity to demonstrate general knowledge. The candidate must not waste too much time on this section because the marks are more easily obtained on the problem sections.

Skeleton Solution

i) Definition of 'domicile' – consideration of the case law on domicile – examination of the shortcomings with domicile – definition of 'habitual residence' – potential comparative benefits – conclusion.

ii) Factual circumstances stage by stage.

Suggested Solution

i) Domicile is the accepted test for many issues in the conflicts of laws and is of great importance with reference to United Kingdom tax legislation. Domicile requires prolonged attachment to a particular state with a long-term intention to remain resident in that state as a permanent home. There is a need for an emotional attachment, almost, to a particular nation state to establish domicile. In many of the cases, discussed below, living in another state while desiring to be in the state of domicile is the determining characteristic in deciding domicile.

The difficulty is in changing domicile in many circumstances. In *Re Clore* [1982] 2 WLR 314 the propositus had been brought to England by his parents from Lithuania and had become a successful businessman in the United Kingdom. For tax purposes he sought to move abroad so that his domicile would no longer be the United Kingdom. He began to sever important ties with the United Kingdom (such as selling his property) and took Monaco as his permanent home. However, despite his moving abroad and expressing this intention, witnesses told the court that they considered that he would eventually move back to England. There were also letters produced which demonstrated that the propositus was unhappy in Monaco. The court found that the domicile of choice in England had not been lost.

In *Buswell* v *IRC* [1974] 2 All ER 520 the propositus was born in South Africa to an English father who had acquired South Africa as his domicile of choice. The propositus moved between education in England and working in India before returning to England to work while his father recovered from ill-health. He intended to return to South Africa, having bought a farm there which he visited for three months in the year, intending it to be his family home. The only evidence to suggest an English domicile was a Revenue questionnaire where the propositus stated that he was an English resident but made no comment as to length of stay. The Court of Appeal found that this was not enough to deny the retention of the domicile of origin.

The role of the domicile of origin is that of a decisive factor in the absence of other evidence. It is difficult for the individual to shake off the domicile of origin, as in *Buswell*. In *Re Clore* the domicile of origin, technically, was England where the propositus's parents brought him when a child. This domicile could not be shaken off despite selling all United Kingdom property and moving abroad.

The test of 'habitual residence' is concerned with the place where the individual ordinarily lives. The advantage of this test is that it allows for greater flexibility. The advantage of flexibility of result is that it pays closer attention to the behaviour of the individual at the time when the subject matter of the case is concerned. Whether or not an individual is resident in a particular state at the date of a divorce is more important than the place where that individual is born. Which system of law is applied to a divorce situation, for example, is more important with reference to the residence of the individual than a domicile of choice. A rule which looks to the habitual residence of the individual would allow greater fairness between the parties.

Where there are children involved, it is better to have a system of law used connected to the residence of the family unit than another system. If the spouse has to leave the jurisdiction, the use of habitual residence can cater for the change of residence without having to look backwards to behaviour since birth. On this basis, it is submitted that greater fairness can be done between parties in all situations where a more flexible test is used.

ii) a) Bibi's domicile of origin was Iran. The issue is as to the application of the rule in *Re Beaumont* [1893] 3 Ch 490 to the situation where Fatima moves abroad to New York. The question is whether Bibi's domicile follows her mother or her father. It would appear from the judgment of Stirling J that the mother has discretion as to the domicile of her child. In this instance there is no evidence that Fatima intends to lose her Iranian domicile – it is only fear of the political situation which has caused her to leave. It would be necessary to show that she intended to return when the trouble was removed.

   In widowhood, Fatima controls Bibi's domicile: *Re Beaumont*. The issue in 1988 is then whether or not the family intends to remain in France with Fatima's new husband. Bibi is unhappy in France and chooses to live in New York. What is important at this stage is whether or not she intends to reside in New York permanently or whether she intends to return to Iran. Such an intention would mitigate her having spent ten years out of Iran.

   When she comes to study in London, this will not affect her domicile unless she forms an intention to live permanently in the United Kingdom. The issue is therefore whether she has an intention to reside permanently in New York as a domicile of choice or to return to Iran, thus retaining the domicile of origin.

   b) Mohammed's domicile of origin is dependent upon Fatima's domicile when she becomes widowed. She intends to return to Iran before her remarriage and therefore Mohammed has a domicile of origin which is Iran. The issue is whether he acquires a domicile in France when his mother moves there to live with Hussein: this would alter the domicile of Mohammed, depending upon her intention.

QUESTION TWO

In 1968 Amy, domiciled in Lilliput, married Boris, domiciled in Erewhon. They set up home together in Erewhon. In 1970 they had a son, Carlos. In 1974 Amy discovered that Boris was having an affair with Mandy. She left Boris and returned to her parents in Saxonia taking Carlos with her. In 1975 she went to work in Erewhon, but Carlos was left with his grandparents in Saxonia.

In 1978 Boris died in Erewhon at the Erewhonian International Airport. He was on his way to start a new life in Latinia with Mandy.

Amy continued to work in Erewhon. She acquired Erewhonian citizenship but said that she would return to Lilliput when she had acquired sufficient money to live on there. Carlos visited her twice a year during this period.

In 1982 Carlos ran away from his grandparents and went to live with Amy in Erewhon. He wanted to join the navy but was not old enough to do so. Between 1982 and 1987 he travelled widely. In 1987 he joined the Erewhon navy and has since been at sea, except for periods of leave which he spent in Saxonia.

Where are Amy and Carlos now domiciled?

University of London LLB Examination
(for External Students) Conflict of Laws June 1989 Q1

General Comment

If the student has a good grasp of the principles in this area, then this question will present no problems. The danger is to look for a simple/straightforward answer. Frequently insufficient information is supplied (deliberately so). This makes the latter half of the question complex, but the effort will be rewarded.

Skeleton Solution

Amy's domicile – domicile of married women before and after 1 January 1974 – domicile of choice – Carlos's domicile – domicile of origin of legitimate children – s4 of the Domicile and Matrimonial Proceedings Act 1973 – *Re Beaumont* inapplicable – domicile of choice.

Suggested Solution

We will trace the domiciles of Amy and Carlos separately and, since Carlos's domicile will in part be dependent upon Amy's, it will be convenient to begin with Amy's domicile.

Amy's domicile

At the commencement of the problem Amy is domiciled in Lilliput. But since she marries (in 1968) before the coming into operation of s1(1) of the Domicile and Matrimonial Proceedings Act 1973, the common law applies. At common law the wife took by operation of law the domicile of her husband as a domicile of dependence: *Lord Advocate* v *Jaffey* [1921] 1 AC 147. And this rule applied even if she is separated from her husband: *Attorney-General for Alberta* v *Cooke* [1926] AC 444. Thus, since Boris is domiciled in Erewhon, Amy is domiciled in Erewhon.

This continues to be the position until 1 January 1974 when the Domicile and Matrimonial Proceedings Act 1973 comes into force and Amy acquires the capacity to obtain a different domicile to her husband (s1(1)). However, s1(2) provides that a married woman was 'to be treated as retaining [her husband's] that domicile (as a domicile of choice, if it is not also her domicile of origin) unless and until it is changed by acquisition or revival of another domicile either on or after the coming into force of this section.' This means that Amy remains domiciled in Erewhon, unless and until she acquires another domicile elsewhere.

Amy, after discovering about the affair with Mandy, leaves Boris in 1974 and goes to live in Saxonia with her parents. Is this enough to change her domicile? Had she become resident in Saxonia with the right state of mind (the intention to remain for ever or, perhaps, indefinitely) she could have acquired a domicile in Saxonia. But there is nothing to indicate that this is what she has done (the onus of proving a change of domicile will rest upon the person alleging that change). *IRC* v *Duchess of Portland* [1982] Ch 314 makes clear that a woman in this sort of position is to be treated as if she had a domicile of choice derived from her husband; and thus all the requirements for abandoning a domicile of choice and acquiring a new one must be established. Similarly, if it were shown that she had cast off her domicile in Erewhon without acquiring another one, her domicile of origin which may be, but is not necessarily, in Saxonia (where her parents live) would revive. (See the discussion of Carlos's domicile of origin below.) However, the evidence is not clear enough to establish any of this; and so notwithstanding her residence in Saxonia, she remains domiciled in Erewhon.

The fact that Amy now returns to Erewhon to work suggests, but does not firmly establish, that she never had the intention to abandon her domicile in Erewhon. So she remains domiciled in Erewhon. This is so, notwithstanding that she develops the intention of returning to Lilliput when she is rich enough. If she is domiciled in Erewhon, then to change that domicile she must cast it off animo et facto (ie both in her mind and in fact by changing her residence); this she cannot do while she remains resident in Erewhon.

However, should I be wrong about the evidence not establishing that Amy did not intend to abandon her domicile in Erewhon when she moved temporarily to Saxonia, then it remains likely that on her return to Erewhon, she reacquired a domicile there. The reason for this is that although in the past the test of the intention necessary to acquire a domicile of choice was strict requiring the intention to settle permanently come what may (*Winans* v *Attorney-General* [1904] AC 287; *Ramsey* v *Royal Liverpool Infirmary* [1930] AC 588) and Amy's intention to leave Erewhon when she is rich enough plainly shows that she did not intend to stay in Erewhon 'come what may', both *Winans* and *Ramsey* concerned not only the intent to acquire a domicile of choice, but were in fact cases where it was sought to be established that the domicile of origin had been cast off (and that is a very onerous task). That is not the case here (unless the evidence shows that Amy's domicile of origin revived when she left Erewhon for the first time). Moreover, even in the old days there were suggestions that some contingent intentions might not prevent the acquisition of a domicile of choice (*Attorney-General* v *Pottinger* (1861) 30 LJE 284), and there is even a case (*Doucet* v *Geoghegan* (1878) 9 Ch D 441) in which an intention to move if he made a fortune (an intent not very different from Amy's) did not prevent a man from acquiring a domicile of choice. And, even more strongly, there are indications in the modern cases that in fact a less onerous test is today being applied: *Re Furse* [1980] 3 All ER 838 and *Re Fuld* [1968] P 675. Anyway, whichever way one approaches it Amy is domiciled in Erewhon as she has been ever since she married Boris.

Carlos's domicile

The rule is that a child takes as his domicile of origin the domicile of his father at the time of his birth (if legitimate) or the domicile of his mother at that time (illegitimate): *Henderson* v *Henderson* [1967] P 77 and *Potinger* v *Wrightman* (1817) 3 Mer 67. Since it seems plain that Carlos is legitimate, he takes as his domicile Boris's Erewhonian domicile.

At common law he will continue to take Boris's domicile as a domicile of dependence as Boris's domicile changes. However, s4 of the Domicile and Matrimonial Proceedings Act 1973 now governs the position where the parents are alive but living apart. The central rule is that if the parents 'are alive but living apart' the child shall take the domicile of its mother if (a) 'he then has his home with her and has no home with his father' or (b) if 'he has at any time had [his mother's domicile by virtue of (a)] and has not since had a home with his father': s4(2).

Thus Carlos while he has his home with his mother in Saxonia will take her domicile in Erewhon. When she returns to Erewhon leaving him in the care of his grandparents the position is a little difficult. There is an old and criticised case, *Re Beaumont* [1893] 3 Ch 490, that holds that at common law the mother can exercise a power to change the domicile of a child that is dependent upon her for its domicile in certain cases. Thus, where the mother changed her domicile but left the child in the care of a relative in its domicile of origin, the child was held to remain domiciled in its domicile of origin.

How does *Re Beaumont* affect Carlos? Probably not at all, first, because he is left in Saxonia not in his domicile of origin, and, second, because the terms of s4(2)(b) seem clear and apply to him; he has had a domicile with his mother by virtue of s4(2)(a) and he has not since had a domicile with his father. Thus, since Amy is domiciled in Erewhon so is Carlos. Carlos remains domiciled in Erewhon for so long as Amy is domiciled there and he has not reached the age at which he could acquire an independent domicile.

He reaches that age in 1986 at the age of 16, but since then he has been at sea save for short periods of leave in Saxonia. It does not seem as if he has done anything that would have the effect of changing his domicile. It may be that during his period of leave he was resident in Saxonia with the necessary intention to acquire a domicile of choice there, but this seems unlikely. Although a domicile of dependence is more easily abandoned than a domicile of choice (and a fortiori a domicile of origin), the necessary intention to settle in Saxonia would sit uneasily with his service in the Erewhonian navy. Thus he remains domiciled in Erewhon.

QUESTION THREE

In 1965, George who was domiciled in Antia set up home in Bogna with Heather, an eighteen year old with a domicile of origin in Carula. In 1968 she gave birth to Iain.

In 1970 George married Heather. By the laws of Carula and Bogna, a child is legitimated by the subsequent marriage of his parents. The institution of legitimacy by subsequent marriage does not exist in Antia.

Immediately after the marriage, George acquired a domicile of choice in England. Heather was not happy in England and longed to return to Carula. In January 1974 she left George. There was a war raging in Carula and, unable to go there, she went to Bogna. She took Iain with her. She became ill and in May 1975 sent Iain to live with her sister Jean in Edenia. Jean soon noticed that Iain missed his father and in December 1975 sent him to live with George in England. In 1979 George was killed in an accident at work. Iain was received into care by a local authority in London.

He is now at University in Scotland. He has no intention of returning permanently to England, and is hoping when he graduates next year to emigrate to the United States or Canada.

Trace Iain's domicile from his birth until today.

University of London LLB Examination
(for External Students) Conflict of Laws June 1985 Q4

General Comment

This is a very similar question to the previous one in terms of the demands placed upon the student. In addition, this requires an appreciation (and correct application) of the Legitimacy Act 1976 and Domicile and Matrimonial Proceedings Act 1973. Patience is essential.

Skeleton Solution

Ian's domicile of origin – domicile of illegitimate children – s3 of the Legitimacy Act 1976 – domicile of married women under the common law – s4 of the Domicile and Matrimonial Proceedings Act 1973 – s1(2) of the same Act – revival of the domicile of origin – inapplicability of *Re Beaumont* – s3 of the same Act – domicile of choice.

Suggested Solution

Iain's domicile of origin

The rule is that a child takes as his domicile of origin the domicile of his father at the time of his birth (if legitimate) or the domicile of his mother at that time (illegitimate): *Henderson* v *Henderson* [1967] P 77 and *Potinger* v *Wrightman* (1817) 3 Mer 67. George and Heather do not appear to be married and so Iain is illegitimate; consequently he takes as his domicile of origin, the domicile of his mother at the time of his birth. But where is Heather domiciled? We are told that her domicile of origin is in Carula but we are not told whether that is where she is domiciled at the time of Iain's birth. However, we are not told anything that suggests that that domicile is not operative at the time of Iain's birth; so it will be assumed that that domicile was operative and that Iain's domicile of origin was therefore Carula.

Iain's domicile of dependence between his birth and the marriage of George and Heather

The general rule is that an illegitimate child takes as his domicile of dependence the domicile of his mother: see the authorities cited above. We are not told of any event that would lead to a change in Heather's domicile at this time and, on the same assumption we made earlier about her domicile of origin being operative, it follows that Iain is domiciled in Carula.

Iain's domicile of dependence after the marriage and before the separation of Heather and George

First, we need to decide whether the marriage of Heather and George had the effect of legitimating Iain. The rule laid down in s3 of the Legitimacy Act 1976 is that where the father is not domiciled in England at the time of the marriage (and this is the case with Iain) the child shall be regarded as legitimated as from the date of the marriage, if at the date of the marriage the father was domiciled in a country by the law of which the illegitimate person became legitimate. Since George seems to have been domiciled in Antia at the time of the marriage (and at the time of the birth), and under the law of Antia legitimation by subsequent marriage does not exist, it appears that Iain is not legitimated. (This would be the case under common law, too.) Consequently, he does not take George's domicile as a domicile of dependence but continues to take that of his mother.

However, since George and Heather marry in 1970 before the Domicile and Matrimonial Proceedings Act 1973 comes into force, the common law will apply and Heather will take as a domicile of dependence the domicile of her husband: *Lord Advocate* v *Jaffey* [1921] 1 AC 147. Thus on marriage she will take George's domicile in Antia. Moreover, since Iain's domicile is dependent upon Heather's, he too will take a domicile in Antia when his parents marry. (This proposition is subject to what is said below about the case of *Re Beaumont* [1893] 3 Ch 490.)

Furthermore, when George (in 1970) acquires a domicile in England so does Heather, and, through Heather, so does Iain. Iain remains domiciled in England until January 1974.

Iain's domicile after the separation of George and Heather and before the death of George

After 1 January 1973 the provisions of the Domicile and Matrimonial Proceedings Act 1973 apply. But it may be that the provisions of s4(2) do not apply to this case, because s4(4) of that Act provides that 'nothing in this section prejudices any existing rule of law as to the cases in which a child's domicile is regarded as being, by dependence, that of his mother'. This is interpreted (by Dicey and Morris, Rule 15 (exception)) as preserving the common law rules as far as illegitimate (such as Iain) children are concerned. Not too much turns on this as either through the common law or through the operation of s4(2), Iain will continue to take the domicile of his mother.

And here the Domicile and Matrimonial Proceedings Act 1973 is important for in terms of s1 Heather acquired the capacity to obtain a domicile separate from that of her husband. Section 1(2) provides that where immediately before 1 January 1974 a married woman had her husband's domicile by dependence (as is the case with Heather) 'she is to be treated as retaining that domicile (as domicile of choice if it is not also her domicile of origin) unless and until it is changed by acquisition or revival of another domicile'. So Heather remains domiciled in England.

However, soon after leaving George she moves to Bogna. It seems clear that at this stage she wishes to settle in Carula, but since she has not taken up residence there she cannot obtain a domicile of choice there. Plainly she does not acquire a domicile of choice in Bogna; her residence there is of a contingent and temporary nature. Given though that she is not 'happy in England' she has probably cast off her domicile in England. Hence her domicile of origin revives: *Udny v Udny* (1869) LR 1 Sc & Div 441. She is thus domiciled in Carula; and, since Iain's domicile is dependent upon her, he too is domiciled in Carula.

Now, however, Heather falls ill and sends Iain to live with Jean in Edenia. What effect does this have? It is time to discuss *Re Beaumont*. This case holds that at common law the mother can exercise a power to change the domicile of a child that is dependent upon her for its domicile in certain cases. Thus where the mother changed her domicile but left the child in the care of relatives in its domicile of origin, the child was held to remain domiciled in its domicile of origin. Does this exception to the ordinary rule apply in Iain's case? It seems not. First, Iain is not sent to his domicile of origin but to Edenia. Second, it may be that *Re Beaumont* does not apply to illegitimate children such as Iain, since their domicile of origin is already derived from their mother, not from their father. Hence the better view is that Iain continues to take Heather's domicile as a domicile of dependence, even though he goes to live with his father in England. This is artificial, but it seems to be the law; and his father's death makes no difference. Of course, were Iain legitimate (and s4(2) applied) then he would take his father's domicile through operation of law when he had a home with his father. Should Iain be legitimate, then on the death of his father his domicile would again be determined by his mother (and she is still domiciled in Carula).

Iain's domicile after the death of George

Whether s4 applies or not once George dies it is clear that Iain's domicile is determined by his mother until he reaches the age of 16 in 1984: s3 of the Domicile and Matrimonial

Proceedings Act 1973. As far as we can tell during this period she remains domiciled in Carula, so Iain is too.

On reaching the age of 16 Iain has the capacity to acquire his own domicile anywhere he likes. But has he done so? He has certainly not settled in Scotland and whatever his intentions he has never been resident in the USA so he cannot obtain a domicile there. If he ever had a domicile in England, he seems to have abandoned it since he 'has no intention of returning permanently to England'. Hence his domicile of origin must have revived and, according to our earlier assumption, he is domiciled in Carula.

QUESTION FOUR

In 1967, Ali, a Muslim domiciled in Pakistan, married Bibi, domiciled in India. In 1969, a son, Mohammed, was born to them. In 1979, Ali died in local fighting.

Bibi decided to return to India to her family. However, she could not leave Pakistan until she had wound up Ali's affairs there. Concerned for Mohammed's safety, she sent him to her brother's in Calcutta in India, intending to follow herself as soon as possible. In 1984, Bibi, having sold all her property in Pakistan, started on the journey for Calcutta. Unfortunately, the train on which she was travelling crashed just before crossing the border and Bibi was killed.

Mohammed remained at his uncle's home in Calcutta. In 1987, he got a job working for the local jute mill. Mohammed's interest in the jute trade stemmed from the fact that his paternal grandfather owned a very large jute mill in Pakistan. Mohammed hoped that if he were to get experience in the business, then his grandfather would select him to take over the management of the mill in Pakistan in preference to his older cousins.

In December 1991, Mohammed heard that his grandfather had chosen one of his cousins to take over the jute mill. He was bitterly disappointed. In January 1992, he received a letter from an old friend, who had settled in England, offering him a place in his successful textile business near Bradford. Mohammed decided to take up the offer in the rather vain hope that the experience in England would persuade his grandfather to change his mind. He arrived in England in February 1992 and rented accommodation in Bradford.

In March 1993, Mohammed returned for a holiday to see his uncle in India. While he was there he married Fatima in a Muslim ceremony. In Muslim law, as applied in India and Pakistan, a man is allowed to take more than one wife.

a) Trace Mohammed's domicile from his birth to the date of his marriage.

b) Discuss how, if at all, the validity of the marriage is affected by your conclusions about his domicile.

University of London LLB Examination
(for External Students) Conflict of Laws June 1993 Q1

General Comment

A rather more demanding question as it combines the relatively straightforward principles of domicile with the area of marriage (essential and formal validity). Students must ensure that sufficient (ie detailed) discussion of (b) is included in their answer. Time management is essential.

Skeleton Solution

a) The leading cases, especially *Udny* v *Udny* and *Re Beaumont*, must be noted, and their relevance to the question must be quickly established – contrast between Bibi and Mohammed's case and *Re Beaumont* – how an independent domicile of choice is acquired.

b) Essential and formal validity of a potentially polygamous marriage – recognition, or otherwise, of such a marriage by English law.

Suggested Solution

a) Domicile is 'an idea of law': *Bell* v *Kennedy* (1868) LR 1 Sc & Div 307. Its significance is that it gives rise to 'that legal relationship between a person ... and a territory subject to a distinctive legal system which invokes [that] system as [his] personal law': *Henderson* v *Henderson* [1967] P 77 and cited by Scarman J in *Re Fuld* [1968] P 675. In the leading case on domicile, *Udny* v *Udny* (1869) LR 1 Sc & Div 441, Lord Westbury said 'it is an established principle that no man shall be without a domicile.' Accordingly, at every stage of his life, Mohammed will have a domicile, whether it be of origin, of dependence, or of choice. In determining Mohammed's domicile at the various stages of his life, it is to be noted that, as a general rule, domicile is determined according to the English concept of domicile and not that of a foreign law: *Lawrence* v *Lawrence* [1985] Fam 106.

That Mohammed was born a legitimate baby means that 'the law attribute[d] to him as soon as he [was] born the domicile of his father ... This has been called the domicile of origin and is involuntary': per Lord Westbury in *Udny* v *Udny*. Accordingly, Mohammed has a Pakistani domicile of origin and domicile of dependence: *Re Duleep Singh* (1890) 6 TLR 385. On Ali's death, the general rule would be that Mohammed retains his father's domicile until he reaches the age of 16 when he is able to acquire an independent domicile of choice: s3(1) Domicile and Matrimonial Proceedings Act (DMPA) 1973. However, as Mohammed was aged ten when his father died in 1979, he would first of all acquire the domicile of his mother, if different, as a domicile of dependence: *Potinger* v *Wrightman* (1817) 3 Mer 67. In 1979 Bibi's Pakistani domicile, which she acquired as a domicile of dependence at the time of her marriage in 1967, was replaced by a deemed Pakistani domicile of choice: s1(2) DMPA 1973. At this stage, then, there would appear to be no change in Mohammed's domicile of dependence (his domicile of origin will change only if he is adopted: Children Act 1975, s8 and Schedule 1).

However, when, in 1979(?), Bibi sends Mohammed to her brother in Calcutta, India, it is uncertain whether the act, performed out of concern for his safety, will change Mohammed's domicile of dependence from Pakistani to Indian. What has to be ascertained is whether the principle in *Re Beaumont* [1893] 3 Ch 490 applies.

In *Re Beaumont* Mrs B, a widow domiciled in Scotland with four infant children, remarried and took three of her children to live in England with her new husband, whereupon they all acquired English domiciles. However, one daughter, Catherine, remained in Scotland where she had lived from the time of her father's death, which was 13 years before her mother remarried. When Catherine died soon after reaching the age of majority, it became necessary to determine where she was domiciled in order to decide who could benefit from her share in a trust fund. Stirling J decided that:

> ' ... the domicil of [a minor] which may follow from a change of domicil on the part of the mother, is not to be regarded as the necessary consequence of a change of the mother's domicil, but as the result of the exercise by her of a power vested in her for the welfare of the [minor], which in [the minor's] interest she may abstain from exercising, even when she changes her own domicil.'

Thus, it is submitted that *Re Beaumont* can be distinguished from Bibi and Mohammed's case in at least two major respects, firstly in respect of the acquisition of a new domicile of choice, which is effected by residing in a new country (factum) and having the intention to reside there 'indefinitely' (animus): *Re Fuld*. Whereas in *Re Beaumont* Mrs B had both factum and animus to acquire a new domicile (which was of dependence), Bibi lacked factum. That she had the clear intention of abandoning her domicile of choice in Pakistan was ineffective since she did not succeed in leaving the country: *In the Goods of Raffenel* (1863) 3 Sw & Tr 49. Consequently, Bibi died domiciled in Pakistan. Secondly, in *Re Beaumont*, Mrs B, who as noted had acquired a new domicile, abstained from exercising her power to change Catherine's domicile, ie Catherine's domicile was preserved. Bibi, in contrast, who failed to change her own domicile, aimed to change Mohammed's.

It would appear to accord with principle that Bibi's action in sending Mohammed to live with her brother in India was a bona fide exercise of her power effected for the sole purpose of promoting the welfare of Mohammed. Whether this would effect a change in Mohammed's domicile of dependency from Pakistan to India when Bibi's domicile has not changed is uncertain although, in the absence of authority, it may be presumed that Mohammed's domicile has not changed.

However, irrespective of any change of domicile of dependence between 1979 and 1984, in 1988 when Mohammed was 16 years of age, he was able to acquire a domicile of choice in India: s3(1) DMPA 1973. He would keep this domicile on arrival in England in 1992 because it is clear that he hoped to return to Pakistan to manage the large jute mill. This would prevent his acquisition of the animus necessary for a change of domicile: *Winans* v *Attorney-General* [1904] AC 287 and *IRC* v *Bullock* [1976] 1 WLR 1178.

b) As to the validity of Mohammed's marriage to Fatima in 1993, the fact that it might
    well have been formally and essentially valid under the lex loci celebrationis (India)
    does not ensure its validity under English law.

From the information given, there is no reason to presume other than that
Mohammed's marriage was formally valid by the lex loci celebrationis, that both
he and Fatima had the capacity to marry, and that they consented to the marriage,
thus giving the marriage essential validity by the 'dual domicile' test. However, that
by Muslim law Mohammed is allowed to take more than one wife is a principle
that does not accord with the English idea of marriage as defined by Lord Penzance
in *Hyde* v *Hyde* (1866) LR 1 P & D 130 where he said that it was a 'voluntary union
for life of one man and one woman to the exclusion of all others'.

Accordingly, it appears that Mohammed has contracted a potentially polygamous
marriage. The law in this area has been clarified by the Private International Law
(Miscellaneous Provisions) Act (PIL(MP)A) 1995. Section 5(1) of the Act provides
that a marriage entered into outside England between a couple, neither of whom is
married, is not void under the law of England because it is solemnised under a law
which permits polygamy, even if one of the parties, or both, is domiciled in
England. Therefore marriages which are potentially polygamous will be recognised
as valid as long as neither party in the relationship has previously married.

This may be contrasted with the common law position prior to the PIL(MP)A 1995.
According to the common law it was for the lex loci celebrationis to determine the
nature and incidents of the marriage and then for English law to decide whether the
union is a monogamous or a polygamous marriage: *Lee* v *Lau* [1967] P 14. Whether
or not Mohammed exercises his privilege of entering into another marriage
contemporaneously is irrelevant from the point of view that English law places an
actually polygamous marriage and a potentially polygamous marriage in the same
category: *Hyde* v *Hyde*.

However, if Mohammed and Fatima later acquire an English domicile, it may be
that from the time they established the animus (intention) to remain in England
their marriage will be recognised as monogamous: *Ali* v *Ali* [1968] P 564. The
apparent uncertainty of this decision is, perhaps, matched by the surprise decision
which would have been the likely outcome had Mohammed been domiciled in
England and married in India a woman, such as Fatima, who was domiciled in
India. He would not have contracted a potentially polygamous marriage; as the
personal law of each spouse would not permit him or her to take another spouse
during the substance of their marriage a valid monogamous marriage would have
been contracted: *Hussain* v *Hussain* [1983] Fam 26.

Unless there is some good reason why Mohammed's (potentially) polygamous
marriage should not be recognised in England, and there doesn't appear to be any
such reason, the general rule is that English law will recognise it and other
polygamous marriages: *Mohammed* v *Knott* [1969] 1 QB 1. The marriage will be

recognised for purposes which include it being a bar to a subsequent monogamous marriage. Thus if a second 'marriage' was contracted, the second wife would be entitled to a decree of nullity based on bigamy: *Srini Vasan* v *Srini Vasan* [1946] P 67. Such a second 'marriage' would not, apparently, lead to Mohammed being indicted for bigamy: *R* v *Sarwan Singh* [1962] 3 All ER 612, though he might be liable for perjury if he claimed to be a single man and to know of no impediment to his marriage.

QUESTION FIVE

Trace the domicile of George from his birth until his death last week.

He was born in 1915 to Nicole, an unmarried French domiciliary. His father, Jock, who was domiciled in Scotland, was a soldier in the British Army serving in France in the First World War. In 1918 Jock returned in the Britain and got an apprenticeship in England. George remained with his mother in France. In 1920 Nicole joined Jock in England. She left George with her sister who had married a Belgian domicilary and was living in Brussels. In 1922 Nicole and Jock married and established their matrimonial home in England. George was brought up by his aunt and uncle in Belgium. He spent a month with his parents in England each year. In 1927 Jock became unemployed and went to Canada in search of a job. He found another woman and in 1929 divorced Nicole and married her. Although happy in British Columbia he always wanted to return to Scotland. However, he was killed in an accident in 1930. In 1929 Nicole remarried and she and her new husband emigrated to Australia settling in New South Wales.

At the age of 18, George joined a French missionary order. He was ordained as a priest, took vows of poverty, chastity and obedience and disposed of all his property. He was sent by his order to minister to the poor of Paraguay. He returned to France in 1939. In 1940 when German forces invaded France, he escaped to England and spent the war as a chaplain to the Free French Forces in England.

After the war he left the missionary order and became a Protestant clergyman in England. He served as a priest in England for the next 40 years (apart from a brief secondment to a community in the Falkland Islands between 1981–1984).

In 1986 George became seriously ill and retired. He went to live in a religious community in France. Earlier this year, told by his doctor that he only had a few months to live, decided to move to a warmer climate where he believed he would feel better. The religious community arranged for him to join a monastery in Spain, where he stayed until he died.

University of London LLB Examination
(for External Students) Conflict of Laws June 1998 Q9

General Comment

This is an ideal question for the well-prepared and knowledgeable student. There are a few issues which should be kept in mind with this type of question though. First, it should be noted that George is the focus of the question. Therefore any analysis of other individuals must be related back to him. Second, do not simply choose the easiest solution. It may be that there is no correct answer at any one stage – which necessarily complicates latter sections of the question. Finally, this question demands patience.

Skeleton Solution

Domicile of origin – domicile of choice and special cases – domicile of dependence – the age of majority – legitimated children.

Suggested Solution

The question commences by stating that George was born to Nicole, an unmarried French domiciliary. Consequently, we may immediately deal with George's domicile of origin. According to the case of *Udny* v *Udny* (1869) LR 1 Sc & Div 441, if a child is illegitimate then he shall be attributed the domicile of his mother. In this case it is France. It should be noted that George will never lose this domicile of origin and it will revive at any time that he loses a subsequent domicile of choice and does not immediately replace it: *Harrison* v *Harrison* [1953] 1 WLR 865.

We are told that George remains with his mother in France between 1915 and 1920. It should be noted that the activities of Jock (his father) do not have a bearing on George's domicile during this time. It should also be noted that throughout this period and until George reaches the age of majority, he would have a domicile of dependence. As a general rule the domicile of such person will be the same as, and changes with, the domicile of the person on whom they are legally dependent. In the case of illegitimate children this person will be the mother: *Potinger* v *Wrightman* (1817) 3 Mer 67. As such, George's domicile of dependence will be that of France throughout this period. However, in 1920, Nicole leaves France in order to join Jock in England. This raises a number of issues.

First of all, according to the rule noted above, George's domicile of dependence will change when Nicole's domicile changes. Therefore, does Nicole acquire a domicile of choice in England when she joins Jock in 1920? The general rule is that every independent person can acquire a new domicile by his or her own actions. The requirement is that Nicole must take up residence in the new state with the intention of remaining there permanently. Therefore, according to cases such as *Bell* v *Kennedy* (1868) LR 1 SC & Div 307 we need to look at Nicole's state of mind at this particular time. There is actually very little information provided in the question which invites us to make assumptions. In this instance it may be suggested that: (a) Nicole leaves George with her sister in Brussels (Belgium) (as such she would appear to cut links with France in terms of family); (b) Nicole went to England in order to live with Jock (the father of her child); and (c) she eventually marries Jock in 1922 and they establish their matrimonial home in England – though this will have other implications. Consequently, it may be suggested that she acquires a domicile of choice in England.

The second question is whether or not this affects George's domicile of dependence during this period. This invites consideration of the case of *Re Beaumont* [1893] 3 Ch 490 which involved a Scottish widow leaving her child behind in Scotland in the care of her aunt whilst she moved to England to set up home with her second husband. It was held that a change in domicile of an infant was 'not to be regarded as a necessary consequence of a change of the mother's domicile'. Rather, such a change may result from the exercise of a power vested in the mother that she may abstain from exercising. The question is what effect the decision in *Re Beaumont* would have on this present scenario. As with any problem question, the answer is not always straightforward or indeed certain. The fact that Nicole moved George to Belgium to live with her sister (as opposed to leaving him in the original country with a family member) may have a bearing on the outcome. It is far from certain whether a mother may only preserve a domicile that would otherwise change (ie France) or whether by sending the child away she may change the domicile of the child (ie Belgium).

In any event, Nicole and Jock marry in 1922 and set up their matrimonial home in England. This has implications for both Nicole and George.

a) Prior to the Domicile and Matrimonial Proceedings Act 1973, at common law a married woman took the domicile of her husband as a domicile of dependence. As her husband changed his domicile so her domicile changed – irrespective of her wishes and irrespective of whether she continued to live with him: see *Lord Advocate v Jaffey* [921] 1 AC 147. Therefore, from this point onwards we may state that Nicole, as a married woman, has a domicile of dependence – which may be that of England. (See (b) below.)

b) This also has a bearing on George's domicile. Although there is no authority on the matter, Morris (*The Conflict of Laws* (2000), 5th ed at p40) states that it seems likely that 'the domicile of a legitimated child would be dependent on that of its father … if the legitimation was effected by the subsequent marriage of the parents.' Consequently, following the marriage of Jock and Nicole in 1922, George's domicile of dependence is then reliant on Jock. At this stage Jock's domicile may be that of England. Once again the question must be posed as to whether Jock has lost his domicile in Scotland (we are not informed whether this is a domicile of origin or choice) and acquired one in England. As noted above this is dependent on the two key issues of physical presence – which is satisfied since 1918 – and intention to reside there permanently. The latter issue may pose problems: see cases such as *Ramsey* v *Royal Liverpool Infirmary* [1930] AC 588 and *Winans* v *Attorney-General* [1904] AC 287. Both of these cases illustrate the problem faced by the courts when attempting to determine an individual's state of mind. However, as per *Drevon* v *Drevon* (1834) 34 LJ Ch 129, 'there is no act, no circumstance in a man's life, however trivial it may be in itself, which ought to be left out of consideration in trying the question whether there was an intention to change domicile.' The fact that Jock has: lived in England since 1918; worked in England of his own free will during this time; married Nicole in England and set up a matrimonial home with her there; and remained there until he became unemployed in 1927, may suggest that he acquired a domicile of choice in England. Otherwise, it would remain that of Scotland. This in turn dictates George's domicile of dependence during this period.

In 1927 Jock leaves England and travels to Canada in search of work. As with the discussion outlined above, the question as to whether he acquires a domicile of choice in Canada is far from simple. We are not provided with sufficient information as to whether he intends to return to England – the fact that Nicole remains there suggest that he may return – or whether he intends to bring Nicole to Canada once he has found a job. We are told later on in the scenario that although he is happy in Canada (British Columbia) that he wishes to return to Scotland. This would appear to indicate a lack of intention to reside there permanently. As such, it may be suggested that he failed to acquire a domicile of choice there and remains domiciled in England (or Scotland depending upon the outcome of our earlier discussion). This needs to be linked back to George who is still classified as a dependent.

However, we are told that by 1929 Jock divorces Nicole and marries another woman. In this particular case we need to consider the following issues.

First, the general rule is that George's domicile of dependence should follow that of his father, despite the fact that he has separated from Nicole. However, there is the possibility of a common law exception – *Hope* v *Hope* [1968] NI 1 (no English authority exists) – which suggests that where a father has totally abdicated his responsibility for the child and custody has been granted to the mother, the child should cease to follow the father's domicile. If this is the case, then George's domicile of dependence may follow that of Nicole as opposed to that of Jock. (Given the general lack of contact between father a son over the past 12 years and Jock's remarriage in Canada, it would appear to support this exception.)

Second, prior to the divorce Nicole's domicile of dependence follows the domicile of Jock. However, following the divorce she is capable of acquiring her own domicile again. However, given the fact that she remains in England until her remarriage in 1929, this will not alter. On her remarriage she will adopt another domicile of dependence which, following her emigration to New South Wales (Australia), will be that of New South Wales so long as both issues of residence and intention are satisfied.

It should be noted that until 1 January 1970 a domicile of dependence applied to everyone under the age of 21: s1 Family Law Reform Act 1969. Therefore, George does not reach the age of majority until 1936 in this question and as such these changes in Nicole's domicile will affect George's domicile of dependence. (This is especially so following Jock's death in 1930 – see earlier discussion.)

We are told that George is ordained as a priest at the age of 18 and subsequently sent to minister in Paraguay where he remains until 1939. The question arises as to whether

George acquires a domicile of choice in Paraguay. As per our discussion earlier, he certainly satisfies the requirement of residence – living in Paraguay until his return to France in 1939. However, the scenario demands that we focus on the requirement of intention. Rather than analysing the general rule, it is worth commencing our discussion with a consideration of the various exceptions and special cases. These include prisoners, refugees, fugitives, invalids and the final category of employees, diplomats and soldiers. The traditional view was that service and residence abroad by diplomats, employees and service personnel would not normally give rise to a change of domicile as the residence was linked to duties that were intended only to last for a limited period of time: *Attorney-General* v *Rowe* (1862) 1 H & C 31. However, this has gradually changed to become an issue of nature and degree, in that an individual may acquire a new domicile if there is evidence that he intends to settle there once he becomes free from his obligation to reside there: *Donaldson* v *Donaldson* [1949] P 363. It may be suggested that since George took vows of 'poverty, chastity and obedience', then he falls within the former category – his presence in Paraguay is due to his vocation and as such he has no intention of residing there. If this fails then, under the general rule, he also fails to satisfy the requirement of intention. As noted in the first paragraph of this answer, where George loses a domicile and does not acquire a new one, his domicile of origin will revive in order to fill the gap (that of France).

In 1939 he returns to France but in 1940 escapes to England where he works with the Free French Forces. This invites us to consider another one of the special cases when dealing with the possible acquisition of a domicile of choice – refugees. Such cases will depend upon the circumstances. If George intends to return to France once conditions change then he would not acquire a domicile in England: *Re Lloyd Evans* [1947] Ch 695. However, if George gives up hope of returning to France and intends to settle in England, he may very well acquire a domicile there: *May* v *May* [1943] 2 All ER 146.

Whilst it is difficult to make any comment as to whether George acquires a domicile of choice in England between 1940 and the end of the war, there is evidence that he falls within the *May* v *May* example when he decides to remain in England as a Protestant clergyman. This is lent support by the fact that he remains in England for the next 40 years. However, the possibility that George never satisfies the requirement of intention should not be overlooked, especially given cases such as *Ramsey* v *Royal Liverpool Infirmary* (above). This is a distinct possibility given the fact that when he becomes ill and eventually retires in 1986 he goes to live in France.

George continues to live in France until 1998 (the date of the question), a period of 12 years. Once again, if he had acquired a domicile of choice in England between 1945 and 1986, then the question should be posed as to whether he has replaced this with a domicile in France. However, if he had not acquired a domicile in England, his presence in France will have little practical effect on his domicile, given that his domicile of origin is that of France. Finally, he moves to Spain due to his health. The question needs to be posed as to whether this is a situation similar to that of *Winans* v *Attorney General* (above).

QUESTION SIX

Ann and Bishan have recently died leaving movable property in England. By what law is this to be distributed?

Ann married Gyorgy in 1967 in London. He has a domicile of origin in Hungary but fled to England after the 1956 revolution. She has a domicile of origin in California. He has said he would always like to return to Budapest, but has now built up a large business in London, and is actively involved in British politics. Ann, though content to live in London, has always hoped to persuade her husband to relocate to California. She has spent a few weeks each year in the last six years in California and on her last visit purchased a luxury mansion for the two of them. Six months ago she persuaded her husband to give California a go and the two of them set out for the United States last week. They died in a plane crash over the Atlantic.

Bishan is the child of Indira and Raj. They were not married when Bishan was born. Raj was brought up in England by parents who were domiciled in India. In 1978, when Bishan was born, Raj was 30 and had made his home in England: unlike his parents he only spoke English. Indira had been brought to England from India when a teenager by parents who settled successfully in Leicester but she had never adapted to the English way of life and yearned to return to India. Bishan's parents married each other in 1981. The marriage was not successful and in 1985 they separated and Bishan was taken by his mother to India. Bishan found India too hot and his mother arranged for him to go and live with an aunt in Toronto. He lived there until his parents divorced in 1990, at which point his aunt sent him to live with his father. He was not happy with his father and ran away to his aunt in Toronto in 1992. He lived in Toronto until late in 1993 when he decided to explore the world as a back-packer. He was in Thailand on his sixteenth birthday when he was kidnapped and taken by guerillas to Indonesia. Converted to their cause, he joined a liberation army in Indonesia. He was killed in an ambush last month.

University of London LLB Examination
(for External Students) Conflict of Laws June 1996 Q8

General Comment

This is a question relating to domicile. But it is confusing at the outset, with the student having to decide which topic is predominant: property or domicile.

Skeleton Solution

Ann: the common law position relating to the domicile of the married woman – s1(1) Domicile and Matrimonial Proceedings Act 1973 – domicile of choice – revival of the domicile of origin.

Bishan: illegitimate child: domicile of mother or father? – domicile of choice – *Re Beaumont*: whether applicable – infringement of freedom of choice by outside factors.

Suggested Solution

Before tracing the domiciles of Ann and Bishan, it is important to note that domicile is a connecting factor of potentially great significance to all individuals. In this case, it will be particularly influential in determining the distribution of their movable property, which at present is in England.

As domicile is a connecting factor, the domicile of both Ann and Bishan will be determined by the lex fori (*Re Annesley* [1926] Ch 692), and 'it is a settled principle that (neither Ann nor Bishan) shall be without a domicile': *Udny* v *Udny* (1869) LR 1 Sc & Div 441.

Ann married in 1967 bringing to her marriage a Californian domicile of origin. She will take her husband's domicile as a domicile of dependence (*Lord Advocate* v *Jaffey* [1921] 1 AC 147) until 1 January 1974, when, under s1(1) Domicile and Matrimonial Proceedings Act (DMPA) 1973, she is able to acquire her own domicile of choice. This section states that:

> 'The domicile of a married woman as at any time after the coming into force of this section [1 January 1974] shall, instead of being the same as her husband's by virtue only of marriage, be ascertained by reference to the same factors as in the case of any individual capable of having an independent domicile.'

Ann will thus be liberated from her domicile of dependence which was relegated to 'the last barbarous relic of a wife's servitude': *Gray (otherwise Formosa)* v *Formosa* [1963] P 259.

Ann will retain her husband's domicile as her domicile of choice until she acquires a new domicile: *IRC* v *Duchess of Portland* [1982] Ch 314. It would appear on the facts, therefore, that Ann will gain an English domicile of dependence, because her husband seems to have acquired an English domicile of choice. But, we are told that her husband has always wanted to return to Hungary and thus he may have lacked the necessary animus (or intention to reside) sufficient to establish an English domicile of choice: *Bell* v *Kennedy* (1868) LR 1 Sc & Div 307.

Whichever domicile of dependence Ann had acquired from 1967–1974, whether Hungarian or English, it is clear that from 1974 she has no indefinite or permanent intention to reside in England. Her residence in England, though lengthy is 'colourless': *Ramsey* v *Liverpool Royal Infirmary* [1930] AC 588. From 1990, she has spent time in California and, in 1996, she abandoned any existing domicile by 'ceasing to reside (in England) and by ceasing to intend to reside there permanently or indefinitely or otherwise': Dicey & Morris (Rule 13).

Ann did not acquire a domicile of choice in California, because of the absence of factum (or residence), but under these circumstances her Californian domicile of origin will revive. Such a domicile is extremely tenacious 'its character is more enduring, its hold stronger and less easily shaken off ': *Winans* v *Attorney-General* [1904] AC 287. Once the previous domicile has been abandoned, it cannot be revived: *In the Goods of Raffenel* (1863) 3 Sw & Tr 49.

Ann dies domiciled in California and her property will be distributed according to this law, being the law of the last domicile.

In tracing Bishan's domicile, it is clear from the outset that he is illegitimate and will therefore take the domicile of his mother at the time of his birth in 1978: *Henderson* v *Henderson* [1967] P 77; *Potinger* v *Wrightman* (1817) 3 Mer 67. The issue now is the domicile of his mother (Indira) at this time. She appears to have an Indian domicile of origin, but an English domicile of dependence. Whereas, at 16, she was capable of acquiring a domicile of choice by her own actions, it appears on the facts that she had insufficient animus to have acquired an English domicile of choice. Whilst in this situation, her Indian domicile of origin will revive: *Bell* v *Kennedy*. At this stage, Bishan will have an Indian domicile of origin and dependence. When he was sent to Toronto, he would retain his Indian domicile, unless his mother had taken positive steps to change it for his benefit: *Re Beaumont* [1893] 3 Ch 490. It is not known whether Re Beaumont would apply here, as Bishan was illegitimate and had been sent from his domicile of origin, unlike Catherine Beaumont, who was legitimate and was allowed to stay in her domicile of origin. Also, Bishan was left with his aunt for a specific purpose and there is no evidence that the arrangement was to be permanent. Between the ages of 12 and 16 his domicile had not changed and at 16 he was able to acquire his own domicile of choice by his own actions, ie by combining animus with factum. It is essential that these elements coincide if the law is to recognise a change in domicile.

There is a problem here, however, in that Bishan is not free to choose his domicile at this time, and it was stated in *Udny* v *Udny* per Lord Westbury that 'there must be a residence freely chosen and not prescribed or dictated by any external necessity'. Thus Bishan's freedom to make a choice was infringed, which would render a Thai domicile invalid. Later, when Bishan became converted to the cause, it is possible that he acquired an Indonesian domicile of choice, which is his domicile at death. This will be largely evidential, but if established Bishan's property will be distributed according to the law of Indonesia, being the law of his last domicile.

Chapter 4

Jurisdiction I – the Common Law Rules

4.1   Introduction

4.2   Key points

4.3   Key cases and statutes

4.4   Questions and suggested solutions

4.1 Introduction

The issue of the jurisdiction of the English courts has been confused by the existence of two separate regimes, one a creation of the common law, the other a creation of statute. The Civil Jurisdiction and Judgments Act 1982, and now Council Regulation 44/2001/EC, radically changed the law relating to jurisdiction but only in relation to defendants domiciled – in the statutory sense of the term – in member states of the European Union. Where the statutory provisions are inapplicable, the common law rules continue to apply.

When considering the common law rules, a thorough appreciation of the concept of forum non conveniens, together with its acceptance into English law, is essential.

4.2 Key points

The concept of jurisdiction in personam in common law

Jurisdiction in personam is the power of the courts to exercise authority over individuals. Put another way, it is the authority of a court to hear a case involving proceedings brought by a plaintiff against a defendant.

Jurisdiction in personam is not determined by reference to the status or otherwise of the plaintiff nor the subject-matter of the dispute. It is the power of the court over the defendant that is the critical issue.

A distinction is usually made between jurisdiction in personam and jurisdiction in rem. Jurisdiction in personam is the authority of the court over particular persons, for example, a defendant in an action for breach of contract. Jurisdiction in rem relates to the court's jurisdiction over physical property, eg a ship.

As a general principle, English law confers jurisdiction on the basis of jurisdiction in personam. There are few exceptions to this general rule, the most notable being Admiralty actions in rem.

The common law rules of jurisdiction

On the whole, jurisdiction in personam in England is relatively straightforward. English courts exercise jurisdiction over any person present within the boundaries of the country on whom a valid claim form (formerly referred to as a writ) has been served within England.

There is no requirement that either of the parties to the proceedings should be resident or domiciled in England. The only requirement regarding residence is that the defendant must be physically located in England when the claim form is served: see *Maharanee of Baroda* v *Wildenstein* [1972] 2 QB 283.

Two additional rules relating to jurisdiction in personam should be noted at this stage:

a) Where a defendant is outside England, a plaintiff may apply to the court for leave to serve the claim form outside the jurisdiction: Civil Procedure Rules (CPR) r6. If the leave of the court to serve the claim form out of the jurisdiction is granted, once again the English courts are willing to exercise jurisdiction.

b) Where the parties voluntarily submit to the jurisdiction of the English courts, the courts have generally been willing to exercise jurisdiction even if neither the dispute nor the parties have any connection with England.

Hence, the jurisdiction in personam of the English courts is extensive and the rules for limiting the exercise of jurisdiction may charitably be described as liberal.

The general rule in common law

At common law, the overriding principle is that a court has jurisdiction in personam over anyone who has been validly served with a claim form in England. As the court observed in *John Russell & Co Ltd* v *Cayzer, Irvine & Co Ltd* [1916] 2 AC 298, 'whoever is served with the King's writ [claim form] and can be compelled consequently to submit to the decree made is a person over which the courts have jurisdiction'.

The principal exception is the case where a defendant has been lured into the territory on some false pretext by the plaintiff: see *Watkins* v *North American Land and Timber Co* (1904) 20 TLR 534.

Service of the claim form on persons

The service of a claim form is essential in establishing jurisdiction in personam. The situation is relatively straightforward when the individual is present in England or submits to the jurisdiction of the English courts, but becomes progressively more difficult when the defendant is abroad when service of the claim form is required.

When the defendant is a private individual physically located in England, claim forms may be served in two main ways:

a) By post (CPR r6.2(1)(b)).

b) By personal service (CPR r6.4).

Personal service is effected on an individual by handing over a copy of the claim form. If the defendant refuses to accept the claim form, it can be simply left near to him after he has been informed of its contents: see *Barclays Bank of Swaziland* v *Hahn* [1989] 1 WLR 506.

If the defendant is a company, the claim form must be properly served within the jurisdiction. Where a company is registered in England, the claim form should be served at its registered office: see s725 of the Companies Act 1985.

Foreign incorporated companies are deemed to be present in England if they carry on business in England. Under ss691 and 695 of the Companies Act 1985, a foreign company must notify the Registrar of Companies of a specific employee and address where service of claim forms may be made and any claim form properly served at that address will be deemed to be valid: see *South India Shipping Co* v *Export-Import Bank of Korea* [1985] 2 All ER 219.

Leave to serve a claim form on persons abroad

Where a defendant is not present in England and has not submitted to the jurisdiction of the court, an application may be made to the court for leave to serve the claim form outside the jurisdiction of the court: CPR r6. (This is sometimes referred to as making an application under RSC O.11, which is the former system governing this area.)

The grant of leave to serve a claim form outside the jurisdiction of the court is discretionary and is a power which is exercised by the courts 'with extreme caution and with full regard in every case to the circumstances': *Cordova Land Co* v *Victor Brothers Inc* [1966] 1 WLR 793. The onus is on the plaintiff to establish that there is a strong case before leave with be granted.

CPR r6.20 states the circumstances on which leave may be granted. Amongst these are the following where:

a) a defendant is domiciled within the jurisdiction of the English courts, leave may be granted: CPR r6.20(1). Domicile in this connection is not the same as the concept of domicile in common law but is the statutory definition contained in ss41–46 of the Civil Jurisdiction and Judgments Act 1982.

b) an injunction is sought ordering the defendant to do, or to refrain from doing, some act within the jurisdiction: CPR r6.20(2).

c) a person is 'a necessary and proper party' in an action against a person duly served within or out of the jurisdiction: CPR r6.20(3) and see *MB Pyramid Sound NV* v *Briese Schiffarts GmbH & Co* [1993] 2 Lloyd's Rep 453.

d) a claim is brought to enforce, rescind, dissolve, annul or otherwise affect a contract, or to recover damages or obtain other relief in respect of the breach of a contract: CPR r6.20(5)–(7) and see *Gulf Bank KSC v Mitsubishi Heavy Industries Ltd* [1994] 1 Lloyd's Rep 323; *Brinkibon Ltd v Stahag Stahl* [1982] 2 AC 34.

e) a contract has been breached within the jurisdiction of the court. It is irrelevant whether the contract was made within or outside the jurisdiction: CPR r6.20(6) and see *Johnson v Taylor* [1920] AC 144 .

f) a claim is founded on a tort and the damage was sustained, or resulted from an act committed within the jurisdiction: CPR r6.20(8) and see *Metall und Rohstoff AG v Donaldson Lufkin & Jenrette Inc* [1989] 3 WLR 563.

g) an action is brought to enforce any judgment or arbitration award: CPR r6.20(9).

h) the whole subject matter of an action relates to property located within the jurisdiction: CPR r6.20(10).

i) the claim is brought to execute the trusts of a written instrument being trusts which ought to be executed according to English law: CPR r6.20(11).

j) a claim is made for the administration of an estate of a person who dies domiciled within the jurisdiction or for any relief or remedy which may be obtained in any such action: CPR r6.20(12).

k) relief is sought in a claim brought in a probate action: CPR r6.20(13).

l) a claim is brought against a defendant not domiciled in Scotland or Northern Ireland in respect of a claim brought by the Commissioners of Inland Revenue: CPR r6.20(16)

It should be stressed that giving permission to serve outside the jurisdiction is discretionary. See discussion below relating to CPR r6.21(2A).

Jurisdiction over defendants who submit to the jurisdiction of the court

Defendants who would not otherwise be subject to the jurisdiction of the English courts may voluntarily submit to the jurisdiction. This may occur in three situations:

a) Where an action is raised by a plaintiff against a defendant, the plaintiff is deemed to submit to any counterclaims instituted by the defendant in response.

b) Where a defendant instructs his solicitor to accept service on his behalf, he or she is deemed to submit to the jurisdiction of the court: CPR r6.4(2).

c) Where the defendant appears in order to contest the action, this will be considered submission to the jurisdiction of the court: see *Boyle v Sacker* (1888) 39 Ch D 842. CPR r11(5) provides that if a defendant files an acknowledgement of service, and does not apply within the period for filing a defence for the court to declare it has no jurisdiction or should not exercise its jurisdiction, he is to be treated as having accepted that the court has jurisdiction. However, there is no presumption of submission when the defendant appears for the sole purpose of contesting the jurisdiction of the court: *Re Dulles' Settlement (No 2)* [1951] Ch 842 and see CPR r11(3).

Submission to the jurisdiction of a particular court may also occur when a contract contains a provision which expressly or impliedly contains consent to jurisdiction. Once a party has consented to the jurisdiction of the English courts, he or she is bound by that agreement: see *British Aerospace plc* v *Dee Howard Co* [1993] 1 Lloyd's Rep 368. Consequently, service can either be effected by any method specified in the contract (CPR r6.15), or on his agent within the jurisdiction (CPR r6.16; *Montgomery, Jones & Co* v *Liebenthal & Co* [1898] 1 QB 487), or an application may be made under CPR r6.20.

Situations where leave is not required to serve the claim form on a defendant who is not present within the jurisdiction

The High Court has power to determine certain claims under statutory powers even though the defendant is not in England. These statutory powers are contained in the following statutes:

a) The Carriage by Air Act 1961 – a passenger has the right to sue a carrier in the courts of the place of the destination of the flight. Where the destination is within England, jurisdiction is conferred over foreign airlines.

b) Carriage of Goods by Road Act 1965.

c) Civil Aviation Act 1982.

Forum conveniens – the position under common law

The fact that an English court may validly exercise jurisdiction does not necessarily imply that it must exercise that power. There are occasions in which the courts will decline to exercise jurisdiction. This mainly occurs in two situations:

a) A court may stay an action raised before it because there is a more appropriate forum where the cases should be heard.

b) A court may refuse to exercise its discretion to allow a claim form to be served out of the jurisdiction on the ground that another court would be a more appropriate forum for initiating proceedings.

These situations are in fact merely different aspects of the same principle, namely that of forum conveniens – the existence of a more appropriate court (forum) for litigation. In the area of conflict of laws, a more appropriate forum is usually that of a court of another state.

The grant of a stay of proceedings

Until very recently, the English courts exercised their power to stay proceedings very sparingly. The general view was that if proceedings had been commenced in the English courts according to the appropriate form, then only in exceptional circumstances should the courts decline to hear the case: see *St Pierre* v *South American Stores* [1936] 1 KB 382 at 398.

Since this case a more disciplined approach has been adopted by the courts. In *MacShannon* v *Rockware Glass Limited* [1978] AC 795 Lord Diplock laid down a two-stage test that had to be satisfied:

> 'In order to justify a stay two conditions must be satisfied, one positive and one negative:
> (a) the defendant must satisfy the court that there is another forum to whose jurisdiction
> he is amenable in which justice can be done between the parties at substantially less
> inconvenience or expense, and (b) the stay must not deprive the plaintiff of a legitimate
> personal or juridical advantage which would be available to him if he invoked the
> jurisdiction of the English court ...'

This was subsequently modified in the case of *Spiliada Maritime Corporation* v *Cansulex Ltd* [1986] 3 WLR 972, in which it was stressed that the term 'conveniens' should be taken to mean 'appropriate' and not 'convenient'. Equally, the second stage of the *MacShannon* test was amended to that of 'special circumstances' as opposed to that of 'legitimate personal or juridical advantage'. For the most recent discussion on the *Spiliada* test: see *Berezovsky* v *Michaels and Others* [2000] 2 All ER 986.

The refusal to grant leave to serve outside the jurisdiction

Even when an application for the grant of leave to serve a claim form falls within the scope of CPR r6.20, the English courts have been cautious in exercising this power. One of the considerations which courts have taken into consideration when exercising this power has been that a foreign forum would be more appropriate to conduct the case. CPR r6.21(2A) provides that:

> 'The court will not give permission unless satisfied that England and Wales is the proper
> place in which to bring the claim.'

In *Amin Rasheed Shipping Corp* v *Kuwait Insurance Co* [1983] 2 All ER 884 Lord Wilberforce established the principle that, when applying for leave to serve outside the jurisdiction, a plaintiff had to show:

> '... good reasons why the service of a claim form, calling for appearance before an English
> court, should, in the circumstances, be permitted on a foreign defendant. In considering
> this question the court must take into account the nature of the dispute, the legal and
> practical issues involved, such questions as local knowledge, availability of witnesses and
> their evidence and expense.'

The application of these factors when considering whether leave to serve outside the jurisdiction is appropriate has been approved in subsequent cases: see, for example, *Spiliada Maritime Corporation* v *Cansulex Ltd* [1986] 3 All ER 843 and *The Nile Rhapsody* [1992] 2 Lloyd's Rep 399.

4.3 Key cases and statutes

- *Amin Rasheed Shipping Corporation* v *Kuwait Insurance Co* [1984] AC 50
  Proper law of contract – leave could be granted under RSC O.11 to serve claim form out of jurisdiction

- *Berezovsky* v *Michaels and Others* [2000] 1 WLR 1004
  Examination of *Spiliada* test – appropriate forum

- *Gan Insurance Co Ltd* v *Tai Ping Insurance Co Ltd* [1999] CLC 1270
  England as appropriate forum – effect of applicable law

- *MacShannon* v *Rockware Glass Ltd* [1978] AC 795
  Forum non conveniens – original two-stage test – replaced by *Spiliada* test

- *Maharanee of Baroda* v *Wildenstein* [1972] 2 QB 283
  Service of claim form within jurisdiction

- *Seaconsar Far East Ltd* v *Bank Markazi Jomhouri Islami Iran* [1993] 3 WLR 756
  Discretion of court to grant leave to serve claim form outside the jurisdiction

- *Spiliada Maritime Corporation* v *Cansulex Ltd* [1987] AC 460
  Two stage test – appropriate forum

- Civil Procedure Rules (CPR) r6 – replaces RSC O.11 – leave to serve a claim form on persons abroad

4.4 Questions and suggested solutions

QUESTION ONE

Joseph, a jeweller in England, agrees to sell some of his goods to Harvey, an American. The sales contract was in an American form and contained provisions requiring the jewellery to be delivered in San Diego and that payment was to be made, in sterling, into Joseph's bank account with the Barclays bank in London within two weeks of delivery.

The jewellery is duly delivered but Harvey is informed by experts that the jewellery is fake. Consequently Harvey refuses to make payment. Joseph talks one of his friends into inviting Harvey to stay with him for the weekend at an English seaside resort. During this weekend, Harvey is served with a claim form claiming payment for the jewellery.

a) Harvey wishes to challenge the jurisdiction of the English court and, in the alternative, to ask the court to stay proceedings if it decides that it has jurisdiction. What is your advice?

b) Would your answer differ if the contract had contained a provision referring all disputes exclusively to arbitration in California?

Question prepared by the Editor

General Comment

A very straightforward question. Students must demonstrate a sound knowledge of the theory of jurisdiction. The temptation is to provide a definite answer/solution to the problem.

Skeleton Solution

Jurisdiction – service within jurisdiction – party induced to enter jurisdiction by fraud – stay of proceedings – *Spiliada* principles– enforcement of foreign exclusive arbitration clause.

Suggested Solution

a) Prima facie, the English court has jurisdiction, as Harvey has been served with a claim form within the territorial jurisdiction of the English court, and it matters not that his visit was for the weekend only: *Colt Industries v Sarlie (No 1)* [1966] 1 WLR 440, *Maharanee of Baroda v Wildenstein* [1972] 2 QB 283. However, Harvey has been tricked into coming within the jurisdiction in order to be served, and this may be a ground for setting aside the service: *Watkins v North American Land and Timber Co Ltd* (1904) 20 TLR 534 and *Colt v Sarlie* (above) at 443–44. The test applied will be, was Harvey enticed here solely in order that a claim form might be served?

Even though the court decides that it has jurisdiction, it may decide to stay the proceedings. The principles upon which it will act in considering an application for a stay are those enunciated in Lord Goff's speech in *Spiliada Maritime Corporation v Cansulex Ltd* [1986] 3 WLR 972. In accordance with these guidelines:

i) There must be another competent court – here a United States court is available, and the case can be tried there suitably for the interests of the parties and the ends of justice.

ii) The burden of proof lies on Harvey.

iii) Harvey must show not merely the inappropriateness of the English court but also that there is one other forum which is clearly appropriate.

iv) The court will look for factors which point to the United States as the forum with which the action has 'its most real and substantial connection'; these include convenience, expense, availability of witnesses – all points which here seem to favour the United States. Also to be considered are the place of business or residence of the parties – which cancel out – and which law governs the transaction. Here, there is no express choice of law, but the circumstances, particularly the fact that the contract was drawn up by an American lawyer, suggest that American law will be, by implied choice or objectively, the proper law of the contract.

Lord Goff's fifth principle is not applicable here; under his sixth principle, it will be open to Joseph to show, if he can, further circumstances against a stay, such as that he will not receive justice in the foreign court. It may reasonably safely be anticipated that he will not succeed.

Thus, Harvey has good prospects of having the English proceedings against him stayed, leaving Joseph to sue if so advised in the United States courts.

b) If the contract contained a Californian exclusive arbitration clause, Harvey's prospects of a stay advance to near certainty. In this event Joseph will bear the burden of persuading the court not to grant a stay, since he is suing here in breach of contract (cf *Trendtex Trading Corp* v *Credit Suisse* [1982] AC 679, though that is not to say that it is impossible for Joseph so to persuade an English court: cf *The Fehmarn* [1958] 1 WLR 159.

QUESTION TWO

George is a businessman in England. He enters a contract with Kyto, a manufacturer of perfumes in Japan, to act as a sole agent for the sale of Kyto's perfumes in England. The agency contract stipulates that all disputes arising out of the contract will be settled exclusively in the courts of Japan.

Not surprisingly the parties had a dispute and Kyto purports to terminate the agency contract. George, who feels aggrieved at this decision, wishes to sue Kyto for breach of contract. He had a claim form served on Kyto when he was in England attending a two day business meeting.

George's lawyer has advised that an action in the courts of Japan will take up to five years to come to trial whereas proceedings will be considerably speedier in England. In addition, his lawyers advise that the courts of Japan will apply the laws of Japan which contain a number of provisions discriminating against Roman Catholics. To add to his miseries, George is informed that Kyto has started an action against George in Japan for breach of contract.

George wishes to have the matter resolved in the English courts whereas Kyto naturally prefers the courts of Japan.

What advice would you give to George?

Question prepared by the Editor

General Comment

Another relatively straightforward problem scenario. Students need to ensure that they include all relevant points and deal with every aspect raised. This demands focus and organisation under examination conditions. Do not overlook the exclusive jurisdiction clause.

Skeleton Solution

Jurisdiction of English courts – service of claim form – stay of proceedings in England – forum (non) conveniens doctrine – injunction to restrain plaintiff in foreign proceedings – when granted – exclusive foreign jurisdiction clause – effect.

Suggested Solution

Here George has served a claim form on Kyto while the latter was in England, and thus founded jurisdiction in the English courts, it being of no significance how short Kyto's visit to England was, or (provided Kyto was not tricked into coming here) why he came: *Maharenee of Baroda* v *Wildenstein* [1972] 2 QB 283 and *Barclays Bank of Swaziland* v *Hahn* [1989] 1 WLR 506.

The issues are: can Kyto get the English court to stay its proceedings, so that the dispute will be litigated exclusively in Japan? Or can George successfully resist such an application and moreover obtain an injunction restraining Kyto from pursuing his case in Japan? And what effect will the exclusive jurisdiction clause in the contract have?

Kyto will presumably apply to the English court, which undoubtedly has jurisdiction, to stay its proceedings. The court has an intrinsic power to do this, and here Kyto will be arguing for its exercise on the grounds that the contract between George and Kyto contained a clause in favour of the exclusive jurisdiction of the Japanese court. This is a powerful submission; the English court will normally honour such a stipulation by the parties, but not absolutely invariably so: see *The Eleftheria* [1970] P 94, where it was held that in such circumstances a stay of the English proceedings will be granted unless a strong case for not staying is shown by the plaintiff.

The court will take into account convenience, expense, availability of evidence, closeness of connection of the parties to the relevant countries, similarity or difference of the applicable law to English law, enforceability, possibility of a fair trial, and whether the defendant truly seeks trial in the foreign country or merely a procedural advantage. See also *The Fehmarn* [1958] 1 WLR 159 and *The Adolph Warski* [1976] 2 Lloyd's Rep 241. In the instant case the evidence will presumably be in England, and it is likely that the applicable law (under the Rome Convention) would be held to be English law, absent a choice of law clause in the contract; also, the circumstances indicate that George might well not obtain a fair trial in Japan. It thus seems likely that the Japanese exclusive jurisdiction clause would not by itself be decisive of the matter.

Generally in considering whether a stay of the English proceedings is appropriate the court will apply the forum non conveniens doctrine as expounded in *Spiliada Maritime Corp* v *Cansulex* [1986] 3 WLR 972 by Lord Goff. In looking to see whether there is some other available forum, having competent jurisdiction, in which the case may be tried more suitably for the interests of all the parties and the ends of justice, the burden of proof will rest on Kyto as the defendant. He should prima facie be able to rely on the exclusive jurisdiction clause to show that Japan has jurisdiction and is appropriate (because selected by the parties); and Japan is clearly unique in these respects.

But the burden now shifts to George to show that England is more appropriate than Japan, and he can do this by reference to such factors as the availability of witnesses (probably most available in England, since the issue in the termination was whether George was properly performing his duties here), the applicable law (in English eyes as we have seen this is probably English law, though the Japanese courts take a different view), and the places at which the parties reside/carry out business (these cancel out – George is resident in England, Kyto in Japan).

Overall it seems fairly clear that George has the better of the argument and a stay should be refused. Even if the court does not take this view of the balance of factors, however, George will still under the *Spiliada* guidelines be able to argue that justice requires that the stay should be refused; the clinching factor is the prejudice against him in Japan on account of his religion. (The delay in trial in Japan, and the relative unfavourableness of Japanese law, are points in the same direction but of less weight.) Thus in any event George should be able to secure trial of his action against Kyto in the English courts.

If that were all, we would have two suits, one in the English and one in the Japanese courts, relating to the same matter, a clearly unsatisfactory situation: cf *The Abidin Daver* [1984] 1 All ER 470. George will therefore ask the English court to grant an injunction restraining Kyto from proceeding with his Japanese action. The principles to be applied are to be found in *Société Nationale Industrielle Aérospatiale* v *Lee Kui Jak* [1987] AC 871; see also *Arab Monetary Fund* v *Hashim (No 6)* (1992) The Times 24 July. The first criterion in that case is satisfied in that England as we have seen is the forum conveniens. The second condition to be met is that the continuance of the foreign proceedings should be vexatious and oppressive of the plaintiff in the English proceedings (George). This is arguable here in view of the element of religious prejudice, while there appears to be no counterbalancing personal or juridical disadvantage to Kyto in the determination of his rights in English proceedings, eg by counterclaiming in George's action. Accordingly, George has a good chance of obtaining such an injunction against Kyto.

QUESTION THREE

In what circumstances will an English court restrain foreign proceedings?

University of London LLB Examination
(for External Students) Conflict of Laws June 1993 Q3(a)

General Comment

The temptation here is to produce a basic description of the circumstances. The better student should focus on the case law, together with a detailed analysis of the area.

Skeleton Solution

Review of law pre and post *Spiliada* – significance of the *Société Nationale Industrielle Aérospatiale* case and later developments.

Suggested Solution

Two points arise from s37 Supreme Court Act 1981 which empowers the High Court to grant an injunction restraining a party 'who has sufficient connection with this country' from commencing or continuing as plaintiff with foreign proceedings. First, the injunction is not to the (foreign) court but to the party engaged in the proceedings (*Love* v *Baker* (1665) 1 Cas in Ch 67); ie the injunction acts in personam and a disobedient party may be liable for contempt of court. Second, the implicit interference with the jurisdiction of the foreign court whenever the English court grants an injunction restraining foreign proceedings means that it is necessary for the English court to exercise its discretion 'with great caution': *Société Nationale Industrielle Aérospatiale* v *Lee Kui Jak* [1987] AC 871.

Within these parameters, Lord Scarman, in the pre-*Spiliada* case of *Castanho* v *Brown and Root (UK) Ltd* [1981] AC 557, said that in relation to the 'criteria [which] should govern the exercise of the court's discretion to impose a stay or grant an injunction [restraining foreign proceedings] … the principle is the same', and that the *MacShannon* test (*MacShannon* v *Rockware Glass Ltd* [1978] AC 795) should apply mutatis mutandis. In effect, this meant that a defendant had to show both that the English court was a forum to which he was amenable and in which justice could be done at less expense and inconvenience than in the foreign court, and that the grant of an injunction to restrain the plaintiff from suing in the foreign court would not deprive him of a legitimate personal or juridical advantage. Lord Scarman did not categorise instances in which the court would exercise its discretion and grant an injunction since 'the width and flexibility of equity are not to be undermined by categorisation'. Accordingly, an injunction would be granted whenever justice so demands.

Whereas two House of Lords decisions, *British Airways Board* v *Laker Airways* [1985] AC 58 and *South Carolina Insurance Co* v *Assurantie NV* [1987] AC 24, affirmed that the *MacShannon test* should apply mutatis mutandis, the majority opinion in the *South Carolina* case was that the earlier House of Lords cases had decided that the power of the High Court to grant an injunction was, in fact, limited to three categories, viz:

a) when there is a choice of forum (of which England is one);

b) where one party, by bringing, or threatening to bring, proceedings abroad, has invaded, or threatens to invade, a legal or equitable right of the other party not to be sued abroad;

c) where the bringing of the proceedings abroad would be unconscionable.

No injunction was granted in the *South Carolina* case because the case did not come within one of the three categories specified and there was no choice of forum. On the facts of the case there was no need to grant an injunction in order to preserve the English jurisdiction.

Furthermore, one result of the decision in *Spiliada Maritime Corporation* v *Cansulex* [1987] AC 460 is that the role of 'legitimate personal or juridical advantage' – a significant factor in *MacShannon* – is much reduced: it has become a factor which 'clearly ... cannot be decisive', per Lord Goff. It could have led to undue emphasis on England being regarded as the natural forum for trial. This would have been the result of injunction being granted too readily.

Although Lord Goff's opinion in *Spiliada* did not make any reference to injunctions restraining foreign proceedings, his view was clarified in the Privy Council case of *Société Nationale Industrielle Aérospatiale* v *Lee Kui Jak* where he said:

> 'Where a remedy for a particular wrong is available both in the English court and in a foreign court, the English court will, generally speaking, only restrain the plaintiff from pursuing proceedings in the foreign court if such pursuit would be *vexatious or oppressive.*'

Clearly, then, there is a distinction between what, in *Casthano*, Lord Scarman had seen as an assimilation of the same principle 'whether the remedy sought is a stay of English proceedings or a restraint or for foreign proceedings'. The decision whether to restrain foreign proceedings is now based on a resurrection of the old ideas of vexation or oppression being combined with the modern idea of the natural or appropriate forum.

In the *Société Nationale* case, the plaintiff, who wished to pursue claims resulting from a fatal helicopter crash, commenced proceedings for damages against two defendants, D1 and D2, in Brunei and Texas. However, it was decided that, since the Texan courts probably had jurisdiction over D1, but not over D2, if D1 were found liable they would have to seek a contribution from D2 in some other country. On that basis the Privy Council granted an injunction restraining the Texan proceedings, holding that Brunei was the natural forum for trial.

Whereas the *Société Nationale* decision is incompatible with the House of Lords decision in the *Casthano* and *South Carolina* cases, it was followed in the Court of Appeal case of *Du Pont* v *Agnew* [1987] 2 Lloyd's Rep 585. Furthermore, although the *Société Nationale* decision was in respect of a case in which there was a choice of forum, and proceedings had been commenced in both of them, the same principles would appear to apply to cases in which there is no choice of forum: *Du Pont* v *Agnew* and *British Airways Board* v *Laker Airways*.

In conclusion, then, it is to be noted that, apart from the incompatibility of the *Société Nationale* case with the two House of Lords cases, the difficulty of specifying the circumstances in which an English court may restrain foreign proceedings is compounded by the uncertainty of the meanings of 'vexation' and 'oppression'. Old case law, decided in a different context, will not elucidate the meaning of these words. This will be a matter for future cases to decide.

QUESTION FOUR

When it comes to deciding whether the English court is the forum conveniens has 'judicial chauvinism' been replaced by 'judicial comity'?

University of London LLB Examination
(for External Students) Conflict of Laws June 1990 Q1

General Comment

This question invites the student to discuss the history of forum conveniens. However, this must deal with the cases (not just the obvious ones) and link in with the specific question posed. The better student will go on to discuss the new Council Regulation 44/2001/EC.

Skeleton Solution

'Judicial chauvinism' and 'judicial comity' – the history of forum conveniens – the decline of chauvinism – the *Spiliada* case – applicable both to stays and to CPR r6.20(1) – the two-stage approach to questions of forum conveniens – comity requires different principles for injunctions to restrain – *Lee Kui Jak* – forum conveniens and Council Regulation 44/2001/EC.

Suggested Solution

The short and general answer to this question is yes: as a result of several decisions of the House of Lords and Privy Council in the second half of the 1980s, 'judicial chauvinism' has been replaced with 'judicial comity' in deciding whether the English court is the forum conveniens or not. But before this answer can be appreciated we will need to explain the terms 'judicial chauvinism' and 'judicial comity'.

The liberality of the English law of jurisdiction in personam, namely, that the court has jurisdiction over anyone duly served with a claim form in England (*Maharanee of Baroda* v *Wildenstein* [1972] 2 QB 283) or who, with leave of the court, is served with a claim form outside the jurisdiction (CPR r6.20(1)), means that cases frequently arise before English courts in which the local court has jurisdiction but there is some other court in which it is more appropriate or convenient for the litigation to be conducted. In these circumstances, a defendant who has been served with a claim form in England may apply to court to stay the action, so that the plaintiff is forced to sue elsewhere. Where the defendant has been served with the claim form outside England he may apply to the English court to have the leave to serve outside the jurisdiction set aside. In both these circumstances the court has a discretion to stay the action or to set aside the grant of leave (and indeed in many cases technically within CPR r6.20(1) it will not grant leave at all). The debate over forum conveniens concerns the principles upon which that discretion will be exercised.

For many years, indeed centuries, the English courts adopted an attitude of 'British (or at least English was best'. If the matter was properly within the jurisdiction of the English courts it was only rarely that the matter would be stayed. This traditional stance of 'judicial chauvinism' may be illustrated by *St Pierre v South American Stores* [1936] 1 KB 382 where the Court of Appeal laid down that 'a mere balance of convenience is not a sufficient ground for depriving a plaintiff of the advantages of prosecuting his action in an English court … The right of access to the King's court must not be lightly refused'. Consequently, before a stay would be granted the defendant (the party seeking a stay) needed to show, first, that it would be 'oppressive or vexatious to him [the defendant] or it would be an abuse of the process of the court' to allow the action to continue in England and, secondly, that a stay would not 'cause an injustice to the plaintiff'.

Whatever might he said in favour of this 'judicial chauvinism' it plainly belongs in a different era. Today, it is not assumed, even by Her Majesty's judges, that justice will not be available elsewhere than in the Queen's courts. Indeed, we recognise that it is far too often not available in them. More to the point, it is difficult to see why the plaintiff (perhaps only able to serve the defendant in England during a fleeting visit) should have the advantage of being able to sue in England without proper consideration of whether that would be fair to the defendant. Hence the attitude of the English judges began to change. Following a speech by Lord Reid in *The Atlantic Star* [1973] 2 All ER 174 in which he disapproved of the traditional approach, the House of Lords in *MacShannon v Rockware Glass Ltd* [1978] AC 795 laid down a test that was less favourable to plaintiffs and made it easier for a stay to be granted. Broadly speaking the requirement that the proceedings were 'oppressive or vexatious' was replaced with the principle of 'substantially less inconvenience or expense' and the requirement of no injustice to the plaintiff was replaced with the principle that a stay would not deprive the plaintiff of 'a legitimate personal or juridical advantage'.

In this way did considerations of convenience slip into English law. But *MacShannon v Rockware Glass* was only the beginning. In *The Abidin Daver* [1984] 1 All ER 470 Lord Diplock expressly referred to the concepts of 'judicial chauvinism' and 'judicial comity' and indicated his preference for the latter. And then in *Spiliada Maritime Corporation v Cansulex Ltd* [1986] 3 WLR 972 Lord Goff of Chieveley in a speech of great power and influence recast the law in a way that made it clear that considerations of which was the most appropriate forum would now be the most weighty in the exercise of the discretion to stay.

I do not believe that a full exposition of the law following *Spiliada* is required within the restrictive compass of this essay. Suffice it to say that Lord Goff envisaged a two-stage procedure. First, there would be an investigation into whether there existed some other available forum which was the appropriate forum for the trial of the action and in which the case could be tried more suitably in the interests of all the parties and the end of justice. Note that the English court will refuse to grant a stay where there is no clearly more appropriate forum. (Thus it is not enough for a stay that the English court is not clearly appropriate.) The factors that will guide the court in deciding whether another forum is clearly more appropriate will include the following: factors affecting convenience and expense (such as the availability of witnesses), the law governing the disputed transaction, the places where the parties carry on business, and the places of residence of the parties. The burden of satisfying the court of these matters lies with the defendant seeking a stay.

Second, however, even if the court concludes that there is another clearly more appropriate forum it may yet refuse a stay if it is shown that the plaintiff will not receive justice in that forum. Here factors rather wider than those mentioned above in determining the natural forum are taken into account, especially matters touching the plaintiff such as that he cannot return to the appropriate forum to litigate there: *Purcell v Khayat* (1987) The Times 23 November. However, in this second stage the onus lies on the plaintiff to establish that a stay should not be granted.

Now these principles have been discussed in the context of a stay but the *Spiliada* makes clear that essentially similar principles govern the decision whether to grant leave to serve outside the jurisdiction (or to set aside leave already granted). Indeed, the *Spiliada* was itself an CPR r6.20 case. However, there remained some differences between stays and CPR r6.20 cases. For instance, while the onus in staying cases is on the defendant (prior to the second stage), the onus is on the plaintiff in CPR r6.20 cases because he has to establish that the case is a proper one for service out of the jurisdiction.

The essential point about the *Spiliada* principles is that they show the declining influence of 'judicial chauvinism'. Now it is much easier to obtain stays and the search is on primarily for the appropriate forum and there are no chauvinistic remarks about keeping the doors of the King's court open to all. In a spirit of 'judicial comity' all legal systems are considered equal and decisions taken accordingly. However, it is should be noted that concepts such as 'legitimate personal or juridical advantages' survive (see *Du Pont v Agnew* [1987] 2 Lloyd's Rep 585), although much attenuated, in the second stage of the proceedings. This is not 'judicial chauvinism' nor is it 'judicial comity' but it is a proper concern with justice to the plaintiff: there remain cases in which there is another clearly appropriate forum so 'juridical comity' might call for a stay, but that it would be unjust to the plaintiff to deny access to the English courts.

The crucial importance of 'judicial comity' underlying these developments in the law may be seen in the related, but different area, of injunctions to retrain foreign proceedings. Here the English court may be persuaded to take steps to ensure that it and not some foreign court hears a particular case. Where the English court has jurisdiction over the plaintiff in the foreign court, it can issue an injunction ordering the plaintiff to withdraw the proceedings in the foreign jurisdiction.

But on what principles should the English court decide whether to grant such an injunction or not? The leading case is the decision of the Privy Council in *Société National Industrielle Aérospatiale v Lee Kui Jak* [1987] AC 871 in which once more Lord Goff delivered a judgment that changed the direction of the law and which is destined to become canonical. Lord Diplock had said in *Castanho v Brown and Root (UK) Ltd*

[1981] AC 557 that the same principles applied to the restraint of foreign proceedings as applied to the grant of a stay. If this were right then after *Spiliada* the same principles would govern the grant of a stay, the grant of leave to serve outside the jurisdiction, and the grant of an injunction to restrain foreign proceedings.

This would certainly simplify the law; but the crux of Lord Goff's judgment is that that would amount to the survival of 'judicial chauvinism' in the area of the restraint of foreign judgments. Applying the principles of forum conveniens to the restraint of foreign proceedings would mean that where the English court concluded that it was the natural forum, it would then grant an injunction to restrain the foreign proceedings. But that, said Lord Goff,

> '... could not be right. It would lead to the conclusion that in a case where there was simply a difference of view between the English court and the foreign court as to which was the natural forum, the English court could arrogate to itself, by the grant of an injunction, the power to resolve the dispute. Such a conclusion would be inconsistent with comity and disregard the fundamental requirement that an injunction would only be granted where the ends of justice so required.'

Thus it is that different and more onerous principles govern the restraint of foreign proceedings than govern the grant of a stay. This is not inconsistent with *Spiliada* but is simply the working out of the principle of 'judicial comity' in different circumstances. (The principles that govern the restraint of foreign proceedings are, very briefly, that before an injunction would be granted the English courts had to be the natural forum and the foreign proceedings had to be vexatious and oppressive (judged by taking into account the injustices to both the plaintiff and the defendant in the respective forums they wish to avoid).)

One final point needs to be made about forum conveniens. It is presently unclear what the precise relationship is between forum conveniens and Council Regulation 44/2001/EC. On one view forum conveniens has no role to play: where more than one court has jurisdiction under the Regulation the court 'first seised' retains jurisdiction and the other declines jurisdiction: arts 27, 28 and 29. However, the question must be posed as to the position where, although the matter falls within the Regulation, the two courts that have jurisdiction are not both in the EC? Suppose (as in *Arkwright Mutual Insurance Co v Bryanstone Insurance Co Ltd* [1990] 3 WLR 75) the English court has jurisdiction under the Council Regulation 44/2001/EC, but the courts of New York have jurisdiction under their own rules. How does one determine which court hears the case? It was hoped that the case of *Re Harrods (Buenos Aires) Ltd* [1991] 3 WLR 397 would resolve this question. Unfortunately, the case was settled and as such no definitive answer has, to date, been forthcoming. It must be said though that, if it is decided that once a matter is within the Regulation forum conveniens no longer applies, this will amount to 'judicial chauvinism' by the EC seeking to ensure that its rules of jurisdiction determine cases elsewhere in the world.

Chapter 5

Jurisdiction II – the Statutory Regime under Council Regulation 44/2001/EC

5.1   Introduction

5.2   Key points

5.3   Key cases and statutes

5.4   Questions and suggested solutions

5.1 Introduction

This is an important area for two main reasons. First of all, it represents the second key topic which forms the conflict of laws – the determination of jurisdiction. Second, it represents a vital and complex area of the law in which European law in the form of Council Regulation 44/2001/EC and, prior to 1 March 2002, the Brussels Convention (in force in the United Kingdom as a result of the Civil Jurisdiction and Judgments Act (CJJA) 1982) makes its influence felt. The importance of this area cannot be stressed enough. The student who is not on top of jurisdiction will be at a grave disadvantage, especially in light of recent developments.

5.2 Key points

The Brussels Convention on Jurisdiction and the Enforcement of Judgments in Civil and Commercial Matters

The common law principles of jurisdiction were substantially supplemented by the (CJJA) 1982 which gives effect in the United Kingdom to the Brussels Convention on Jurisdiction and the Enforcement of Judgments in Civil and Commercial Matters 1968. The Convention is an agreement negotiated among the member states of the European Union. Although the Convention was agreed in 1968 among the original six member states, it applies to acceding member states – including the United Kingdom – by virtue of accession protocols.

The 1968 Convention has been amended on two occasions. The first amendment occurred as a consequence of the Lugano Convention of 1988 which extended the terms of the 1968 Convention to the states of the European Free Trade Association (EFTA) so that the advantages of a uniform law of jurisdiction and enforcement of judgments would extend to these states. The 1988 Convention was given force in the UK by virtue of the CJJA 1991 and came into effect on 1 May 1992.

The second amendment took place on the signing of the San Sebastian Convention of 1989. This Convention made certain adjustments to the 1968 Convention to allow Spain and Portugal to accede to the system. A number of technical amendments were also made to the 1988 Convention in order to improve and streamline the system.

Since the 1968 Convention was negotiated between the original six members of the Community it has a distinctly civil law flavour. Hence, the CJJA 1982 makes a number of radical changes to the pre-existing common law system of jurisdiction.

Since 1 March 2002 Council Regulation 44/2001/EC has superseded the Brussels Convention and it is this set of rules to which the following section will make reference, whilst providing the corresponding articles of the Brussels Convention in brackets as follows – art 22{16} – where art 22 is Council Regulation 44/2001/EC and 16 is the corresponding article of the Brussels Convention).

Characteristics of the previous and current scheme

As noted above, the Brussels Convention was incorporated into United Kingdom law by the CJJA 1982. In this respect, it is worth noting that:

a) The Act itself was essentially a device to facilitate the direct application of the terms of the Conventions into United Kingdom law.

b) Jurisdiction was therefore determined by reference to the terms of the Conventions' articles and the sections of the Act were merely designed to provide the necessary concepts and principles to integrate the Conventions into the United Kingdom jurisdictional system.

c) The interpretation of the Conventions was subject to the principles of interpretation established by the European Court of Justice (ECJ) and not the traditional literal approach used by the English courts at least until recently.

Council Regulation 44/2001/EC has now replaced the Brussels Convention and it is this regime that should be followed by the student. In this respect, it should be noted that:

a) A number of detailed amendments has been made. In addition, and perhaps most confusing from the perspective of the student, the article numbering has changed.

b) The procedure for interpretation has been replaced by the 'ordinary' procedure under art 234 EC. The consequence of this may be that more references are made, given the fact that the power to make a preliminary reference will no longer be confined to courts at the higher levels.

c) The current geographical scope of the Regulation is not the same as the Convention. Aside from Denmark which opted out, the Regulation extends to Gibraltar.

The scope of the Regulation

Article 1{1} of the Regulation defines the scope of its application as simply to 'civil and commercial matters'. Civil and commercial matters are not defined with any degree of clarity in the Regulation, but certain subjects are expressly excluded from the scope of the Regulation. These include:

a) revenue, customs or administrative matters;

b) matters concerning the status or capacity of natural persons, rights in property arising out of matrimonial relationships, wills and succession;

c) bankruptcy proceedings and like matters;

d) social security; and

e) arbitration.

The failure to define civil and commercial matters with a sufficient degree of clarity still handicaps the proper identification of disputes which fall within the scope of the Regulation, as it did with the Brussels Convention: see *LTU* v *Eurocontrol* [1976] ECR 1541.

The key to the application of the Regulation – the Regulation's concept of 'domicile'

The Regulation uses the concept of domicile to link individuals to specific legal systems in order to decide the issue of jurisdiction. Unfortunately, the concept of domicile under the Regulation is not the same as that used in English common law. While the different uses of the term must be distinguished, the Regulation does not provide any assistance in defining the Regulation concept of domicile used in the framework which it establishes.

Instead, the Regulation sets up a two-stage process for establishing domicile in art 59{52}:

Step 1: To determine whether a party is domiciled in the contracting state whose courts are seized of the matter, a court shall apply its internal law.

Step 2: If a party is not domiciled in the State whose courts are seized of the matter then, to determine whether the party is domiciled in another contracting state, a court shall apply the law of the other state.

Hence, a court first applies its own internal law to decide if a person is domiciled within that jurisdiction. If not, the court applies the law of any other contracting state in which the individual may be domiciled. Fortunately ss41–46 CJJA 1982 create rules of English law to assist in determining whether or not an individual is domiciled in the United Kingdom.

Special rules are established to identify the domicile of companies and trusts.

The domicile of a company is where it has its seat, which again is a question to be decided in accordance with national law. Section 42 of the 1982 Act clarifies this point by providing that a company has its seat in the United Kingdom if it is incorporated in the United Kingdom and has its registered office or some other official address in the United Kingdom or if its central management is exercised in the United Kingdom.

The domicile of a trust is decided under special provisions enacted as s45 of the 1982 Act. This specifies, as a general rule, that the domicile of a trust will be the United Kingdom if and only if one of the three legal systems within the United Kingdom is the legal system with which the trust has its closest and most real connection.

Domicile as defined in the 1982 Act

Section 41(2) CJJA 1982 fills the lacunae in the Regulation by creating a definition of domicile for individuals in UK law.

This section states that a person is domiciled in the United Kingdom

'... if and only if –
(a) he is resident in the United Kingdom; and
(b) the nature and circumstances of his residence indicate that he has a substantial connection with the United Kingdom.'

Under s41(6) of the Act a presumption of 'substantial connection' arises where a person has been resident in the United Kingdom for an immediately preceding period of three months. But this presumption may be rebutted by proof that no substantial connection exists.

Since there are three separate legal systems in the United Kingdom – those of England and Wales, Northern Ireland and Scotland – special internal United Kingdom rules are contained in the Act to allow for the proper identification of domicile within these three separate systems. These rules are also contained in s41 of the Act.

The central rule under the Regulation for ascertaining jurisdiction

The central rule regulating jurisdiction under the Regulation, as stated in art 2{2}, is that:

'(1) Subject to this Regulation, persons domiciled in a member state shall, whatever their nationality, be sued in the courts of that member state.'

Therefore, an individual must be sued in the court of his or her domicile as this term is defined in the national laws of the EU countries which are parties to the Regulation. Where an individual is not domiciled in one of the EU states, then the ordinary jurisdictional rules of the state where he is sued are applied to decide the question of jurisdiction. In the case of England, this will be the common law principles: see Chapter 4.

Again the 1982 Act contains detailed provisions for determining in which legal system within the United Kingdom an individual is domiciled: see s16 and Sch 4 of the Act.

There are two separate types of exceptions which deviate from this general principle: cases of special jurisdiction; and cases of exclusive jurisdiction.

Special jurisdictional rules

Article 5{5} of the Regulation specifies seven situations in which a court, other than that of the defendant's domicile, is entitled to exercise jurisdiction. In other words, the defendant may be sued in these jurisdictions in addition to the legal system in which he or she is domiciled.

However, it should be noted at the outset that the defendant must be domiciled, in the sense of the Act, in the European Union before the issue of special jurisdiction can arise.

Contract – art 5(1)

In matters relating to a contract, the courts for the place of performance of the obligation in question have concurrent jurisdiction: see *Jakob Handte GmbH* v *Traitements Mecano-Chimiques des Surfaces* [1993] ILPr 5. It is a matter for national courts, applying their own rules of private international law, to decide where the contract is to be performed: *Tessili* v *Dunlop AG* [1976] ECR 1473 and *Custom Made Commercial Limited* v *Stawa Metallbau GmbH* [1994] ILPr 516.

Similarly, it is for the national courts to decide which of the terms of the contract contain the critical obligation to be performed and to extract this obligation from the collateral rights and duties: see *Barclays Bank pie* v *Glasgow City Council* [1994] 2 WLR 466.

Maintenance – art 5(2)

The courts where a maintenance creditor has his or her domicile or habitual residence have jurisdiction in addition to those of the debtor's domicile.

If the matter in dispute is ancillary to proceedings concerning the status of a person, then the court which has jurisdiction to entertain those proceedings will similarly have jurisdiction over the question of maintenance.

Tort – art 5(3)

Where proceedings relate to tort, delict or quasi-delict, the courts of the place where the harmful event occurred have jurisdiction in addition to those of the defendant's domicile: see *Reichert, Reichert and Kockler* v *Dresdner Bank (No 2)* [1992] ILPr 404.

The major difficulty in applying this principle is that a defendant may have acted wrongfully in one country and the harm caused in another: see *Bier* v *Mines de Potasse* [1976] ECR 1735.

Civil claims in criminal proceedings – art 5(4)

Where a court has jurisdiction to entertain a civil claim in criminal proceedings, it is not precluded from hearing that claim by the terms of the Regulation.

Branches and agencies – art 5(5)

In the case of a dispute arising out of the operation of a branch or agency, the courts of the place in which the branch or agency is situated have jurisdiction to hear the dispute.

The question of the definition of 'branch' or 'agency' has arisen in a number of cases. As a general principle, to constitute a branch or agency for the purposes of the Regulation, the commercial operation must be under the direction and control of the head office of the parent company and the operation must appear as a discernible extension of the parent body: see *Blanckaert & Williams v Trost* [1981] ECR 819 and *New Hampshire Insurance Co v Strabag Bau AG* [1990] ILPr 334.

Trusts – art 5(6)

Disputes between beneficiaries, settlors and trustees under a trust, whether established under statute or by some other means, may be litigated in the courts of the domicile of the trust in addition to the courts of the domicile of the defendant.

This principle does not apply to constructive and resulting trusts. Further, trusts established under wills are excluded under art 1 from the scope of the Regulation.

Salvage of a cargo or freight – art 5(7)

Special and complicated rules have been established to deal with the unique problems created in Admiralty litigation: see *The Deichland* [1989] 3 WLR 478.

As a final point, it should also be observed that a person domiciled in a member state may also be sued: (1) where he is one of a number of defendants, in the courts of the place where any one of them is domiciled (see *The Owners of the Cargo Lately Laden on Board the Rewia v Caribbean Liners* [1993] ILPr 507); (2) as a third party in an action on a warranty or guarantee; and (3) on a counterclaim arising from the same contract or facts on which the original claim was based in the court in which the original claim is pending.

Exclusive jurisdictional rules

Article 22{16} of the Regulation stipulates that, irrespective of the issue of domicile, certain courts retain exclusive jurisdiction over particular matters. Hence, the issue of domicile is not relevant in these cases to establishing the appropriate jurisdiction. This article therefore prevails over any other conflicting provisions of the Regulation.

Immovable property – art 22(1){16(1)}

In proceedings which have as their object rights in rem in immovable property or tenancies of immovable property, the courts of the legal system in which the property is situated have exclusive jurisdiction: see *Webb* v *Webb* [1994] ILPr 389 and *Hacker* v *Euro-Relais GmbH* [1992] ILPr 515.

As an exception to this rule, in actions relating to tenancies of immovable property concluded for temporary private use for a maximum period of six consecutive months, the courts of the legal system in which the defendant is domiciled also have jurisdiction provided that the landlord and the tenant are natural persons and are both domiciled in the same country.

Corporations, legal persons and associations – art 22(2){16(2)}

Companies are creatures of national law and therefore it is not surprising that the Regulation reserves exclusive jurisdiction over disputes concerning their constitution and internal organisation to the countries where they were created.

The Regulation therefore provides that in proceedings which concern the constitution, nullity or dissolution of companies or other legal persons or associations of natural or legal persons, the courts of the state in which the company, legal person or association has its seat exercise exclusive jurisdiction over these affairs.

The seat of a company in United Kingdom law is ascertained by s43 CJJA 1982 Act which stipulates that a company has is seat in the United Kingdom if, and only if, either it was incorporated or formed under the law of a part of the UK or its central management and control is exercised in the United Kingdom: see *Newtherapeutics Ltd* v *Katz* [1990] 3 WLR 1183.

Public registers – art 22(3){16(3)}

Where the validity of entries in public registers is at issue, the courts of the legal system where the register is maintained have exclusive jurisdiction.

Trade marks and patents – art 22(4){16(4)}

In litigation concerning the registration or validity of patents, trade marks, designs and similar rights, the courts of the country in which the deposit or registration has taken place, or in terms of an international Regulation has been deemed to take place, have exclusive jurisdiction.

Actions for the enforcement of judgments – art 22(5){16(5)}

Exclusive jurisdiction is also reserved in the case of proceedings concerned with the enforcement of judgments to the courts of the country in which the judgment has been, or is to be, enforced.

The special rules for consumer contracts and insurance contracts

Due to their special character, consumer contracts and insurance contracts have unique rules to govern the jurisdiction of courts over their interpretation and enforcement. These two types of contracts must therefore be treated as special cases.

Consumer contracts – arts 15–17{13–15}

The reason for having special rules for consumer contracts is to ensure that consumers do not find that they are placed in the awkward position of being forced to sue a supplier of goods in a state other than that where the goods were supplied to the consumer.

Article 16{14} of the Regulation allows a consumer to bring proceedings in respect of consumer contracts in either the court of the supplier's domicile or in the court of his or her own domicile.

However, proceedings against a consumer can only be brought in the consumer's domicile.

There are also complex rules for identifying who qualify as consumers for the purposes of these special rules. A consumer is a person who enters into a contract outside his or her trade or profession, which takes one of the following forms:

a) a contract for the sale of goods on instalment credit terms;

b) a contract for a loan repayable by instalment, or any other form of credit, which has been made to finance the sale of goods;

c) any other contract for the supply of goods or services and which was preceded by a specific invitation to the consumer or advertising and in which the consumer took the necessary steps to conclude the contract in his or her own state.

The Regulation has introduced a number of important amendments:

a) The scope of 'consumer contracts' has been widened to include any contract entered into by a consumer with a person who pursues commercial or professional activities in the state of the consumer's domicile or, by any means, directs such activities to that state and the contract falls within the scope of those activities. This is intended to include the provision of interactve websites accessible in a country – though not simply passive websites containing advertising material.

b) It is no longer necessary for the consumer to take the steps necessary for the conclusion of the contract in the state of his domicile. Contracts made by a consumer induced to visit the other party's place of business in another country will be caught (this brings package holidays and time-share arrangements within the scope of 'consumer contract' provisions).

Insurance contracts – arts 8–14{7–12A}

An insurer domiciled in a member state may be sued in the courts of the state where he is domiciled or in the courts of the country where the policy holder is domiciled.

If an insurer is not domiciled in an EU country, but has a branch or agency in one of these states, then in the case of disputes arising out of the operation of that branch or agency the insurer is deemed to be domiciled in that state.

In addition, in respect of liability insurance or insurance of immovable property, the insurer may be sued in the place where the harmful event occurred.

Finally, irrespective of any other provision, if an insurer brings an action against an insured in the court of his or her domicile that court also has jurisdiction to hear any counterclaim.

Employment contracts – arts 18–21

This is a much welcomed new development under the Regulation, which attempts to resolve a number of difficulties encountered under the Convention: see *Ivenel* v *Schwab* [1982] ECR 1891 and *De Bloos* v *Bouyer* [1976] ECR 1497

Article 19 of the Regulation allows a employee to bring proceedings in respect of a contract of employment in either the court for the place where the employee habitually carries out his work or in the last place where he did so; or if he does not habitually carry out his work in any one country, in the courts for the place where the business which engaged the employee is situated; or in the court of his or her own domicile.

However, under art 20, proceedings against an employee can only be brought in the employee's domicile.

The issue of prorogation of jurisdiction under the Regulation

Private parties can agree to prorogate to the jurisdiction of a particular court and the Regulation acknowledges this freedom in art 23{17}. This allows the parties, if one or more is domiciled in an EU state, to agree that the courts of a particular EU state are to have jurisdiction to settle any disputes which may arise in connection with a particular legal relationship. That court will have exclusive jurisdiction over the dispute.

There are a number of conditions in the Regulation relating to the form of the agreement prorogating jurisdiction. The agreement conferring jurisdiction must be either:

a) in writing or evidenced in writing; or

b) in a form which accords with practices which the parties have established between themselves; or

c) in international trade or commerce, in a form which accords with a usage of which the parties are, or ought to have been, aware and which is widely known in such trade or commerce to parties to contracts of the type involved in the particular trade or commerce.

Where an agreement conferring jurisdiction is made by parties, none of whom is domiciled in an EU state, the courts of other EU states cannot exercise jurisdiction unless the court which has been selected declines to exert jurisdiction: see *Continental Bank NA* v *Akakos Compania Naviera SA* (1993) The Times 26 November.

Lis alibis pendens

Despite the basic principle that a defendant should be sued in the courts of his domicile, the Regulation gives considerable scope to the possibility that proceedings may be raised in more than one court. It is therefore feasible that more than one court may be seized of the same dispute at the same time.

In this situation, the basic rule is contained in art 27{21} of the Regulation. Where proceedings involving the same cause of action and between the same parties are brought in the courts of different EU countries, any court other than the courts first seized may, of its own motion, stay its proceedings until such time as the court first seized of the proceedings has established its jurisdiction.

In the event that the court first seized of the proceedings establishes jurisdiction, courts other than the first court are required to decline jurisdiction in favour of that court: see *Overseas Union Insurance Ltd* v *New Hampshire Insurance Co* [1991] ILPr 495.

5.3 Key cases and statutes

* *Barclays Bank plc* v *Glasgow City Council* [1992] 3 WLR 827
  Council Regulation 44/2001/EC, art 5(1){5(1)}

* *De Bloos* v *Bouyer* [1976] ECR 1497
  Special jurisdiction – place where the obligation which constitutes basis of claim is performed

* *Gascoine & Another* v *Pyrah & Another* [1994] ILPr 82
  Council Regulation 44/2001/EC, art 6(1){6(1)} – co-defendants

* *Harrods (Buenos Aires), Re* [1992] Ch 72
  Council Regulation 44/2001/EC, art 27{21}

* *Industrie Tessili Italiana Como* v *Dunlop AG* [1976] ECR 1473
  Council Regulation 44/2001/EC, art 5(1){5(1)} – words 'place of performance of the obligation' to be determined by law governing obligation

* *Ivenel* v *Schwab* [1982] ECR 1891
  Contract of employment – Council Regulation 44/2001/EC, art 5(1){5(1)}

* *Lloyd's Register of Shipping* v *Société Campenon Bernard* [1995] All ER (EC) 531
  Council Regulation 44/2001/EC, art 5(5){5(5)} – undertakings entered into by

branch do not have to be performed in member state where the branch was established for undertaking to form part of the operations of the branch

- *Republic of Haiti* v *Duvalier* [1989] 2 WLR 261
  Grant of a freezing injunction (formerly a Mareva injunction)

- *Zelger* v *Salinitri* [1980] ECR 89
  Council Regulation 44/2001/EC, arts 5 and 17 {5 and 23}

- Civil Jurisdiction and Judgments Act 1982 – implementing the Brussels Convention 1968, the 1971 Protocol and the 1978 Convention on Accession (still has relevance to new Council Regulation)

- Council Regulation 44/2001/EC – replaced the Brussels Convention 1968 on 1 March 2002

5.4 Questions and suggested solutions

QUESTION ONE

a) Minelli, an Italian company, manufactures a hair dryer at its factory in Rome. It markets it in England and Ann buys one at a shop in London. She uses it whilst on holiday in Wales and, due to a fault in its design, her hair catches fire. She suffers pain and her head is badly scarred.

Can she sue Minelli in England? If so, what law will decide whether she can claim damages for pain and suffering?

b) Yokohira, a Japanese construction company, has a small office in London, which is staffed by two employees, to gather market information. The company is not registered under section 691 of the Companies Act 1985, and the London office has no authority to enter into contracts: potential customers are referred to the head office of the company in Tokyo.

An Israeli company wishes to sue Yokohira because a factory built by Yokohira in Israel was defective.

Will the English courts have jurisdiction if the writ is served on the London office?

Would the position be different if the construction company had been domiciled in Italy?

c) Mr and Mrs Smith, who are domiciled in England and live in Manchester, hired a villa in Greece last summer from Mr Brown who is also domiciled in England and lives in Leeds. They responded to an advertisement placed in the *Trans-Pennine Times* in which Mr Brown described the villa as having 'all mod cons'. The Smiths' holiday was a disaster because there was no running water and no gas or electricity. They wish to sue Mr Brown to recover the rent and their fares to Greece. They propose to sue him in England. Can they do so? Would your answer be different if the villa had been in Miami?

University of London LLB Examination
(for External Students) Conflict of Laws June 1993 Q2

General Comment

The question invites the student to apply the statutory rules applicable to special and exclusive jurisdiction. This is all the more relevant given the new Council Regulation.

Skeleton Solution

a) Article 5(3) Council Regulation 44/2001/EC – rule in *Phillips* v *Eyre* now (post 1990) inapplicable to torts committed in England.

b) Sections 691 and 695 Companies Act 1985 and case law on these provisions – arts 60 and 5(5) Council Regulation 44/2001/EC.

c) Article 22 of Council Regulation 44/2001/EC – exception to the *Mocambique* rule.

Suggested Solution

a) The basic provision relating to jurisdiction over a defendant domiciled in the EU is contained in art 2 of Council Regulation 44/2001/EC which states:

   '(1) Subject to this Regulation, persons domiciled in a member state shall, whatever their nationality, be sued in the courts of that member state.'

   However, art 5(3) provides for special jurisdiction in relation to torts, ie it provides for the courts of a state, other than the member state in which the defendant is domiciled, to have jurisdiction. Accordingly, if the plaintiff sues the defendant in the other member state the jurisdiction of the courts where the defendant is domiciled is ousted.

   The member state other than Italy in which Ann could sue Minelli would be that in which 'the harmful event occurred': art 5(3). Whereas the Jenard Report did not answer the question of whether 'the place where the harmful event occurred' referred to the place where the act which initiated the damage occurred or the place where the damage took effect, the answer that it was 'both' was provided by the decision in *Bier* v *Mines de Potasse* [1978] QB 708. Here the French defendant was alleged to have poured effluents into the Rhine in France, and the ensuing pollution was alleged to have damaged the Dutch plaintiff's property in the Netherlands. Thus, it was necessary to decide where the harmful event occurred if litigation was to proceed. The ECJ held that both the French and the Dutch courts had jurisdiction.

   This decision would indicate that whether the harmful event was regarded as negligence in the manufacture of the hair dryer in Rome, Italy, or the pain and suffering experienced by Ann from using the hair dryer in England and Wales, the

English courts would have jurisdiction if Ann chose to sue Minelli in England. The English courts would have jurisdiction because, for the purposes of the conflict of laws, Wales is not a separate country; it is not a country subject to a distinctive legal system.

English law will decide whether Ann can claim damages for pain and suffering. In essence, and until 1990, this appeared to be a straightforward application of the rule in *Phillips* v *Eyre* (1870) LR 6 QB 1, as amended by *Boys* v *Chaplin* [1971] AC 356. As there is a coincidence of lex fori and lex causae the choice of law would be English law. This applied when two foreign parties had but a tenuous connection with England; as the harmful event occured in England, English law applied. This was illustrated by the case of *Szalatnay-Stacho* v *Fink* [1947] KB 1 in which documents which defamed the plaintiff were published in England. They had been sent by one Czech national to another, both of them being temporarily resident in England during the Second World War. That the harmful event took place in England was sufficient for the Court of Appeal to declare that English law applied. However, following the decision in *Metall und Rohstoff AG* v *Donaldson Lufkin & Jenrette Inc* [1990] 1 QB 391, it was said that where a tort was, in substance, committed in England, the court could entirely disregard the double actionability rule in *Boys* v *Chaplin* and only English law would be applied to resolve the dispute.

b) One purpose of s691 of the Companies Act 1985 is to provide the Registrar of Companies with the name and address of a person resident in Great Britain who is authorised to accept service of process on behalf of the company. Furthermore, a company must have a specific location in England for its business if it is to come within the ambit of s691: *Re Oriel* [1985] 3 All ER 216. Yokohira appears to have this specific location in London, but that it has defaulted on the registration obligation means that the English courts will only have jurisdiction if the writ is served on a place of business established by the company in Great Britain: s695(2) Companies Act 1985. What constitutes an established place of business fell to be decided in *South India Shipping Co* v *Export-Import Bank of Korea* [1985] 2 All ER 219. Here, the bank did not carry on the recognised banking practises of accepting deposits and making loans. What it did have, however, were premises and staff within the jurisdiction; it conducted external relations with other banks; it carried out the necessary line of enquiries prior to obtaining loans for clients; it sought to publicise itself; and it encouraged trade between the United Kingdom and Korea. Ackner LJ held:

> ' ... a company established a place of business within Great Britain if it carried on part of its business activities within the jurisdiction and it was not necessary for those activities to be either a substantial part of, or more than incidental to, the main objects of a company.'

Accordingly, the Export-Import Bank of Korea had established a place of business within Great Britain.

On this basis, it is submitted that Yokohira has established a place of business in

England and that a claim form served on its London office will give the English courts jurisdiction.

If Yokohira had been domiciled in Italy, art 60 of the Council Regulation provides that that is where it would have its 'seat', ie, in essence, its central management and control would be exercised there. Article 5(5) provides for special jurisdiction in that a dispute arising out of the operations of a branch, agency or other establishment may be litigated in the contracting state in which the branch, agency or other establishment is situated. Two points arise from this provision: a branch, etc, must be situated within the member state; and the dispute must arise out of the operations of the branch, etc. Whereas Yokohira would appear to have some form of establishment in London in accordance with the first requirement, it would not appear that the dispute between the Israeli company and Yokohira has arisen out of the operations of that establishment. The ECJ gave a narrow interpretation to 'a dispute arising out of the operations of a branch etc' in *Somafer* v *Saar-Ferngas* [1978] ECR 2183 where they identified only three types categories of action as being appropriate, viz: managerial 'such as those concerning the situation of the building … or the local engagement of staff to work there'; actions relating to undertakings entered into in the name of the parent in the place where it (the branch etc) is situated and which must be performed there; and non-contractual actions arising from the activities of the intermediary. As none of these actions applies to the facts of the Yokohira case, it is submitted that the Israeli company would have to sue them where they have their seat, ie in Italy.

c) Article 22(1) of the Council Regulation 44/2001/EC permits a plaintiff to commence an action where:

> '… in proceedings which have as their object tenancies of immovable property concluded for temporary private use for a maximum period of six consecutive months, the courts of the member state in which the defendant is domiciled shall also have jurisdiction, provided that the tenant is a natural person and that the landlord and tenant are domiciled in the same member state'.

This jurisdiction is in addition to the jurisdiction of the state in which the immovable property is situated (if this produces a different result from that of the second part of art 22(1)). Thus, notwithstanding the provision is contained in art 22, which provides for exclusive jurisdiction, it is, in essence, a form of special jurisdiction. However, the courts of one country will have exclusive jurisdiction on the basis that art 29 provides that a court other than the one first seized of the motion must decline jurisdiction.

In relation to 'proceedings which have as their object tenancies of immovable property', it was decided in *Rosler* v *Rottwinkel* [1986] QB 33 – a case decided under art 16(1)(a) of the Brussels Convention (now art 22(1) Council Regulation 44/2001/EC) but which, it is submitted, provides authority for the same term in art 16(1)(b) (now art 22(1) EC Council Regulation) – that this was confined to disputes concerning the respective obligations of the landlord and tenant under the agreement and this would include, inter alia, actions for unpaid rent. However, actions which only indirectly concerned the use of the property, such as a claim for damages for lost enjoyment of a holiday in the property let and for travel expenses, were held to fall outside the scope of art 16(1)(a) (art 22(1) of Council Regulation 44/2001/EC).

As the agreement involved a short-term holiday let, and the Smiths and Mr Brown are natural persons and are domiciled in the same contracting state, England, then they can sue under art 22, at least in respect of the rent. In *Hacker v Euro Relais GmbH* [1992] IIPr 515, the Advocate-General was also of the opinion that where art 22 applied then claims for ancillary damages also came within its ambit. This would prevent a multiplicity of claims in respect of what was, essentially, one and the same dispute. This would appear to be an extension of the provision in art 6(4) which permits, in certain circumstances, an action in contract to be combined with matters relating to rights in rem in immovable property and to be heard in the courts of the member state where the property is situated (the lex situs). Even if this combined action should be rejected by the English courts, they still have jurisdiction to hear an action in contract against Mr Brown as he would be sued in the courts of his domicile: art 2.

If the situs of the villa was Miami, then the provisions of the Regulation would not apply. Instead, recourse would be had to be an exception under the common law rule in the *Mocambique* case (see below). Whereas the general rule at common law is that English courts have no jurisdiction to entertain an action for the determination of the title to, or the right to possession of, any immovable situated outside England (*British South Africa Co v Comphania de Mocambique* [1893] AC 602), the first exception to this rule (as noted in the *Mocambique* case itself) provides that, in the case of Mr Brown, as the English court would have jurisdiction in personam over him by virtue of his presence in England when the claim form was served on him, they would have jurisdiction to entertain an action against him in respect of a contract or an equity affecting foreign land. This rule had its origins in the case of *Penn v Baltimore* (1750) 1 Ves Sen 444 where specific performance of a contract was ordered to settle boundaries between the provinces of Pennsylvania and Maryland. Thus, the English courts would have jurisdiction to hear an action against Mr Brown.

In summary, the Smiths would be able to sue Mr Brown in England irrespective of whether the villa was in Greece or Miami. In respect of the latter, however, the exception to the common law rule would appear to have a wider ambit than its counterpart(s) under Council Regulation 44/2001/EC.

QUESTION TWO

a) Scott, domiciled in Belgium, sends a letter from Belgium to Sandra, domiciled in France, in which he has written defamatory statements concerning Adrian, a

Canadian resident in England. Sandra makes a photocopy of the letter and adds that she agrees with its contents. She then sends it to Richard, a friend of Adrian, who is also resident in England. Richard shows the letter to Adrian.

Is Adrian entitled to sue both Scott and Sandra for libel in England?

b) Manuel Ltd is a company incorporated in Mexico. It has its central management and control in Spain. Manuel Ltd employs Cyril, an Englishman, to work in the Netherlands, under a written contract which provides that any dispute arising out of its terms shall be determined only by the Luxembourg or the Portuguese courts at either party's option.

Manuel Ltd wrongly terminates Cyril's employment contract. Cyril, understandably, wishes to sue the company but is not sure in which country proceedings may be raised.

What is your advice?

Question prepared by the Editor

General Comment

This question focuses on the aspects of Council Regulation 44/2001/EC that deal with tort and joint actions and also includes discussion of the domicile of corporations under the Regulation. Application to the facts of the question are essential though.

Skeleton Solution

a) Council Regulation 44/2001/EC – tort, art 5(3) – joinder, art 6(1).

b) Council Regulation 44/2001/EC – domicile and seat of corporations – prorogation of jurisdiction, art 23 – defendants not domiciled in a member state, art 4.

Suggested Solution

a) Adrian's actions will be for tort, thus 'civil and commercial' within the meaning of Council Regulation 44/2001/EC, art 1, and none of the exceptions in art 1 apply. Also, both potential defendants are domiciled in member states (Belgium and France respectively), thus jurisdiction will be determined by the provisions of the Regulation.

The primary rule is contained in art 2: the defendants are to be sued in the courts of their states of domicile, Belgium for Scott and France for Sandra. These provisions are mandatory and unless an alternative ground of jurisdiction can be found within the four walls of the Regulation, the English courts would be bound to declare of their own motion that they had no jurisdiction: art 26. This need not worry Adrian if Scott/Sandra are willing to be sued in England and enter appearances to Adrian's writs, since by art 24 'a court of a member state before which a defendant enters an appearance shall have jurisdiction' (unless the appearance is purely to protest the jurisdiction or the matter is within art 22 – as this case is not).

Are there any applicable grounds of jurisdiction in the more likely event of Scott/Sandra not wishing to be sued here? Taking Scott first, the only relevant head of jurisdiction is art 5(3), namely, 'in matters relating to tort ... in the courts for the place where the harmful event occurred'. In *Bier* v *Mines de Potasse d'Alsace* [1976] ECR 1735 the European Court held that these words cover both the place of the injurious conduct (here Belgium) and the place where the injury is suffered. The principle is of general application to torts, though Lasok and Stone, *Conflict of Laws in the European Community*, p232 speculate that it does not preclude the adoption by the court of a specific rule that the relevant place for defamation is that of the publication to the third person. Be that as it may, art 5(3) as interpreted in *Bier* will only avail Adrian if the publication took place in England, ie if Sandra received the letter here, and we are not instructed on this point; it would seem more likely that Sandra received Scott's letter in France, so that art 5(3) will not help Adrian.

As regards action against Sandra, in this case the publication (of Scott's letter as copied by Sandra, and of Sandra's own comments) appears to take place in England (assuming Richard received the letter here) and therefore art 5(3) will permit the English court to assume jurisdiction, provided that Adrian has not already commenced proceedings in France, which would be a bar to English jurisdiction: art 27.

It is worth pointing out that it will not be possible, even if Sandra is amenable to the jurisdiction, to bring Scott in by the use of the 'joinder' provision, art 6(1), since this is confined to cases in which the action is depending in the courts of the domicile of one of the defendants, and neither Scott nor Sandra is domiciled in England.

b) Here again the subject matter of the proposed suit is within art 1 of the Regulation. As for the defendant company, the position is summarised by Dicey and Morris, Rule 24(2)(c):

> '... a corporation has its seat [and is therefore domiciled for Regulation purposes] in a State other than the United Kingdom if ... (ii) its central management and control is exercised in that State, provided that it shall not be regarded as having its seat in a member state if by the law of that State it does not have its seat there.'

Thus it will be necessary to ascertain whether Spanish law regards Manuel Ltd as having its seat in Spain in these circumstances: arts 59 and 60, and Civil Jurisdiction and Judgments Act 1982 s42(1), (6) and (7).

i) Suppose that it does; then the Regulation will be applicable. Cyril's contract contains a written submission to the jurisdiction of the Luxembourg or Portuguese courts. This is a valid prorogation of jurisdiction, art 23, and Dicey and Morris, Rule 31. Only the Luxembourg or Portuguese courts will have jurisdiction, though if Cyril sues in another member state and Manuel Ltd submits to its jurisdiction, it will be able to take the case: art 24. (The wording of art 23 refers only to the choice of a single forum, but it is apprehended that this will apply to a choice in the alternative, as here; once either party sues in either Luxembourg or Portugal, the other country will, it is thought, be excluded. See *Meeth* v *Glacetal* [1978] ECR 2133, where the European Court held that the singular in art 23 could not exclude the right to agree on two or more courts in a form based on widespread commercial practice.)

ii) Suppose now that Spanish law does not regard Manuel Ltd as having its seat in Spain. We are no longer dealing with a defendant 'domiciled in a member state' (art 2), and art 4 applies, so that (since art 22 has no bearing here) the jurisdiction of the courts of each member state is domiciled by the law (the national conflicts law) of that state; however, the resulting judgments will be enforceable in other member states under the provisions of the Regulation.

Thus Cyril can take advice as to which member state it will be most advantageous for him to sue in. As far as England is concerned, the English courts would normally refuse to enforce a foreign judgment obtained in breach of a contractual submission to the Luxembourg or Portuguese courts. However, the Regulation takes priority and a judgment required under the Regulation to be enforced will be enforced here even though it is obtained, in breach of the agreement, in a different member state. Note however that if Cyril were to sue in Mexico, for instance, the resulting non-member state judgment would in general be unenforceable here.

QUESTION THREE

Franz, the owner of a timber estate in Germany, discovers that his trees are dying as a result of acid rain falling on them. He believes that he can prove that the acid rain is the result of pollution emanating from a power station in England owned by Cheap Electricity plc. Dick Pratt, the managing director of Cheap Electricity plc, in response to Franz's complaints about the acid rain, wrote to Houtkaufer AG, one of the main purchasers of wood from Franz, saying that Franz was a trouble-maker and 'nutter' and they should not buy any more wood from him as he was unreliable. The letter was posted in England but read by Houtkaufer AG in Germany.

Franz wishes to sue Cheap Electricity plc for the damage to his trees and also Pratt for the defamation. Advise him which courts have jurisdiction.

Question prepared by the Editor

General Comment

Another question demanding the student to focus on art 5(3) of Council Regulation 44/2001/EC. It is a relatively straightforward problem scenario, but students are advised to focus on the case law and not to seek an immediate/simple solution to the question.

Skeleton Solution

Civil and commercial matter – art 2 jurisdiction – special jurisdiction: art 5(3) – locus of the tort.

Suggested Solution

Franz *v* Cheap Electricity plc

The matter is plainly 'civil and commercial' thus in principle the rule of art 2 of Council Regulation 44/2001/EC applies: the defendant must be sued in the court of his domicile (presumably Cheap Electricity plc is domiciled in England). However, there may be special jurisdiction, ie jurisdiction in the courts of another member state in addition to the court of the defendant's domicile. If there is such jurisdiction it will be found in art 5(3) of the Regulation which provides that 'a person domiciled in a member state may, in another member state, be sued in matters relating to tort, delict or quasi-delict, in the courts for the place where the harmful event occurred'.

Plainly the dispute between Franz and Cheap Electricity plc relates to 'tort' and they are both domiciled in member states, so the court where 'the harmful event occurred' has jurisdiction. But is that event the emission of pollutants into the air in England or the falling of the acid rain in Germany? The European Court in *Bier* v *Mines de Potasse* [1976] ECR 1735 gave an authoritative interpretation of art 5(3) and held that the phrase 'harmful event' must be understood as being 'intended to cover both the place where the damage occurred and the place of event giving rise to it'. Thus in our example both the English courts and the German courts have jurisdiction under art 5(3). Hence Franz will be able to sue Cheap Electricity plc in Germany.

Franz *v* Pratt

Franz v *Cheap Electricity plc* was a relatively straightforward application of the jurisprudence of the European Court to art 5(3). However, *Franz* v *Pratt* is more difficult. Obviously, the domiciliary court has jurisdiction but the question is again whether there is special jurisdiction under art 5(3); and that depends upon where the 'harmful event' occurred. In *Shevill and Others* v *Presse Alliance SA* [1992] 1 All ER 409 the Court of Appeal considered the similar issue of the locus of a defamation. Defamatory matter had been published about the plaintiff in a French newspaper which regularly sold a few copies in England; did the English court have jurisdiction? Purchas LJ held that the libel had been published in England. This was not because of any special rule of English law but simply because the cause of action for libel arose when and where the publishee reads the publication. Since the publication had been read in England, the harmful event took place in England; and any member state where the publication was read would have art 5(3) jurisdiction (although the damages would not be extensive where only a few copies were read there). Note that this is not really an application of *Bier* v *Mines de Potasse* [1978] QB 708; England was both the place where the event giving rise to the harm occurred (reading the paper) and where the damage was suffered.

If *Shevill* is right then Franz has no difficulty since the letter was read by Houtkaufer in Germany. However, it does not stand alone. In the German case of *Re Unauthorised Publication of Approved Photographs* [1991] ILPr 468 the German courts held that unless the publication circulated to a significant extent in Germany the German courts lacked jurisdiction. After all, the German courts reasoned practically any publication in the world is, after a delay, available in Germany; that could not mean that the German courts had jurisdiction over all cases of injury caused by publication anywhere in the world. Ultimately, this issue will have to be sorted out by the European Court.

However, even if *Shevill* is wrong Franz may be able to establish special jurisdiction by arguing that even if the event that caused the harm (posting the letter) took place in England, the damage to his reputation amongst his customers took place in Germany, so under a *Bier* v *Mines de Potasse* approach he suffered harm in Germany; and so the German courts have art 5(3) jurisdiction.

QUESTION FOUR

Discuss the requirement in art 23 of Council Regulation 44/2001/EC that jurisdiction agreements must be in writing or evidenced in writing. What is the purpose of the requirement and how has it been interpreted?

Adapted from University of London LLB Examination
(for External Students) Conflict of Laws June 1993 Q8(b)

General Comment

A question that can tempt students to simply write all they know about the subject. The key to success lies in the second part of the question and requires analysis of case law and additional opinion.

Skeleton Solution

What art 23 permits – case law which has addressed aspects of formality under review.

Suggested Solution

Prorogation of jurisdiction, as provided for in art 23 of Council Regulation 44/2001/EC, refers to the ability of the parties to a contract to confer exclusive jurisdiction on the courts of a particular contracting state in the event of any legal disputes 'which have arisen or which may arise' between them. However, one of three requirements as to form has to be complied with in order to satisfy this agreement. The one that is a focal point of this question is that the jurisdiction agreement must be in writing or evidenced in writing.

In essence the purpose of art 23 in relation to form is that it contains specific requirements which have to be met in order to prove the consensus of the parties. However, the strictness of a specified formality may need to be tempered by standard commercial practice, if different. If such a situation arises this becomes a 'balancing act' on which the ECJ has to formulate appropriate principles.

In the case of a written contract containing a choice of jurisdiction clause, it was decided by the ECJ in *Colzani* v *Ruwa* Case 24/76 [1976] ECR 1831 that where the clause is contained in general conditions on the back of a signed contract there must also be express reference to the general conditions within the text of that contract. A further measure of the ECJ which reinforces its determination not to have a contracting party overlook this requirement of form is to provide that if only one party has signed the contract then the other must signify its consent in a separate document: *Partenreederei Russ and Russ* v *Haven and Vervoerbedrijf 'Nova' and Goeminne Hout* Case 71/83 [1984] ECR 2417. The intention of these measures is to ensure that the choice of jurisdiction clause does not go unnoticed.

In the case of an oral contract being confirmed in writing, initially the ECJ decided, in Case 24/76, that the party receiving the written contract containing the choice of jurisdiction clause had to have it accepted in writing by the other party. This was deemed necessary as, otherwise, there was no contract evidenced in writing. However, a relaxation of emphasis on form and a more practical approach towards balancing form with standard commercial practice was the outcome of the decision in Case 71/83. Here the ECJ held that a written choice of jurisdiction clause in a bill of lading could be regarded as written confirmation of an initial orally-communicated agreement between the parties in which there was express reference to that clause. Similarly, the recipient of a written contract, a term of which confirmed an earlier oral contract and which expressly agreed to a jurisdiction clause, was held to have satisfied the evidential requirements of art 23 when he raised no objection to the clause: *Berghoefer* v *ASA SA* [1986] 1 CMLR 13.

QUESTION FIVE

The European Court has held that the concepts 'matters relating to a contract' in Article 5(1) of Council Regulation 44/2001/EC, and 'matters relating to tort, delict or quasi-delict' in art 5(3) of the same Council Regulation 44/2001/EC are both required to be given an independent community meaning.

Explain, with reference to the cases, what this means.

Adapted from University of London LLB Examination
(for External Students) Conflict of Laws June 1995 Q1

General Comment

This is uncomfortably close to a 'write all you know about' type of question.

Skeleton Solution

Article 5 of Regulation 44/2001 in context – explanation of meaning of terms by reference to decisions of the European Court of Justice.

Suggested Solution

The basic jurisdictional rule under Council Regulation 44/2001/EC is contained in art 2 which provides that persons domiciled in a member state, whatever their nationality, must be sued in the courts of that state alone. However, art 5 provides for seven occasions of special jurisdiction, ie occasions on which a court other than that of the defendant's domicile shall have jurisdiction. It is for the plaintiff to elect where to sue the defendant when faced with the choice of jurisdiction.

Given that art 5 provides for a derogation from the basic jurisdictional rule, then this provision for special jurisdiction takes effect only if the defendant is domiciled in a member state and its terms must be interpreted strictly.

The two specified situations provided for in art 5 requiring explanations of their terms are 'matters relating to contract' in art 5(1) and 'matters relating to tort, delict or quasi-delict' in art 5(3).

Peters v *ZNAV* [1983] ECR 987 illustrated that the words 'matters relating to contract' have been given an autonomous community meaning. In this case, where a consequence of Peters' success in obtaining a contract for construction work was that it had to pay a sum of money to an association of which it was a member, the European Court of Justice (ECJ) held that:

> 'Obligations in regard to the payment of a sum of money which have their basis in the relationship existing between an association and its members by virtue of membership are "matters relating to a contract" within the meaning of art 5(1) of the [Brussels] Convention 1968 [now superseded by the Council Regulation] … It makes no difference whether the obligations in question arise simply from the act of becoming a member or from that act in conjunction with one or more decisions made by organs of the association.'

In essence, then, this community or Council Regulation meaning is wide enough to cover any matter having its basis in an agreement. This is well illustrated in the later case of *Arcado SPRL* v *Haviland SA* [1988] ECR 1539 where the ECJ held, that 'Proceedings relating to the wrongful repudiation of an independent commercial agency agreement and the payment of commission due under such an agreement are proceedings relating to a contract'. Moreover, in *Effer* v *Kanter* [1982] ECR 825 the ECJ held that the plaintiff could invoke special jurisdiction in accordance with art 5(1) 'even when the existence of the contract on which the claim is based is in dispute between the parties'. The English Court of Appeal has affirmed this approach in *Tesam Distribution* v *Schuh Mode Team GmbH* (1989) The Times 24 October.

With regard to the place of performance of the 'obligation in question' in 'matters relating to contract', the ECJ held in *Tessili v Dunlop AG* [1976] ECR 1473 that it is for the national courts of the member states of the EC to use their own rules of private international law to determine where the contract is to be performed. Whereas this approach does not appear to be in accord with a 'community concept', it is an approach which was not departed from in *Custom Made Commercial Ltd v Stawa Metallbau GmbH* [1994] ILPr 516.

Ivenel v Schwab [1982] ECR 1891 and *Shenavai v Kreischer* [1987] ECR 239 determined and affirmed, respectively, that with regard to contracts of employment, the 'obligation in question' is the 'characteristic performance' of such a contract, that is, it refers to the place where the employee habitually works. The identification of a single place of performance is meant to protect the employee by enabling the mandatory rules of employment legislation of the place of his work to be incorporated into his contract, irrespective of the proper law of the contract. That this protection is confined to contracts of employment was confirmed in *Mercury Publicity v Wolfgang Loerke GmbH* (1991) The Times 21 October where it was held that a contract engaging a company as an advertising agency was not of the personal master-servant nature and so outside the scope of *Ivenel v Schwab*.

In *De Bloos v Bouyer* [1976] ECR 1497 the ECJ held that the meaning of 'obligation in question' referred to 'the obligation forming the legal basis of the legal proceedings, namely the contractual obligation of the grantor which corresponds to the contractual right relied upon by the grantee in support of the application'. In other words, this means that it is the defendant's non-performance in the place of performance of the obligation imposed on him by his contract with the plaintiff which enables the latter to invoke the special jurisdiction provision of art 5(1) of Council Regulation 44/2001/EC. Limiting the 'obligation' to that which constitutes the plaintiff's claim ensures the avoidance of a multiplicity of courts having special jurisdiction.

In *Shenavai v Kreischer*, the ECJ decided that where more than one obligation was being sued on, it would be the courts for the place of performance of the most important of the contractual obligations on which any of the claims are based which would have jurisdiction. However, it is for the national courts to determine the principal obligation, an approach followed by the House of Lords in *Union Transport plc v Continental Lines SA* [1992] 1 Lloyd's Rep 229. If, or where, it would be artificial to select one obligation as the principal obligation, then *Shenavai* does not impose any demand on the national court to do so. Thus, the competence conferred on the latter by *De Bloos* is retained.

'Matters relating to tort' are provided for in art 5(3) of the Council Regulation. In *Kalfelis v Schroder, Munchmeyer, Hengst & Co* [1988] ECR 5565 the wide, community meaning given to this expression was said by the ECJ to include any action which calls a defendant's liability into question and which does not involve matters relating to a contract.

As to where the 'harmful event' occurs was a matter which fell for the ECJ to decide in

Handelskwekerij GJ Bier BV v *Mines de Potasse d'Alsace SA* [1978] QB 708 where it was held that it incorporated both the place where the defendant acted and the place where the plaintiff experienced the harm. The approach in *Bier* was applied in *Shevill and Others* v *Presse Alliance SA* (1995) The Times 6 April where it was held that a defamatory statement was published in England via the circulation of approximately 250 copies of a newspaper which had a circulation of about 200,000 copies in France. However, in *Re the Unauthorised Publication of Approved Photographs* [1991] ILPr 468, a German court held that it would be necessary for a newspaper to circulate to a significant extent or be distributed regularly before the 'harmful event' could be said to have occurred in Germany.

Moreover, a plaintiff seeking to invoke the special jurisdiction provisions of art 5(3) has to experience 'direct' harm. Accordingly, the ECJ has held in *Dumez France and Tracoba* v *Hessiche Landesbank (Helaba) and Others* [1990] ECR 49 that a parent company could not invoke the jurisdiction provisions in France to claim compensation for economic loss when its subsidiary company had been harmed in Germany.

The wording of art 5(3) has been held to include a claim for an infringement of a patent (*Molnlycke* v *Procter & Gamble Ltd* [1992] 1 WLR 1112), but not for restitution of monies paid under a contract which, in an earlier court case, had been declared to be void: *Barclays Bank plc* v *Glasgow City Council* [1994] 2 WLR 466.

It will be observed that the lack of definitions of terms within the Council Regulation has led to judicial interpretation, largely by the ECJ, which, of course, is to be expected if a single community meaning is to develop in relation to each of the terms analysed. However, the fact that a teleological interpretation is employed, ie, an interpretation which attempts to divine the purpose and spirit of the meaning, may appear to detract from the precision and consistency ideally expected of a literal approach to legislative terminology.

QUESTION SIX

'Has the Brussels Convention achieved what it was intended to achieve?'

University of London LLB Examination
(for External Students) Conflict of Laws June 2001 Q3

General Comment

This is an ideal question for the well-prepared and knowledgeable student to produce an excellent answer. Whilst it appears quite focused, the question requires the student to comment on two out of the three main issues of private international law: (a) jurisdiction; and (b) recognition and enforcement under the traditional rules and Convention rules. The student needs to keep in mind the purpose of the Convention and resist the temptation to describe the two sets of rules.

Skeleton Solution

Two main aspects of private international law – jurisdiction of the courts, recognition and enforcement of judgments – purpose of the Brussels Convention – Council Regulation 44/2001/EC – comparison with the traditional rules of jurisdiction.

Suggested Solution

It may be suggested that the subject of jurisdiction is now the most important aspect of private international law. The reasons for this are twofold. First, the development of the doctrine of forum non conveniens has had a significant impact on the traditional rules. Second, the establishment of statutory scheme on jurisdiction, the Brussels Convention 1968, introduced into English law by the Civil Jurisdiction and Judgments Act 1982.

Jurisdiction concerns the competence of a state's courts to hear a case with an authority that will make the decision binding and enforceable within their own system, as well as capable of recognition and enforcement by the courts of other states. Whilst this sounds perfectly straightforward, the question arises as to whether the approach adopted by a particular court to determine its competence is acceptable or unacceptable to the courts of another state, as this will have an impact on recognition and enforcement. For instance, if a jurisdiction's rules are too lax, then they may encourage 'forum shopping', with cases being brought before the open forum which have little, if no, connection with the state. This in turn will have an impact on whether other states will recognise and subsequently enforce the resultant judgments of these cases. By contrast, if they are too restrictive, then this may result in a denial of justice with cases being turned away.

Traditionally, English law adopted an open forum policy for personal actions. The result was an influx of personal actions which had little or no connection with England. Whilst this was good business, the liberal approach to jurisdiction impacted on the respect attached to judgments granted by the English courts. Over time, the courts adopted the principle of forum non conveniens – recognising/acknowledging the fact that a more appropriate court for litigation existed: *Spiliada Maritime Corporation* v *Cansulex Ltd* [1986] 3 All ER 843. Whilst this represents a more disciplined and restrained approach towards the exercise of jurisdiction by the courts, it nevertheless still represents the English approach towards this aspect of private international law. Consequently, the question remains as to whether another country's courts will recognise the competence of the English courts and as such their willingness to recognise and enforce any resulting judgment.

Under the Treaty of Rome 1957, the original members of the EEC entered into a Convention on Jurisdiction and the Enforcement of Judgments in Civil and Commercial matters in 1968. This was the original Brussels Convention and it entered into force in 1973.

The original object of the Convention was to provide for the free circulation of judgments within the Community as it was seen as an important aspect of European integration and growth of the 'Common Market'. However, it was felt that this free circulation of judgments would not be accepted unless the courts of member states had confidence in the claims to jurisdiction made by the courts of other states. In order to resolve this potential difficulty, it was seen as necessary to unify the law on international jurisdiction in member states. In this respect, the Convention set out to regulate two of the main issues in private international law: the jurisdiction of courts and the recognition and enforcement of judgments rendered in other member states.

Each enlargement of the EC led to changes/amendments to the original Convention. Until Council Regulation 44/2001/EC, there were five versions of the Brussels Convention. Whilst each version provided the opportunity to fine tune the content of the Convention, it nevertheless resulted in the question as to which version was relevant to the dispute in question.

The UK signed an instrument of Accession to the Brussels Convention in 1978 and it was given effect into domestic law via the Civil Jurisdiction and Judgments Act (CJJA) 1982. Consequently, from this date, the English courts were bound to abide by the Convention's rules on jurisdiction in cases falling within its scope.

Article 1 outlines the scope of the Convention, stating that it applies in civil and commercial matters. Unfortunately, the Community definition of the concept of 'civil and commercial matters' does not sit easily with the English courts: *LTU v Eurocontrol* [1976] ECR 1541. In addition, certain subjects are expressly excluded from the scope of the Convention, such as revenue and administrative matters, arbitration and bankruptcy. Those matters, which fall outside the scope of the Convention, are governed by the traditional common law rules discussed above.

The fundamental principle of the Brussels Convention on the international jurisdiction of courts in member states is that when the defendant is domiciled in a member state, then he is subject to the jurisdiction of that state: art 2. Consequently, the Convention uses the concept of domicile to link individuals to specific legal systems in order to decide the issue of jurisdiction. In this respect, s41 CJJA 1982 contains the definition of domicile for individuals in United Kingdom law.

However, there are two types of exceptions to this general principle: special jurisdiction under art 5 and exclusive jurisdiction as provided for in art 16. Article 5 contains specific provisions in relation to contract, maintenance, tort, branches and agencies, trusts and admiralty. Article 16 deals with exclusive jurisdiction, the main heading being art 16(1) which provides that in proceedings which have as their object rights in rem in immovable property, the courts of the legal system in which the property is situated have exclusive jurisdiction: *Webb v Webb* [1994] ILPr 389.

In addition to this, arts 13–15 make special provision for consumer contracts. Article 14 provides that a consumer is permitted to bring proceedings in either the court of the supplier's domicile or his own domicile. Likewise, arts 7–12 make provision for insurance contracts. It should be noted at this point that the new Council Regulation 44/2001/EC has added to this by including specific provisions regarding contracts of employment. This has been in response to a number of difficulties faced by the courts of member states when trying to apply the Brussels Convention to this area.

It may be seen from this brief discussion of the Convention that it created a complex set of rules designed to determine the competence of a member state's court to hear a case. Consequently, once the Convention allocates jurisdiction to an English court, it has no discretion to try the case (given the fact that the doctrine of forum non conveniens does not apply). However, this has two beneficial effects. First, these rules are identical in all member states. Therefore, if the Convention indicates that the English courts have jurisdiction, the courts of other states would have reached a similar conclusion. Second, the enforcement of judgments has been improved across other member states in terms of procedure, cost and time.

By contrast, whilst the traditional rules under the common law have curbed their open forum approach through the adoption of the doctrine of forum non conveniens, recognition and enforcement by another state's courts is by no means guaranteed. The traditional rules still represent the English court's approach (as opposed to the Convention's collective approach) towards its competence to hear a case, which in turn may either be viewed as acceptable or unacceptable by the courts of another state. Consequently, the process of enforcing a judgment may prove to be burdensome, costly and uncertain.

As such, it may be said that the Brussels Convention has achieved what it set out to achieve. Subsequent versions of the 1968 Convention have attempted to improve its mechanics up until the implementation of the new Council Regulation 44/2001/EC which represents the latest approach towards this area.

Chapter 6

Contract

6.1 Introduction

A contractual obligation cannot exist in a vacuum. There must be a legal system from which that contract can draw its binding force. In this chapter we are concerned with the rules that are used to determine what that legal system is (often called 'the proper law of the contract') in any particular case. This is an important topic both from the point of view of the examination and for practical and commercial reasons. In addition, other aspects will be examined including capacity to contract and the formalities of the contract which are not necessarily governed by the proper law.

The law in this area underwent a fundamental change with the enactment of the Contracts (Applicable Law) Act 1990, which enacted into English law the Rome Convention 1980 and that now dominates the law in this area. However, the student should note that the common law (which has now been largely superseded) and the Convention contain similar principles, most importantly that of party autonomy to select the law applicable to the contract.

6.2 Key points

The distinction between the common law position and the statutory regime

In common with the subject of jurisdiction, a two-tier system of law operates in relation to choice of law in contractual relationships.

The common law principles regulating the choice of law in contracts have been largely superseded by a statutory regime introduced by the Contracts (Applicable Law) Act 1990 which itself gave effect to the EC Convention on the Law Applicable to Contractual Obligations 1980 (known as the Rome Convention). Once again, this Convention is an agreement negotiated among the member states of the European Union with a view to co-ordinating and harmonising this aspect of law among the member states.

The statutory regime dominates this area of the law since the scope of the Convention to which the statute gives effect is extensive. The common law principles only continue to apply to those situations where the Convention regime is inapplicable. These are two-fold:

a) the Convention is not retroactive and the common law will continue to apply to regulate contractual relationships entered into before the Convention came into force, namely 1 April 1991;

b) the Convention itself excludes certain subjects from its scope and these matters will continue to be regulated by the common law.

The common law rules – general principles

The common law rules revolve around a system for the selection of the proper law of a contract. The proper law of a contract is simply the legal system which regulates the contractual relationship between the parties to the contract. From a strict legal perspective, the proper law has been defined as:

> '... the substantive law of the country which the parties have chosen as that by which their mutually legally enforceable rights are to be ascertained': *Amin Rasheed Shipping Corp* v *Kuwait Insurance Co* [1983] 2 All ER 884.

Unfortunately, there is no single overriding legal principle in English law which allows the proper law of a contract to be deduced.

On the other hand, if there is a general principle applied by the English courts for the selection of the proper law of the contract it is that the parties are free to select the law which they wish to regulate their contractual relationship. In the absence of an express choice, the courts will even try to construe their intentions by examining the terms of the contract in order to ascertain if a legal system is the proper law by implication.

It should be observed at this point that the proper law is the law which applies to the application, construction and enforcement of the terms of the contract subject to two limitations:

a) a contract will normally have only one proper law, but in certain cases, two or more proper laws may be found to exist to regulate different terms of the contract.

b) the proper law of a contract does not regulate all aspects of the contractual relationship. Certain aspects are reserved for the laws of legal systems other than that of the proper law. For example, capacity to contract is not considered to be an issue for the proper law but rather for the law of the domicile of the parties.

Process for the determination of the proper law

Lord Atkin has spelled out the applicable process for the determination of the proper law in the following terms:

> 'The legal principles which are to guide an English court on the question of the proper

law of a contract are now well settled. It is the law which the parties intend to apply. Their intention will be ascertained by the intention expressed in the contract, if any, which will be conclusive. If no intention be expressed, the intention will be presumed by the court from the terms of the contract and the relevant surrounding circumstances': *R v International Trustee for the Protection of Bondholders* [1937] AC 500.

The methodology which a court will follow is therefore three-fold. The proper law of the contract is the law expressly selected by the parties. In the absence of an express selection, the law will be that of the legal system which is implied by the parties. If no such system is implied, the court will assign a proper law to the contract.

Express choice of law

If the parties have specified in the contract a particular law to govern their agreement then, almost invariably, this choice will be upheld by the courts and will be the proper law of the contract: see *Vita Food Products Inc v Unus Shipping Co Ltd* [1939] AC 277.

The parties must express their intention in precise and unambiguous terms. Provided that the intention expressed is bona fide, legal and there is no reason for refusing to give effect to the choice on grounds of public policy, this intention will be conclusive. These are the main three grounds on which a court may rule that an express choice of law will be ineffective.

The requirement of bona fide

A choice of English law as the proper law of a contract will remain bona fide even though the parties have no obvious connection with England. For example, in *Vita Food Products* (above) the court held that the selection of English law in a contract between a Canadian company and an American company was valid since English law has established effective and renowned legal principles in the area of law which concerned the contract.

A choice will not be bona fide, however, if the parties select a particular law for the sole purpose of evading their obligations under a legal system. This possibility is becoming increasingly more remote due to the growth of mandatory requirements in certain legal systems. These are statutes which provide that regardless of the proper law, certain contractual terms will not be enforced.

For example, the Employment Protection (Consolidation) Act 1978 provides that where an employee ordinarily works in the United Kingdom, for the purposes of the statute, it is immaterial whether the law which governs that person's employment is the law of the United Kingdom or not, because certain statutory rights cannot be taken away.

Similarly, the Unfair Contract Terms Act 1977 states that where it appears to a court that a choice of law has been imposed wholly or mainly for the purpose of enabling the party imposing it to evade the operation of the Act, the statute will continue to apply.

The requirement of legality

Similarly, contracts which are illegal will not be enforced by the English courts. This is simply an extension of the same doctrine which applies in English contract law. Diplock LJ ably stated the scope of this rule in *Mackender* v *Feldia AG* [1966] 3 All ER 847 where he made three propositions in this connection:

a) English courts will not enforce an agreement, whatever its proper law, if it is contrary to English law, whether statute or common law.

b) English courts will not enforce, even though it is not contrary to English law, a contractual term if it is void for illegality under the proper law of the contract.

c) English courts will not enforce performance or give damages for non-performance of an act required to be done under a contract, whatever be the proper law of the contract, if the act would be illegal in the country in which it is required to be performed: see *Howard* v *Shirlstar Container Transport Ltd* [1990] 3 All ER 366.

Public policy

Although there are very few reported cases whereby an English court has refused to apply a rule of foreign law as the proper law on the grounds of public policy this possibility has been alluded to in a number of cases: see *R* v *International Trustee for the Protection of Bondholders* [1937] AC 500.

Implied choice of law

Where the parties fail to nominate an express choice of law, the courts will attempt to identify which proper law is implied in the terms of the contract. Unfortunately this is not always an easy task and, to a large degree, depends on the facts and circumstances surrounding the negotiation of the contract.

The following factors have been taken into consideration by the courts in ascertaining the implied choice of law:

a) where the parties provide that any disputes should be submitted to adjudication or arbitration in a particular country, this is a significant indication that the law of that country is the proper law by implication: see *Compagnie Tunisienne de Navigation SA* v *Compagnie d'Armement Maritime SA* [1971] AC 572;

b) the language in which the contract is drafted;

c) the place the contract is to be performed and the place payment is to be made;

d) the locations and places of business of the parties;

e) the currency in which payment is to be made;

f) the maturity of the legal principles in a particular legal system over the relative infancy of another. For example, the English laws of marine insurance have a special value in international trade and reference to terms in the English terminology is a strong factor in favour of the selection of English law: see *Amin Rasheed Shipping Corp* v *Kuwait Insurance Co* [1983] 2 All ER 884.

Obviously not all these factors have equal weight. It is a question of balancing all the facts and circumstances of the case against each other in order to arrive at the proper law of the contract.

The absence of an express or implied choice of law

It is not impossible for a situation to arise in which the parties did not contemplate that a particular law should apply to their contractual relationship. In such situations, the court must assign a proper law to the contract.

Originally, the general principle in this situation was as follows. Where there was no choice of law, either express or implied:

> '... the court has to impute an intention or to determine for the parties the proper law which, as just and reasonable persons, they ought to or would have intended if they had thought about the question when they made the contract': *Mount Albert Borough Council* v *Australasian Assurance Society Ltd* [1938] AC 224.

In modern law, this test has been boiled down to principle that the proper law in such circumstances under the common law is 'that with which the transaction has its closest and most real connection': *Amin Rasheed Shipping Corp* (above).

This is a process of weighing up the wide range of factors connected to the contract and is an exercise of judgment and weighing of a multitude of factors. There is no limit to the number of factors which can be taken into consideration, provided that they have some bearing on the transaction.

Again the place of contracting, the place of performance, the places of residence or business of the parties, as well as the nature and subject matter of the contract are all matters which must be taken into consideration.

The application of the proper law to the terms of the contract

Not all contractual matters are governed by the proper law. Some are governed by the laws of other legal systems depending on the particular issue under consideration.

Formation of the contract

The formation of a contract usually involves issues such as the need for consideration, offer and acceptance, mistake, misrepresentation, duress and undue influence. The putative proper law – ie the law which would be the proper law if the contract was validly concluded – is generally applicable to the resolution of these matters: see *Mackender* v *Feldia* [1967] 2 QB 590.

Formal validity

The formalities required for the valid conclusion of a contract are regulated by either the lexi loci contractus or the putative proper law. The question has never been definitively resolved and opinion on the matter is evenly split among writers between these two options.

Capacity

As far as decisions concerning the law applicable to the determination of capacity to contract are concerned, again there is no established definitive view. Some cases support the application of the lex domicilii, but the majority of these cases concern capacity to marry: see *Sottomayor v de Barros (No 1)* (1877) 3 PD 1. Other cases, including the most recent relevant English case, indicate a tendency towards the selection of the objective proper law of the contract: *Bodley Head Ltd v Flegon* [1972] 1 WLR 680. Also see *Cooper v Cooper* (1888) 13 App Cas 88. A further alternative is to allow the lex loci contractus to determine capacity to contract.

The upshot of all this is that, as Morris points out (see *The Conflict of Laws* (2000), 5th ed at p288), the actual law that would be applied in a matter of capacity to contract before an English court is 'anyone's guess'. However, from a practical perspective, it may be suggested that application of the objective proper law offers the most logical choice.

Essential validity of the contract

The essential validity of a contract is to be decided by reference to the proper law of the contract: see *Dimskal Shipping Co SA v International Transport Workers' Federation* [1991] 4 All ER 871.

Discharge of the contract

It is generally recognised that the matter of the discharge of a contract is an issue for the proper law of the contract: see *Jacobs v Credit Lyonnais* (1884) 12 QBD 589.

Performance

Again, the proper law of the contract governs the substance of the obligation: *Mount Albert Borough Council v Australasian Assurance Society Ltd* [1938] AC 224.

Interpretation

The most common term in a contract referring to a choice of law is a term specifying which law is to apply in the interpretation of the provisions of a contract. Where such a term has been incorporated, the courts will give effect to the intention of the parties: *Forsikringsaktiesekapet Vesta v Butcher* [1986] 2 All ER 488.

The Rome Convention on the Law Applicable to Contractual Obligations 1980

In an ambitious effort to harmonise the conflict of laws rules of the member states of the European Union as far as these concern contractual relations, the Rome Convention on the Law Applicable to Contractual Relations 1980 was negotiated. This international agreement was incorporated into English law by the Contracts (Applicable Law) Act 1990 which came into force on 1 April 1991. The majority of relevant principles are contained in the Convention as opposed to the statute itself.

The Rome Convention has been added to by the First Protocol on the Interpretation by the ECJ of the Convention Applicable to Contractual Relations which creates a mechanism to allow national courts to apply to the European Court of Justice for guidance in the interpretation of the terms of the Convention itself.

On the question of interpretation, the Convention expressly provides in art 18 that, in interpreting the rules of the Convention 'regard shall be had to their international character and to the desirability of achieving uniformity in their interpretation and application'. This principle requires the English courts to take into consideration not only the jurisprudence of the European Court, but also the decisions of other national courts of the Convention countries.

The scope of the Convention

It is important to grasp the extent of the scope of the Convention. Article 1(1) of the Convention stipulates that:

> 'The rules of this Convention shall apply to contractual obligations in any situation involving a choice between the laws of different countries.'

The application of the Convention is not therefore restricted to situations involving a selection between the laws of two or more EU states; it applies to any situation involving a choice between the laws of different countries, whether European Union member states or otherwise. It is the existence of a need to make a selection between competing legal systems in the course of litigation in the English courts that gives rise to the application of the Convention.

The world-wide scope of application of the Convention gives rise to some difficulties regarding the interpretation of art 1(1):

a) Which legal system is to be used to determine whether a particular disputed relationship amounts to a contractual obligation or not? Article 8(1) of the Convention gives some guidance by providing that the validity of a contract 'shall be determined by the law which would govern it under this Convention if the contract were valid'.

b) While the Convention used the term 'countries', it is relatively clear that this means legal systems. Article 19(1) of the Convention establishes the rule that where states consist of 'several territorial units' with different legal systems, 'each territorial unit will be considered as a country for the purposes of identifying the law applicable under the Convention'.

It should also be pointed out at this stage that, according to s2(3) of the Contracts (Applicable Law) Act 1990, the Convention applies to disputes concerning a selection of the applicable law from the laws of England and Wales, Scotland and Northern Ireland.

Although the ambit of the scope of the Convention is broad, there are certain matters expressly excluded from its range. These are specified in art 1(2) and (3) and include questions relating to:

a) the capacity and status of natural and legal persons;

b) contractual obligations relating to wills and succession, matrimonial property and other family law matters;

c) obligations arising under most aspects of negotiable instruments;

d) arbitration agreements and agreements on the choice of courts;

e) company law, agency, trusts, evidence and procedure; and

f) insurance.

One additional exception should also be mentioned: art 21 provides that the Convention shall not prejudice the application of international conventions to which a member state is, or becomes, a party.

The basic principles of the Convention

Party autonomy

Like the common law, the Convention recognises the autonomy of contracting parties to select the legal system which will govern their contract: art 3(1). This choice must be express and demonstrated with reasonable certainty by the terms of the contract or the circumstances of the case. The parties can select a law applicable to the whole of the contract or only to a part of it.

The parties are also free at any time, even after the contract has been concluded and when litigation is pending, to agree to subject the contract to another law other than that previously agreed: art 3(2).

The issue of how to determine whether the choice of law clause is valid is addressed in art 3(4) which provides that:

> 'The existence and validity of the consent of the parties as to the choice of the applicable law shall be determined in accordance with the provisions of Articles 8 [material validity], 9 [formal validity] and 11 [incapacity].'

Limitations on party autonomy

The Convention limits the choices of the parties to select particular legal systems for specific types of contracts:

a) Consumer contracts – a choice of law by the parties shall not have the effect of depriving the consumer of the protection afforded to him by the mandatory rules of the law of the country in which he is habitually resident: art 5.

b) Employment contracts – the rights of employees are not to be rendered illusory by a choice of law foisted by an employer on an employee: art 6.

c) General mandatory requirements – where the parties have made an express choice of law but all the other localising elements of the contract are connected with another country, the choice of law will not be allowed to prejudice the application of the laws of that country which cannot be derogated from by contract: arts 3(3) and 7.

The principle of closest connection

Where no express choice of law has been made by the parties, the contract is governed by the law of the country with which it is 'most closely connected': art 4(1).

Article 4(2) creates a presumption of closest connection. It stipulates that:

> '... it shall be presumed that the contract is most closely connected with the country where the party who is to effect the performance which is characteristic of the contract has, at the time of the conclusion of the contract, his habitual residence, or, in the case of a body corporate or unincorporate, its central administration.'

The doctrine of 'characteristic performance', which is critical to the operation of this principle, is open to the criticism that it is not always a straightforward process to determine what the characteristic performance of a contract may be.

At the same time, the application of the doctrine is clear in some circumstances, eg, in a contract of sale, the characteristic performance is the delivery of the goods which have been sold; in a contract of employment the characteristic performance is the work itself.

The presumption of closest connection is slightly modified for some types of contract including the following:

a) contracts made in the course of a party's trade or profession – the country of closest connection is the country in which the principal's place of business is situated (art 4(2);

b) contracts for the carriage of goods – the country of closest connection is the country in which the carrier has its principal place of business (art4(4));

c) contracts relating to immovable property – the country of the closest connection is that of the location of the property (art 4(3)).

Finally, art 4(5) makes it clear that the rules set out in the preceding three paragraphs are only presumptions. Consequently, they 'shall be disregarded if it appears from the circumstances as a whole that the contract is more closely connected with another country.'

Particular aspects of the contract

Material validity

Article 8(1) of the Convention provides that the validity of a contract is to be determined by reference to the law which would govern it under the Convention if the contract was valid. In other words, it is the putative proper law which is applicable.

This principle is, however, qualified by art 8(2) which allows a party to rely on the law of his habitual residence to establish his consent if it would not be reasonable to determine the effect of his conduct in accordance with the putative proper law.

Formal validity

Where the parties are in the same country when the contract is concluded, formal validity is tested either by the law of the country with the closest connection or the law of the country where the parties are located: art 9(1).

Where the parties are in different countries, then the law of either of the countries where the parties are located is applicable: art 9(2)

Incapacity

Article 11 of the Convention provides that where the parties are in the same country, then a natural person can only invoke an incapacity arising out of another law if the other party knew of the incapacity or was unaware of it through his negligence.

The scope of the applicable law as determined under the Convention

Article 10 specifies the matters which are to be governed by the applicable law. These are: interpretation, performance, the consequences of breach (including damages), the extinguishing of obligations, limitation of actions and the consequences of the nullity of a contract.

It should also be noted, as a final point, that renvoi does not apply under the Convention.

6.3 Key cases and statutes

• *Amin Rasheed Shipping Corporation* v *Kuwait Insurance Co* [1984] AC 50
  Implied choice of law to govern contract

- *Assunzione, The* [1954] P 150
  Common law – determining the proper law of contract – no express choice

- *Boissevain* v *Weil* [1950] AC 327
  Giving effect to proper law of contract – overriding statute cannot be ignored

- *Definitely Maybe (Touring) Ltd* v *Marek Lieberberg Konzertagentur GmbH* [2001] 2 Lloyd's Rep 455
  Article 4 – place of performance

- *Dubai Electricity Co* v *Islamic Republic of Iran Shipping Lines* [1984] 2 Lloyd's Rep 380
  Floating applicable law is not usually valid

- *Egon Oldendorff* v *Liberia Corporation* [1995] 2 Lloyd's Rep 65
  Putative proper law will govern issues of material validity

- *Gan Insurance Co Ltd* v *Tai Ping Insurance Co Ltd* [1999] CLC 1270
  Pre-existing contract/course of dealings – express choice of law

- *Hollandia, The* [1983] 1 AC 565
  Particular statutes from lex fori may override an express choice of law

- *Vita Food Products Inc* v *Unus Shipping Co Ltd* [1939] AC 277
  Common law – party autonomy – express choice of law

- Contracts (Applicable Law) Act 1990 – implements the Rome Convention on the Law Applicable to Contractual Obligations 1980

- The Giuliano Lagarde Report – guidance as to the interpretation of the Rome Convention (see above)

6.4 Questions and suggested solutions

QUESTION ONE

i) What autonomy does English law give to parties to choose the law to govern their contract?

ii) X and Co, a Utopian company, enter into a contract with Y and Co, a Ruritanian company, to purchase Ruritanian timber. The contract provides that the timber be shipped aboard Erewhonian ships and paid for in Erewhonian currency in Erewhon. Before the timber reaches Utopia, the Utopian government bans the import of Ruritanian timber because, so it says, this is cut by slave labour. Y and Co has to sell the timber at an auction in Erewhon for a knock down price. Y and Co has sued X and Co, in England, where X and Co has a place of business. Advise Y as to its chance of success.

University of London LLB Examination
(for External Students) Conflict of Laws June 1991 Q3

General Comment

Whilst the second part of this question is relatively simple, the student must focus upon addressing the first part appropriately. Students should not be tempted to discuss art 4 of the Rome Convention within this section of the question.

Skeleton Solution

Party autonomy: art 3(1) of the Rome Convention – art 7(1); s2(2) Contracts (Applicable Law) Act 1990 – limits on the principle of party autonomy – where there is no choice: art 4 – illegality: art 10(1)(b), etc.

Suggested Solution

i) Article 3(1) of the Rome Convention 1980 spells out the basic rule that the parties may by their express or implied choice choose the governing law of the contract. Article 3 provides that:

> 'A contract shall be governed by the law chosen by the parties. The choice must be express or demonstrated with reasonable certainty by the terms of the contract or the circumstances of the case. By their choice the parties can select the law applicable to the whole or only part of their contract.'

Furthermore, the Rome Convention is not restricted to contracts that are in some way connected to the EC, for art 1 provides that the Convention applies 'to contractual obligations in *any* situation involving a choice between the laws of different countries'; and art 2 makes it clear that '*any* law specified by this Convention shall be applied whether or not it is the law of a Contracting State.'

So the basic principle is that under the Rome Convention the parties have a very considerable autonomy to choose the law applicable to their contract. However, art 3(3) does limit this party autonomy to a certain degree. It provides that the choice of a foreign law

> '... where all the other elements relevant to the situation at the time of the choice are connected with one country only, [shall not] prejudice the application of rules of the law of that country which cannot be derogated from by contract, hereinafter called "mandatory rules".'

Several other articles may restrict the autonomy of the parties. The most prominent of these is art 7(1) (although as we shall see it does not apply in the United Kingdom). Article 7 provides that 'effect *may* be given to the mandatory rules of the law of ... [a country other than that of the chosen law] with which the situation has a close connection ... in so far as ... those rules must be applied whatever the law applicable to the contract'. Many civilian legal systems recognise that there are rules from neither the lex fori nor the lex causae that should be taken into account. However, the United Kingdom entered a reservation to this article and subsequently provided in s2(2) of the Contracts (Applicable Law) Act 1990 that art 7(1) 'shall not have the force of law in the United Kingdom'.

The other articles that should be noted are arts 5 and 6. Article 5 deals with consumer contracts and provides that an art 3 choice of another law 'shall not have the result of depriving the consumer of the protection afforded to him by the mandatory rules of the law of the country in which he has his habitual residence.' This principle is restricted to contracts connected in a range of ways with his country of habitual residence. Secondly, art 6 limits party autonomy in the context of individual contracts of employment. Once more the employee cannot be deprived of the protection of the mandatory rules of the legal system that would otherwise apply.

Where there is no choice in terms of art 3, then the principles laid down in art 4 apply.

ii) Since there is plainly no art 3 choice, art 4 applies to determine the governing law of the contract. The basic principle is that 'the contract shall be governed by the law of the country with which it is most closely connected.' (Note that we are here talking about a *country* whereas we saw earlier that at common law the search is for the legal *system* with which the contract is most closely connected.)

The task of determining this law is aided by the presumption in art 4(2) that the contract is presumed most closely connected with the law of the country in which the party who is to carry out the 'characteristic performance' of the contract is habitually resident. However, a different rule applies where the contract is entered into during the course of that party's (ie the party performing the characteristic performance) 'trade or profession'. In these circumstances, the presumption of closest connection leads to 'the country in which the principal place of business is situated'.

Now Y and Co in shipping the timber performs the 'characteristic performance'. (X and Co's obligation to pay can hardly be characteristic.) Thus the presumption is that Ruritanian law (apparently Y and Co's place of business) is that with which the contract is most closely connected. It may be that this presumption can be displaced (and if this contract is a contract for 'the carriage of goods' the presumption does not apply: art 4(4)). However, let us follow the presumption and assume that Ruritanian law is the governing law.

The remaining question is the effect of the illegality under Utopian law. There is plainly no scope for the application of art 3(3) or art 7(1) discussed above. But the illegality may be relevant in two ways:

First of all, art 10 while providing that the governing law (in our case Ruritanian law) shall govern 'performance' (art 10(1)(b)), also provides (art 10(2)) in relation to 'the manner of performance ... regard shall be had to the law of the country in which the performance takes place'. This is awkward. Obviously, the court is not bound to apply the lex loci solutionis but what then is the judge supposed to do? The authors of the Giuliano-Lagarde Report say that the judge has a discretion but give little guidance on how to exercise that discretion.

But, second, whatever way the English judge chooses to exercise his discretion in terms of art 10(2), art 16 says that 'a rule of the law of any country specified by this Convention may be refused only if such application is manifestly incompatible with the public policy of the forum.' Since as we have seen, public policy (*Ralli Bros* v *Compagnia Naviera Sota y Aznar* [1920] 2 KB 287 aside) seems to underlie the lex loci solutionis principle in English law, this may provide a route by which the English court may refuse enforcement because of the illegality under the law of Utopia.

QUESTION TWO

In June 1990, Steve, domiciled and resident in South Africa, agreed to sell to Rio Tinto, domiciled and resident in the Netherlands, 100 tonnes of copper ore from Steve's mine in Namibia. The bargain is struck by the exchange of letters which state that the contract is to be governed by Namibian law. The stipulated price is 1,000 US dollars per tonne and the price is payable in South Africa in Rands. The consignment is to be transported by ship from Namibia and delivered to Rio Tinto in Rotterdam. All disputes arising from the terms of the agreement are to be determined by the English courts.

By South African law, South African producers are forbidden to sell copper for less than 2,000 US dollars per tonne. By Dutch law, but no other law, a contract to import copper into the Netherlands must be registered with an advokat. This requirement has not been satisfied. While the vessel carrying the copper is on the open seas, the South African government passed a statute boycotting deliveries of copper by South African residents to the Netherlands.

Rio Tinto tendered payment to Steve in South Africa of the equivalent in Rands of 100,000 US dollars. Steve refused to accept payment saying that the agreement was invalid under both South African and Dutch law. The ship's captain obeys Steve's order not to deliver the copper at Rotterdam. Rio Tinto wishes to sue Steve for non-delivery.

How would you advise Rio Tinto?

Question prepared by the Editor

General Comment

Problem questions can frequently appear rather daunting to students. However, if the student has a sound understanding of (in this case) the common law principle regulating the proper law of a contract, then such scenarios are no problem.

Skeleton Solution

Contract – illegality – illegality by lex loci solutionis – public policy.

Suggested Solution

Since the contract was entered into prior to 1 April 1991, the common law rules regulating the selection of the proper law of contract will apply.

This problem raises issues of illegality of contract. It is well settled that a contract will not be enforced in the English courts if it is illegal by its proper law (applicable law), or if it is contrary to an 'overriding' English statute or to English public policy. In the instant case there is no relevant English statute, and the contract is not illegal by Namibian law which is the applicable law selected by the parties. It is not clear where the contract was made, but in any event illegality by the lex loci contractus is immaterial. (In terms of formalities, there is nothing to object to the contract which is valid by the formalities requirements of its proper law.)

The important questions in the instant case are whether the contract is illegal by the law of its place of performance and whether such illegality renders the contract unenforceable in the English courts. The contract requires the transportation of copper by ships from Namibia, a performance to be effected in Namibia, and it seems not illegal by Namibian law either as to substance or as to incidents eg price of the copper. Delivery however is to be in the Netherlands and the contract has not been registered with a solicitor as required by Dutch law. However it is unclear what the effect of non-compliance with this requirement is under Dutch law, and it may be that non-compliance would not be such a default as to make the contract unenforceable in the English courts even assuming illegality by the lex loci solutionis to afford a defence. (Further it may be relevant that Steve has not even attempted performance as regards delivery.)

Admitting for argument's sake that the contract is illegal and unenforceable by the law of the Netherlands, the question whether such illegality renders the contract one which cannot be sued upon in England is an open one: see Dicey and Morris, Rule 177 and Exceptions. There is no direct authority on the point, once it has been distinguished from situations where the contract is also illegal by English domestic law or by its proper law, and there are dicta pointing either way in *Kahler* v *Midland Bank* [1950] AC 24 and *Zivnostenska Banka* v *Frankman* [1950] AC 57. Dicey and Morris tentatively adopt the view that such a contract is unenforceable but admit that the contrary view 'both on practical and on theoretical grounds has much to commend itself'.

Illegality by South African law, with the original illegality as to the price and subsequent law, is not directly material. A similar (or rather converse) price law was upheld in *Ralli Bros* v *Compagnia Naviera Sota y Aznar* [1920] 2 KB 287, but there the contract was governed by English law. An English court will not allow a contracting party to refuse performance on the grounds that performance would infringe the law of his own country, where that is neither the proper law nor the law of the place of performance and enforcement would not be contrary to English public policy: *Kleinwort* v *Ungarische Baumwolle* [1939] 2 KB 678.

It remains to consider whether enforcement may be refused on the grounds of conflict with English public policy: Dicey and Morris, Rule 177 and Exceptions. The objection would be that enforcement would involve the court in lending support, in effect, to an endeavour to perform in a foreign and friendly country some act which is illegal by the law of that country (cf *Foster* v *Driscoll* [1929] 1 KB 470, and the recent case of *Euro-Diam* v *Bathurst* [1990] 1 QB 1), so as to offend the conscience of the court. Here illegality by South African law is not germane in this respect and the only illegality by Dutch law is unlikely in its nature to attract such judicial criticism. It may be concluded that Rio Tinto's chances of success depend largely on the nature and effects in its own system of the Dutch registration rule. If this rule renders the contract illegal and unenforceable in the Netherlands, then it is likely but not certain, depending on the view taken by the court of 'pure' illegality by the lex loci solutionis, that the English court will refuse enforcement. No other law in the case is likely to provide Steve with a defence to Rio Tinto.

QUESTION THREE

The following contracts were concluded after April 1, 1991. What law is applicable to regulate each of them?

a) Mawali, a Malaysian exporter, sent a telex to the offices of Cut Price Clothing Ltd, an English textile manufacturer, offering to sell quantities of jute. The consignment was due to be delivered at the Spanish warehouse of the English company and payment of the price was to be made in US dollars into Mawali's bank account in London. Cut Price Clothing Ltd accepted the terms of the offer by telex sent from England to Malaysia.

b) Laver, a French manufacturer of washing machines, advertised a new model of washing machine in English newspapers. Customers were asked to place orders by post to the company in France together with their cheques for 2,000 French francs. In terms of the advertisement, Laver undertook to deliver the washing machines to the customers' homes.

   Persil, a customer resident in England, sent the company the money together with her letter requesting a new machine.

c) Mitsubisi, a Japanese corporation, engaged John to work in Ireland for the company. Mitsubisi has a place of business in the Netherlands while John is habitually resident in England. John is to be paid in pounds sterling and his pay and expenses are to be paid directly into his current account with a bank in London.

Question prepared by the Editor

General Comment

These questions relate to contracts falling within the remit of the Rome Convention. This requires an application of the relevant articles to the facts presented. Given the nature of the question, time management is essential.

Skeleton Solution

Contract – applicable law – applicable law in the absence of choice by the parties – general rule and presumptions – performance characteristic of the contract – consumer contracts – individual employment contracts – Rome Convention, arts 4, 5 and 6.

Suggested Solution

The three contracts for consideration are all made after 1 April 1991 and none of them falls within the topics excluded from the scope of the Rome Convention 1980 by art 1 thereof; thus all are governed by the Convention.

a) Mawali offers and Cut Price Clothing Limited accepts a contract for the sale of jute, without any express choice of law, which if made would have determined the applicable law: art 3(1). Nor, it would seem, is there any *implied* choice of law; there is nothing in the geographically dispersed elements of the transaction to point to an implied selection by the parties of a law to govern their contracts, still less to any such choice being such as would be said to be 'demonstrated with reasonable certainty by the terms of the contract or the circumstances of the case': art 3(1). Thus, absent any choice express or implied by the parties, we must fall back on the provisions of art 4 to determine the 'applicable law in the absence of choice'.

The contract will be governed by the law of the country with which it is most closely connected: art 4(1). However, the Convention lays down presumptions to be employed to determine the most closely connected country, and the relevant presumption here (since this is not a contract in relation to immovable property, carriage of goods, a consumer contract or an employment contract) is that prescribed by art 4(2). Applying this, it is first necessary to determine which party is to effect the performance which is characteristic of the contract.

The Convention does not define this concept, but with the aid of the Giuliano-Lagarde Report it may confidently be asserted that, where one party to a contract is to pay money in return for a non-monetary counter-performance by the other party, the non-monetary performance is that which is characteristic of the contract. Thus here Mawali's delivery of jute is the characteristic performance. As Mawali is an exporter, the contract would appear to be entered into in the course of his trade or profession, thus the country with which the contract is most closely connected will be taken to be that in which Mawali's principal place of business is situated – presumably Malaysia – unless by the terms of the contract performance was to be through another place of business (but we have not been informed that Mawali has any other place of business eg in Spain).

Even if Mawali did not make the contract in the course of his trade or profession, the contract would be presumed most closely connected with his country of residence, again Malaysia. Thus the law applicable to this contract is almost certainly Malaysian law. By art 4(5) the presumption in art 4(2) which we have applied 'shall be disregarded if it appears from the circumstances as a whole that the contract is more closely connected with another country', but the non-Malaysian facts are divided between Spain and England, and no one other country has a stronger connection than Malaysia.

b) As in the previous case, there is no express choice of law to govern this contract; nor, given the distribution of the facts between England and France, can it be said that there is an implied choice. The contract between Persil and Laver satisfied the conditions prescribed in art 5: the object is the supply of goods (washing machines) to Persil for a purpose outside her trade or profession (assuming she is not a seller of washing machines!) (art 5(1)), and in England, the country of Persil's habitual residence, the conclusion of the contract was preceded by advertising, and Persil, by sending her letter by post from England enclosing her remittance, took in England all the steps necessary on her part for the conclusion of the contract: art 5(2), first alternative. Thus, in the absence of a choice of law in accordance with art 3, the contract is governed, under art 5(3), by the law of England as the country of Persil's habitual residence. Note that this is not a case of a *presumption* in favour of English law, as with the presumption operative in problem (a); art 5(3) makes the law of the country of habitual residence automatically operative in the absence of a choice of law, assuming, art 5(4), that the contract is not one of carriage or for services to be supplied exclusively in another country.

c) Again an absence of choice of law, express or implied. This is a contract of individual employment, accordingly art 6(2) applies. We are told that John was engaged to work 'in Ireland'. Assuming that he was to work only in Ireland, by art 6(2)(a) the law of Ireland (presumably the Republic of Ireland is meant) will govern the contract. However, this is not a prescriptive rule but a presumption, the closing proviso of art 6(2) allowing the contract to be governed by the law of a different country if it is more closely connected with that country: cf art 4(5) and contrast art 5(3). It is just about possible to argue here that the contract is more closely connected with England than with Ireland; John is habitually resident in England and is to be paid in English currency into an English bank account. If other features of the contract presently unknown to us bear out the English connection, English law may apply.

Alternatively, if John is to work not only in Ireland but also elsewhere, so that he does not habitually carry out his work in one country, then by art 6(2)(b) the contract will be governed by the law of the country in which the place of business through which he was engaged is situated, ie presumably Dutch law if he was engaged through Mitsubisi's place of business in the Netherlands, though in this case it would certainly appear likely that the contract of employment will be more closely connected with another country, displacing the presumption.

QUESTION FOUR

i) The Portland Shipping Company, a company incorporated in England with a head office in Southampton, contracts with a Dutch company to carry goods from Rotterdam to Buenos Aires in a British-registered ship. The contract is negotiated by telex between London and Rotterdam. It is in the English language and the freight is payable in sterling. There is no choice of law clause. What is the applicable law?

ii) On the facts in (i) above, assume that half the freight is payable in Argentina on delivery of the goods. After the contract is made, but before delivery, Argentina passes a law imposing maximum rates of freight for such contracts. Would an English court apply that law in determining how much freight is payable?

iii) Frank AG, a German company, employs construction workers from all over the world to work on its oil rigs off the coast of Norway. One such employee is Bill, an English domiciliary. The standard contract which is in German excludes liability for any injury sustained by employees if, in the opinion of the company, the employee has not taken reasonable care. The contract contains a clause referring all disputes to the district court of Hamburg. Bill, who was injured when not wearing a hard hat, wishes to sue Frank AG for failing to provide a safe system of work. He wants to do this in the courts of England. Do they have jurisdiction? Which law would they apply?

University of London LLB Examination
(for External Students) Conflict of Laws June 1995 Q8

General Comment

This question is more testing than may at first be apparent. Not only are provisions of both the Rome Convention 1980 and Council Regulation 44/2001/EC to be analysed, but elements of public policy and some case law is required to construct a satisfactory answer to this question.

Skeleton Solution

Applicability of Rome Convention to the problem – brief references to arts 1 and 3 and a more detailed account relating to art 4 – supervening illegality and analogy with *Ralli Bros* case – public policy and other provisions of the Rome Convention – employment contracts and the provisions of arts 18–21 of Council Regulation 44/2001/EC – jurisdiction and choice of law.

Suggested Solution

i) The Contracts (Applicable Law) Act 1990, which came into force on 1 April 1991, has given the force of law to the Rome Convention on the Law Applicable to Contractual Obligations 1980. Since art 1(1) of the Convention provides that the rules of the Convention apply to 'contractual obligations in any situation', and the contract between the Portland Shipping Company and the Dutch company for the carriage of goods by sea does not come within the scope of contracts expressly excluded by art 1(2) of the Convention, the law governing the contract will be determined by applying the provisions of art 4, given that the companies have not availed themselves of the opportunity to choose the applicable law under art 3 and that it cannot be said that the choice of law has been expressed with reasonable certainty.

Article 4(1) provides that in the absence of a choice of law, in accordance with art 3, 'the contract shall be governed by the law of the country with which it is most closely connected'. The country with which the contract is most closely connected is then ascertained by adopting the presumption in art 4(2) that the party who is to effect the performance which is characteristic of the contract has, at the time of the conclusion of the contract, his habitual residence or, in the case of a corporate body such as the Portland Shipping Company, the country shall be 'the country where the principal place of business is situated'.

The party which is to effect the performance of the contract is the one which is to receive the payment in consideration of providing the services rendered. Accordingly, the Portland Shipping Company is the relevant party. It was acting in the course of its trade or profession and, given that its principal place of business is in England, it may be deduced that English law will govern the contract. That the contract was written in the English language, and the freight was payable in sterling, are almost inconsequential factors under the Rome Convention.

ii) The limitation on freight rates imposed by the Argentinian Government after conclusion of the contract is a case of supervening illegality, an aspect of material validity which, under art 8 of the Rome Convention, is governed by the applicable law of the contract presuming, of course, the contract is valid. However, it would appear that art 16 of the Rome Convention preserves the traditional English rules on public policy, which means that the English courts are very unlikely to enforce a contractual obligation if its commission abroad, in this case Argentina, would constitute a criminal act on the date of its performance. It is not clear if the Argentinian law imposes criminal liability, but as the contract is governed by English law, and it is subjected to supervening illegality, its performance will be pro tanto frustrated and discharged. Thus, the situation under the Rome Convention would mirror the common law decision in *Ralli Bros v Compagnia Naviera Sota y Aznar* [1920] 2 KB 287 where the Court of Appeal held that a Spanish decree prohibiting the payment of freight above a specified limit prevailed over the rate agreed under the proper law of the contract.

iii) Under Council Regulation 44/2001/EC, the general rules of jurisdiction are that a plaintiff who wishes to sue in contract or tort has the option to choose whether to comply with the general rule of jurisdiction contained in art 2 of the Regulation and sue the defendant in the courts of the latter's domicile or to exercise the special jurisdiction provisions of art 19 which states that an employer may be sued in another member state (a) where the employee habitually carries out his work, or the last place he did so; or (b) in the courts of the place of business which engaged the employee or was situated.

In relation to individual contracts of employment, the special provisions to protect the employee as the weaker party are contained within art 6 of the Regulation and they are expressed in substantive, as opposed to territorial, terms. That is, if there is no express choice of law or one which can be determined with reasonable certainty under art 3, then art 6(2) provides for the ascertainment of the applicable law to the exclusion of art 4. The rebuttable presumptions in art 6(2) are that: (a) the applicable law is the law of the country in which the employee habitually carries out his work in performance of the contract, even while he is temporarily employed in another country; or (b) if the employee does not habitually carry out his work in one country, then the applicable law is the law of the country in which the place of business through which he was engaged is situated. However, these are rebuttable presumptions: they may be displaced, if it appears from the circumstances as a whole, by the law of the country most closely connected with the contract.

Application of the principles of jurisdiction indicates that the courts having jurisdiction are the German or the Norwegian courts: see art 19 above. With regard to the applicable law of the contract, given that Frank AG recruits employees from all over the world, that there is no evidence that the contract with Bill was made in England or through an English agency, that the language of the contract was German and German jurisdiction was provided for, then the law of the country most closely connected with the contract appears to be German. There is, moreover, no evidence to suggest that Bill habitually carries out his work in performance of his contract in England. Accordingly, it would appear that Bill would be unable to invoke the mandatory provisions of English law, and that he is no more likely to succeed in a claim under English law than the plaintiff in *Sayers* v *International Drilling Co NV* [1971] 1 WLR 1176. Accordingly, he will have to rely on mandatory provisions of German law (if any) for protection of his bodily integrity if he is to pursue his claims for compensation in the German or Norwegian courts.

QUESTION FIVE

'The business community looks to private international law to deliver it freedom, flexibility and certainty'. Has the Rome Convention delivered?

University of London LLB Examination
(for External Students) Conflict of Laws June 2000 Q2

General Comment

This is actually quite a demanding question despite the fact that is appears very straightforward. The question requires two main issues to be examined: (a) a discussion of party autonomy – freedom to select the law governing the contract – and any restrictions; and (b) an analysis of whether or not the Rome Convention achieves freedom, flexibility and certainty as compared with the common law prior to 1991.

Skeleton Solution

Party autonomy – freedom to negotiate terms of the contract such as choice of law clause – the need for certainty – forum shopping – the common law regime – Rome Convention – process under each.

Suggested Solution

The Rome Convention 1980 was brought into force in the Contracts (Applicable Law) Act 1990. The objective of the Rome Convention is to harmonise the choice of law rules in contract and as such reduce forum shopping and increase confidence and certainty in the process to be applied when determining the applicable law of a contract. This may be contrasted with the common law regime, which had as its focus the principles of party autonomy and freedom of contract as opposed to the harmonisation of choice of law rules in contract. However, it may be noted that the Convention rules are not drastically different from the common law approach.

Article 1(1) of the Rome Convention provides that it shall apply to 'contractual obligations in any situation involving a choice between the laws of different countries.' Consequently, whilst the Convention is centred on the EU, its application is not restricted to situations involving a selection between the laws of two or more EU states. The only real limitation that is placed on the scope of the Convention is contained in art 1(2) and (3) which provides for matters expressly excluded from its range. These include questions relating to capacity and status of natural persons, family law matters and arbitration agreements. Consequently, the Rome Convention attempts to provide the business community with a clear idea of its precise legal and geographical scope.

Progressing to the basic principles of the Convention, it should be noted that like the common law the Convention recognises the autonomy of contracting parties to choose the law governing their contract. Article 3(1) provides that the choice must be either express or may be demonstrated with reasonable certainty by the terms of the contract or the circumstances of the case. Where the contract is severable, then the choice of law may apply to certain parts of that contract. Consequently, there would appear to be no restriction to the choice of law. As per art 2, there does not even have to be any connection between the legal system and the contract.

However, it should be noted that this apparent freedom is subject to specific limitations for certain types of contracts. Under art 3(3) the Convention provides that where the parties have made an express choice, but all the other localising elements of the contract are connected with another country, then the parties' choice will not be allowed to interfere with the application of the laws of that country 'which cannot be derogated from by contract', ie the mandatory rules of that country. Article 7(1) goes on to provide that effect may be given to the mandatory rules of another country with which the contact has a close connection, though it should be noted that a number of countries, including the United Kingdom, have opted out of this provision. Nevertheless, art 7(2) remains applicable and states that the courts may apply the mandatory rules of the forum in which the case is heard. Consequently, it would appear that the parties' choice is subject to the application of two separate sets of mandatory rules. These in turn may be said to restrict party autonomy and freedom to contract. However, the Convention does set down the instances when such rules may be applied, and as such, may be said to provide a certain degree of certainty to the business community.

There are two other types of contract under which party autonomy is limited. Article 5 provides that in consumer contracts a choice of law shall not deprive a consumer of the protection afforded to him by the mandatory rules of the law of the country in which he is habitually resident. Similarly, art 6 provides that employment contracts are automatically protected by the mandatory rules of the place where the employee habitually carries out his duties.

It may be argued that whilst the English common law has taken into account the situations provided for under arts 3 and 7, the content of arts 5 and 6 could be said to be a difference between the Convention and the common law. Furthermore, it could be suggested that whilst these provisions have introduced a certain degree of protection for both consumers and employees, they have restricted the freedom and flexibility of parties to make an express choice in these types of contract.

Turning to art 4 of the Convention, this provides for instances where there is no choice of law clause or agreement identifiable from the circumstances surrounding the contract. Consequently, art 4 sets down the process whereby the courts may ascertain the law of the country with which the contact is 'most closely connected'. In many respects, this appears to be very similar to the common law approach, which seeks to ascertain the legal system with which the contract has the closest and most real connection. However, art 4 goes on to provide a series of rebuttable presumptions which are intended to assist the court in ascertaining the closest connection. Article 4(2) sets down the presumption that the law of the party who has to effect 'the performance which is characteristic of the contract' will apply to the contract as the law which has the closest connection. This is generally the place where the individual is habitually resident.

In many respects, it may be said that art 4 represents a quite different approach to that under the common law. It provides greater certainty as to the process to be adopted by the courts, as opposed to the common law under which the court had far greater discretion in determining the system of law which had the closest and most real connection. However, if one considers the potential effect of art 4(5), then this provides for a country which is more closely connected to the contract, despite conclusions reached under the presumptions. In many respects, it may be said that this returns to the English common law approach outlined above in that the court may exercise its discretion in certain circumstances; never a ideal situation for certainty.

Once again, art 4 is subject to the specific provisions relating to mandatory rules, together with consumer and employment contracts. However, it is also perhaps worth mentioning at this point the effect of art 8, which deals with the material validity of the contract. This article provides that a party may rely on the law of his habitual residence to establish his lack of consent. Once again, this represents a difference between the Convention and common law, which may be attributed to the international focus of the former regime.

Finally, if one considers any interpretation of the Convention, then art 1 of the Brussels Protocol states that the ECJ shall have the final word in such matters. In many respects this may be linked back in with the issue of harmonisation and as such certainty for the business community.

To conclude, it may be stated that the Convention reflects a number of the characteristics of the common law in that it recognises the desirability of, and attempts to provide for, principles of party autonomy and freedom of contract. Consequently, it ensures the freedom of the business community to continue to negotiate contractual terms, a part of which is the determination of the applicable law. However, this freedom is subject to a number of limitations, some of which are present in the common law, others which are not. Consequently, this apparent freedom is subject to considerations relating to mandatory rules, consumer and employment contracts, as well as issues such as consent. Nevertheless, these restrictions are on the whole set down in a logical and accessible manner. As such, it may be argued that whilst there is less freedom under the Rome Convention, there is certainty as to the scope and applicability of these limitations. In addition, the Convention has harmonised the choice of law rules in this area. Therefore, it could be said to have delivered some, if not all, of the features outlined in the question.

QUESTION SIX

'The Rome Convention has followed the English notion of the proper law of the contract very closely.'

Discuss.

University of London LLB Examination
(for External Students) Conflict of Laws June 1996 Q4

General Comment

Whilst it may appear innocuous on a 1996 paper, it must be remembered that as time progresses much less information, let alone analysis, of the old common law rules of contract is available in the textbooks used by undergraduates. Indeed, the 13th edition of Cheshire and North's *Private International Law*, published in 1999, focuses almost exclusively on contract under the Rome Convention. Accordingly, fewer students would have been taught the old law in any detail in 1995/96.

Skeleton Solution

Purpose of ascertaining the proper law – the position at common law – integrate a comparative analysis of the position under the Rome Convention as the answer is developed; analysis to include express and 'implied' proper law and scope of proper law – concluding commentary.

Suggested Solution

'The English notion of the proper law of the contract' at common law must be discussed in order that the notion of the applicable law under the Rome Convention on the Law Applicable to Contractual Obligations 1980 may be compared and the assertion underlying this question evaluated.

In *Amin Rasheed Shipping Corp* v *Kuwait Insurance Co* [1984] AC 50, Lord Diplock described the proper law of a contract as 'the substantive law of the country which the parties have chosen as that by which their mutually legally enforceable rights are to be ascertained'. Most aspects of a contract are governed by the proper law.

The absence of a generally applicable connecting factor in English law ascertaining the proper law of the contract led to the principle of party autonomy, ie, 'the proper law of the contract ... is the law which the parties intended to apply', per Lord Atkin in *R* v *International Trustee for the Protection of Bondholders* [1937] AC 500. The principle of party autonomy has been preserved in the Rome Convention, art 3(1) providing that: 'A contract shall be governed by the law chosen by the parties.' However, to be effective, this choice 'must be expressed or demonstrated with reasonable certainty by the terms of the contract or the circumstances of the case'.

One would expect the principle of party autonomy to carry great weight in the determination of the proper law and to be followed very closely in the Rome Convention if party expectations are not to be undermined. This, indeed, is the case subject to the qualifications noted. Moreover, as elements (terms) of certain types of contract are excluded from the Rome Convention and, as such, must be decided under the traditional rules, one would not expect much deviation from the traditional rules for the particular terms in question.

A couple of points are worthy of note, however. First, it was uncertain whether a subjectivist or an objectivist approach prevailed in the determination of the proper law. In *Amin Rasheed*, the reference in Lord Diplock's speech to the 'necessary implication from the language used [by the parties to evince] a common intention as to the system of law by reference to which their mutual rights and obligations under it are to be ascertained', could be interpreted as supporting the subjectivist approach. By contrast, the 'seek[ing] [of the] system of law with which the contract has its closest and most real connection' has to be interpreted as an objectivist approach.

The subjectivist approach prevailed where the parties had expressly chosen the law to govern their agreement: *Vita Food Products Inc* v *Unus Shipping Co Ltd* [1939] AC 277. Moreover, party autonomy based on the subjectivist approach prevailed even if the parties had [chosen] a law which had no obvious connection with the contract: the choice still could be 'bona fide and legal', per Lord Reid in *Whitworth Street Estates Ltd* v *James Miller and Partners Ltd* [1970] AC 583. This principle is now enshrined in art 2 of the Rome Convention which provides that 'any law specified by the Convention is to be applied whether or not it is the law of a Contracting State'.

The subjectivist approach also prevailed where the parties had impliedly chosen the proper law: *Tzortzis* v *Monark Line A/B* [1968] 1 WLR 406 and *Amin Rasheed Shipping Corp* v *Kuwait Insurance Co*, though in the latter case it was made clear that resolution of what is the impliedly chosen law requires taking into account 'the rest of the contract and the relevant surrounding facts'.

If the parties to a contract have not expressly chosen the law to govern their contract but the terms of the contract or the circumstances of the case can be 'demonstrated with reasonable certainty', then, again, implied party autonomy prevails.

However, the major differences occur in the resolution of the applicable law in the absence of a chosen law, ie, where the objectivist view prevails. First, under the traditional rules, the implied proper law was determined by reference to the system of law having the closest and most real connection with the case. By contrast, art 4(1) of the Rome Convention provides that 'the contract shall be governed by the law of the country with which it is most closely connected'. Thus the 'law of the country' under the Convention represents a different and unconvincing departure from the 'legal system' under the traditional rules.

Moreover, ascertaining the implied proper law under the Convention is by way of a series of rebuttable presumptions: art 4(2)–(5). Remarkably, it is nearly 25 years since Megaw LJ in the *Coast Lines Ltd* v *Hudig & Veder Chartering NV* [1972] 2 QB 34 said that: 'Presumptions, once fashionable during the earlier development of English private international law, are now whether for good or ill, out of fashion and rejected'. Indeed, Cheshire and North (*Private International Law* (1999)) state that the re-introduction of presumptions by the Rome Convention 'turns the clock back as far as English law is concerned'.

Perhaps the major departure from the traditional rule is expressed in art 4(2) which provides for the application of the characteristic performance of the contract. To ascertain the applicable law via such an innovative presumption is a radical departure from the traditional rules since 'characteristic performance' has no necessary connection with the place of performance, a presumption recognised by English law. Collins ((1986) 25 ICLQ 35, at 45–46) also questions whether reference to a personal connecting factor such as that contained in art 4(2) – habitual reference – is appropriate in the context of commercial contracts.

The Rome Convention follows the English notion of putting limitations on the notion of party autonomy. Whereas certain statutory provisions override the proper law of the contract under the traditional rules, eg s153(5) Employment Protection (Consolidation) Act 1978 provides a degree of protection to an employee who ordinarily works in Great Britain irrespective of any foreign law which governs his contract of employment, the Rome Convention provides for 'overriding' mandatory provisions providing 'all the elements relevant to the situation [are] connected with one country only': art 3(3). (See also, inter alia, art 7(1) – which doesn't have the force of law in England – and art 7(2) which does.)

With regard to the scope of a contract, the applicable law under the Rome Convention again follows the traditional rules to a fair extent. This means, however, that neither system is very convincing with its guidance in the proper/applicable law that would govern a contract if that 'agreement' were valid. Moreover, whereas the formal validity of a contract under the traditional rules was probably validated either by the lex loci contractus or the putative law, formal validity of a contract under the Rome Convention may be via the law of the country where it is concluded, or perhaps the law of either the countries where the parties are located (if they are in different countries at the time the contract was concluded) or even the applicable law: see arts 8 and 9.

Both the traditional rules and the Rome Convention exclude the application of renvoi.

In conclusion, the many similarities between the Convention and the traditional rules of contract under English private international law are in sharp contrast with the dissimilar provisions which apply in ascertaining the proper law when there has been no express choice and a proper law cannot be demonstrated with reasonable certainty by the terms of the contract or the circumstances of the case.

Chapter 7

Tort

7.1   Introduction

7.2   Key points

7.3   Key cases and statutes

7.4   Questions and suggested solutions

7.1 Introduction

It is quite possible for a wrongful act to be performed in one country but to be litigated in another, eg where the plaintiff, who is injured in a motor accident in France, sues the English driver of the other vehicle in England. This may be due to matters of convenience or, more likely, the likely size of damages to be awarded. Inevitably this leads to the question as to which law is to govern in these circumstances. Would the English courts apply French law or English law?

7.2 Key points

The original basic rule

The original basic rule in English law for the selection of the applicable law to an action in tort was stated by Willis J in *Phillips* v *Eyre* (1870) LR 6 QB 1. In deciding whether an action for an alleged wrongful act committed in Jamaica by the Governor of Jamaica was actionable in England, Willis J observed:

> 'As a general rule, in order to found a suit in England for a wrong alleged to have been committed abroad, two conditions must be fulfilled. First, the wrong must be of such a character that it would have been actionable if committed in England ... Secondly, the act must not have been justifiable by the law of the place where it was done.'

If this language is examined closely, it is clear that two conditions must be satisfied before a plaintiff will be successful in an action raised in England:

a)   the wrongful act must be actionable under the law of the lex fori, namely England; and

b)   the act which gave raise to the claim must not have been justifiable under the law of the place the act was carried out.

The wrongful act must be actionable in English law

This requirement was a reiteration of a condition developed in an earlier case, *The Halley* (1868) LR 2 PC 193, where Selwyn LJ made the much criticised statement that it was:

> '... alike contrary to principle and to authority to hold that an English Court of Justice will enforce a foreign municipal law and will give a remedy in the shape of damages in respect of an act which, according to [English law] principles, imposes no liability on the person from whom damages are claimed.'

This approach has been described as both provincial and chauvinistic. Quite simply, if this approach applied in other areas of conflict of law, it would effectively mean that if a dispute is actionable in English law, English law applies to the exclusion of all other legal systems.

This requirement did, however, receive unanimous endorsement in the House of Lords in *Boys* v *Chaplin* [1971] AC 356, which we shall look at in more detail later although the principle was criticised by Lord Wilberforce.

The act which gave rise to the claim cannot be justified in the law of the place where it was done

The difficulty in applying this condition has evolved around the construction of the term 'justifiable'. Does this mean the same as actionable or does the term have a wider meaning?

This question arose in *Machado* v *Fontes* [1897] 2 QB 231, where the Court of Appeal had to consider whether an action could be raised in England for a libel published in Brazil when the law of Brazil did not allow a claim for damages on the ground of libel. The court considered that the plaintiff had to establish that the libel was not criminal under the law of Brazil. Naturally, this implies that the term 'justifiable' means something wider than merely actionable. Indeed, Lopes LJ explained that for the defendant to succeed the act had to be 'innocent in the country where it was committed' and he equated 'not justifiable' with 'wrongful'.

This interpretation has also been subject to immense criticism frequently by the courts themselves: see *Canadian Pacific Railway* v *Parent* [1917] AC 195 and *McElroy* v *M'Allister* 1–949 SC 110. Eventually, this second part of the test came under the scrutiny of the House of Lords in *Boys* v *Chaplin* (above). The majority in this case (Lords Hodson, Wilberforce and Guest over Lords Donovan and Pearson) held that instead of requiring that the act should have been 'not justifiable', it must be actionable under the lex loci delicti.

Thus, the requirement for establishing liability under the *Phillips* v *Eyre* rule has been rewritten as the need to establish the actionability of the act giving rise to the claim under both the lex fori and the lex loci.

The reformulated rule established in **Boys v Chaplin**

The rule, following from the House of Lords decision in *Boys v Chaplin*, can be stated as follows: in order for a plaintiff to raise a successful action in tort in the courts in England, he or she must demonstrate that the act which gave rise to the claim is actionable in both the laws of the lex fori and the lex loci delicti. So, there are two dimensions to such a claim:

a)   actionability in the law of the lex fori (English law); and

b)   actionability in the law of the lex loci (the law of the place the act occurred).

The House of Lords, in *Boys v Chaplin*, elaborated considerably on both branches of this requirement. However, the ratio decidendi of the case itself is not crystal clear due to the inability of the judges hearing the case to agree on a unanimous decision. Even the courts themselves are having difficulty in extracting the ratio: see *Church of Scientology of California v Commissioner of the Metropolitan Police* (1976) 120 SJ 690 and *Coupland v Arabian Gulf Petroleum Co* [1983] 2 All ER 434.

But, at least in the leading opinion, Lord Wilberforce introduced a third element into the test for whether or not an action can be raised in England for tortious acts committed in foreign countries, namely 'flexibility'. All three of these concepts must be considered in further detail.

Actionability in English law

There is a certain degree of consensus that it is Lord Wilberforce's speech in *Boys v Chaplin* that has proved to be the prevailing judgment.

Lord Wilberforce was clearly concerned that the rule regarding the lex fori in *Machado v Fontes* (above) 'ought to be overruled' since it was illogical and offered inducements to 'forum shopping'. Forum shopping is simply the phenomenon whereby plaintiffs select the place where the action will be raised based on the prospect of greater or more attractive damages than would be obtained under the legal system of the lex loci delicti.

Unfortunately, Lord Wilberforce did not go this far and the requirement of establishing that an act is actionable in English law remains more or less unchanged.

Actionability in the law of the place where the act occurred

Lord Wilberforce dedicated a considerable part of his judgment to the concept of actionability in the lex loci. He concludes his examination of this topic with the following summary:

> 'I would, therefore, restate the basic rule of English law with regard to foreign torts as requiring actionability as a tort according to English law, subject to the condition that civil liability in respect of the relevant claim exists between the actual parties under the law of the foreign country where the act was done.'

It is now plain that 'civil liability' is the key to this branch of the *Phillips* v *Eyre* test as opposed to tortious liability under the lex loci. Thus, presumably, liability can be contractual, quasi-contractual, quasi-delictual, proprietary or sui generis, as well as tortious. At the same time, it is obvious that there is no doubt that mere criminal liability is not sufficient.

Flexibility

Lord Wilberforce expressed his concern that some degree of flexibility should be introduced into the orthodox double actionability rule in the interests of individual justice. He formulated a new third principle in the following terms:

> 'I think that the necessary flexibility can be obtained from the principle which represents a common denominator of the United States decisions, namely, through segregation of the relevant issue and consideration whether, in relation to that issue, the relevant foreign rule ought, as a matter of policy ... to be applied.
>
> For this purpose it is necessary to identify the policy of the rule, to inquire to what situations and to what contacts, it was intended to apply; whether or not to apply it, in the circumstances of the instant case, would serve any interest which the rule was devised to meet.'

His statement of the rule of flexibility is not a model of clarity. Essentially, Lord Wilberforce is saying that a flexible approach should be adopted when as a matter of policy a foreign rule of law ought not to apply. He did not elaborate which are the relevant grounds of public policy but did specify that the approach should be adopted where the lex loci delicti either limits or excludes damages for personal injury. At the same time, this single ground for flexibility does not exhaust all the possibilities for introducing flexibility into the application of the double actionability rule: see *Red Sea Insurance Co* v *Bouygues SA and Others* [1994] 3 WLR 926.

To summarise, the double actionability rule devised by the House of Lords in the *Boys* v *Chaplin* decision, which itself interpreted the earlier decision of *Phillips* v *Eyre*, remains the principal test for establishing whether or not a claim can be brought in an English court for a tort committed in a foreign country.

This rule is modified slightly to the extent that the courts will bear in mind the overall need to maintain an element of flexibility to avoid injustice, particularly in cases whether damages are excluded or limited for personal injury. There has, however, been a statutory replacement of these rules which sweeps away the common law rules for choice of law in tort.

The statutory modification of the common law rules

Section 10(a) of the Private International Law (Miscellaneous Provisions) Act (PIL(MP)A) 1995 abolishes the common law rule of double actionability. In other words, the rule in *Phillips* v *Eyre* (1870) LR 6 QB 1 is abolished. Section 10(b) goes on to abolish the exceptions to the standard 'double actionability' rule that 'allow ... for the law of a single country to be applied for that purpose'.

Section 11(1) states the general rule under the Act is that the applicable law in cases of tort involving a foreign jurisdiction is that 'of the country in which the events constituting the tort or delict in question occur'. In other words, where all the events giving rise to culpability occur in a single country, the law of that country is to be the applicable law.

Under s11(2), where elements of the factual events giving rise to culpability arise in different countries, the relevant rules are as follows:

a) for a cause of action in respect of personal injury caused to an individual or death resulting from personal injury, the applicable law is the law of the country where the individual was when he sustained the injury (s11(2)(a));

b) for a cause of action in respect of damage to property, the applicable law is the law of the country where the property was when it was damaged (s11(2)(b)); and

c) in any other case, the applicable law is the law of the country in which the most significant element or elements of those events occurred: s11(2)(c).

The Act then goes on to introduce a new rule of flexibility which may, in appropriate circumstances, displace the newly formulated general rule. Under s12 the courts are instructed to consider two elements:

a) the significance of the factors which connect a tort with the country whose law would be the applicable law under the general rule; and

b) the significance of any factors connecting the tort with another country.

After comparing both these dimensions, if a court decides that it is 'substantially more appropriate' for the applicable law for determining the issues arising in the case to be the law of the other country, the general rule may be displaced. This would allow the applicable law for determining those issues to be the law of that other country. The factors to be taken into account in such a determination include those factors relating to the parties, any of the events that constitute the tort, or any circumstances or consequences of those events.

The new rules will apply to all cases where acts or omission giving rise to a claim occurred after the commencement of the Act.

To date there is little case law to illustrate the Act, which has not helped to resolve the division of academic opinion as to the potential effectiveness of the new provisions. Students should be familiar with the following cases: *Edmunds* v *Simmonds* [2001] 1 WLR 1003; *Glencore International AG* v *Metro Trading International Inc* [2001] 1 Lloyd's Rep 284; *Hulse* v *Chambers* [2002] 1 All ER 812; *Roerig* v *Valiant Trawlers Ltd* [2002] 1 All ER 961.

The application of foreign law to torts committed in England

Throughout this chapter, the question has been whether or not foreign torts (ie torts committed outside England) are actionable in England and, if so, which is the proper law to apply. The alternative scenario is when two persons resident in the same foreign country are involved in a tortious action in England. What account would the English courts take of the foreign element involved in such a situation? The answer is probably that English law would take little or no account of the foreign element and would apply English law to a tort committed in England. This approach was confirmed in *Metall und Rohstoff AG* v *Donaldson Lufkin & Jenrette Inc* [1989] 3 WLR 563, where it was held that where a tort was in substance committed in England, then only English law would be applied. The double actionability requirement elaborated in *Boys* v *Chaplin* would not be applied.

The boundary between contract and tort: exclusion clauses

The area in which contract law and the law of tort clash most obviously is when exclusion clauses have been inserted into contracts. These clauses attempt to exclude liability under tort by way of contractual undertakings. Often, such clauses may be valid under the proper law of the contract, but may be invalid under either the lex fori or the lex loci delicti.

The case *Sayers* v *International Drilling* [1971] 1 WLR 1176 provides a good illustration of the scenario in which this problem occurs. An English domiciled worker was employed by a Dutch company on an oil rig in Nigerian waters. He suffered injury through the negligence of a fellow employee, but his employment contract excluded liability on the part of his employers for injury caused in such circumstances. The court held that the proper law of the contract was Dutch law and under Dutch law exclusion clauses were valid and enforceable. Under English law, as the lex fori, clauses exempting employers from liability in these circumstances were void by virtue of sl(3) of the Law Reform (Personal Injuries) Act 1948. Hence, if the issue was one of contract, the plaintiff would lose, whereas if it was one of delict, then subject to a similar rule in Nigerian law, as the lex loci delicti, the English rule would allow the plaintiff to prevail.

The majority of the Court of Appeal considered that the case concerned a matter of contract and not tort. Salmon and Stamp JJ concluded that the proper law of the contract was Dutch and because the clause was valid by Dutch law, the employer was entitled to rely on the clause. Section 1(3) of the 1948 Act was irrelevant to the facts under consideration. Lord Denning agreed with this result but for completely different reasons.

A rather different approach to the issue of exemption clauses was taken in the Scottish case of *Brodin* v *A/R Seljan* 1973 SLT 198. See also *Coupland* v *Arabian Gulf Petroleum Co* [1983] 2 All ER 434 and *Canadian Pacific Railways* v *Parent* [1917] AC 195.

7.3 Key cases and statutes

- *Boys* v *Chaplin* [1971] AC 356
  Rule of double actionability – flexible approach

- *Edmunds* v *Simmonds* [2001] 1 WLR 1003
  Appropriate forum and quantification of damages – ss11 and 12 PIL(MP)A 1995

- *Glencore International AG* v *Metro Trading International Inc* [2001] 1 Lloyd's Rep 284
  Application of s11 PIL(MP)A 1995

- *Hulse* v *Chambers* [2002] 1 All ER 812
  Assessment of damages – s14 PIL(MP)A 1995

- *Machado* v *Fontes* [1897] 2 QB 231
  Not necessary for act to be subject of civil proceedings in the foreign state

- *Phillips* v *Eyre* (1870) LR 6 QB 1
  Rule of double actionability

- *Red Sea Insurance Co Ltd* v *Bouygues SA and Others* [1994] 3 WLR 926
  Exception to general rule of double actionability

- *Roerig* v *Valiant Trawlers Ltd* [2002] 1 All ER 961
  Section 12 PIL(MP)A 1995 – displacement of general rule

- *Tolofson* v *Jensen; Lucas* v *Gagnon* (1995) 120 DLR (4th) 289
  In inter-provincial cases there is to be no exception to the lex loci delecti commissi rule

- Private International Law (Miscellaneous Provisions) Act 1995 – replaced the common law rule of double actionability (together with exceptions) with new statutory framework

7.4 Questions and suggested solutions

QUESTION ONE

Holiday Homes plc, an English company, owned a holiday village in Algarvia. The village consisted of chalets which Holiday Homes planned to rent to tourists. In order to promote the village, the company offered a free two week holiday for two to the person who could write the best advertising jingle for the village. The competition was won by Ann, an English domiciliary, who went on the holiday with her friend, Simon, an Algarvian domiciliary, who was studying law in London for three years.

When they returned from their holiday, both suffered from severe vomiting and headaches. It has been proved that these symptoms were caused by the inhalation of gas which had escaped from the flue of the water heating system installed in the chalet, and that the escape was the result of negligent installation by Tom, an Algarvian domiciliary, employed by Holiday Homes. Robert, an Algarvian domiciliary, employed by Holiday Homes as caretaker of the village, has died from inhalation of gas in the chalet in the village which he occupied in the course of his duties.

By Algarvian law damages cannot be recovered for pain and suffering; an employer is not liable for the torts of his employees; and where negligence causes death the tortfeasor is liable to pay triple damages to the estate of his victim.

Advise Ann, Simon and the executor of Robert's estate who intend to commence proceedings in England.

University of London LLB Examination
(for External Students) Conflict of Laws June 1991 Q5

General Comment

The majority of questions in this area are as per this format. An application of the basic rule is required. In this instance an emphasis has been placed on both the common law rules and the framework under the Private International Law (Miscellaneous Provisions) Act 1995, so as to compare the two systems.

Skeleton Solution

Contract between Ann and Holiday Homes – jurisdiction of the English courts – CPR r6.20(8) – *Boys* v *Chaplin* – flexibility – irrecoverability of penal damages.

Suggested Solution

We shall advise Ann, Simon and Robert's executor separately.

Ann

In setting up the competition Holiday Homes plc is plainly making an offer to all the world; and Ann, by writing the jingle, is accepting their offer. Thus there is a contract between Ann and Holiday Homes plc. The proper law of that contract is, it is submitted, English law, since both parties were English, and the contract seems to have been made in England and the purpose of the contract was to promote the holiday village in, it seems, England; the only factor pulling in the direction of Algarvia is the fact that that is where the prize holiday was to be taken. That lone factor is insufficient to outweigh the other factors. So in the absence of a choice by the parties the contract is governed by English law. This would be the position under either the common law or under the Rome Convention 1980: art 4. English law would have little difficulty in holding that Holiday Homes plc impliedly warranted that the chalets were fit for their purpose, that chalets that subjected the guests to gas poisoning were not fit for their purpose and that consequently damages should be paid even if they were difficult to quantify: *Jarvis* v *Swans Tours Ltd* [1973] 1 QB 233 and *Cox* v *Philips Industries* [1976] 1 WLR 638.

There will be no difficulty with jurisdiction: Ann should simply serve the claim form on

Holiday Homes plc, a company incorporated in England, in the ordinary way, namely, by leaving the claim form either at its registered office or posting it to that office. Unless it turns out that Holiday Homes plc is insolvent or in liquidation, the remedy against them should be adequate for Ann's purposes. Should this not be the case, she will have to consider suing Tom; in these circumstances her position will, mutatis mutandis, be the same as Simon's.

Simon

Simon plainly has no contractual link with Holiday Homes plc or the other possible defendant, Tom. So he will have to sue them in tort.

a) Jurisdiction

Before dealing with the English choice of law rules in tort let us deal briefly with the question of jurisdiction. There should be little difficulty in serving Holiday Homes plc with a claim form but Tom is, presumably, in Algarvia so leave will have to be sought to serve the claim form on him outside the jurisdiction. Fortunately, under CPR r6.20(8) it is provided that leave may be granted where 'the claim is founded on a tort and the damage was sustained, or resulted from an act committed, within the jurisdiction'. While Tom's negligent act took place in Algarvia, it seems that the only damage to Simon was that sustained once they had returned to England. This brings Simon's case within the rule, thus the court has a discretion to order service outside the jurisdiction. Although this is a discretion that is sparingly exercised it is submitted that this is a proper case for it to be exercised. But one cannot be certain that the court would exercise its discretion in favour of Simon.

In the alternative, reliance may be able to be placed upon CPR r6.20(3) which allows leave to be granted where 'a person [who is] a necessary and proper party' in an action against a person 'duly served within or out of the jurisdiction'. Since Holiday Homes plc will have been duly served within the jurisdiction, service on Tom may fall within this sub rule. There is a danger here, however: if the action against the first defendant (Holiday Homes plc) is bound to fail then leave to serve on the 'necessary and proper party' (Tom) will be refused: *The Brabo* [1949] AC 326. Now the action against Holiday Homes plc may fail (see below); and yet that would be the only circumstance in which the action against Tom would be vital. So it is probably more prudent to rely on CPR r6.20(8) rather than r6.20(3).

b) Choice of law in tort

Applying the general principle of s11(1) of the Private International Law (Miscellaneous Provisions) Act 1992, the law of Algarvia will apply since that is the law of the place where the injury was sustained by Simon. The problem for Simon in raising an action is that the law of Algarvia does not recognise the liability of an employer for the negligent acts of his or her employees. In order to be successful, Simon would therefore have to rely on the special circumstances rule set out in s12(1) of the 1995 Act, to show that English law is more appropriate.

In the particular factual circumstances given in this case, Simon would probably not be able to displace the general rule. First, Simon is an Algarvian domiciliary who was only resident in England to complete his studies. Second, the tortious act occurred in Algarvia and can be attributed to Algarvian nationals. Third, there are no factors connecting the law of England to the tortious act and, in the circumstances of this case, a court could not be justified in law in displacing the law of Algarvia with the law of England.

The basic rule under the common law is the interpretation adopted by Lord Wilberforce in *Boys* v *Chaplin* [1971] AC 356 of the rule first laid down in *Philips* v *Eyre* (1870) LR 6 QB 1. That rule is a rule of 'double actionability', namely, that before there could be recovery in England for a tort committed abroad the wrong had to be 'actionable as a tort according to English law, subject to the condition that civil liability in respect of the relevant claim exists between the actual parties under the law of the foreign country where the action was done', ie there had to be actionability under both the lex fori and the lex loci delicti commissi.

The words cited in the previous paragraph come from Lord Wilberforce's speech in *Boys* v *Chaplin*. Although all five law lords gave judgment in that case and their reasons are very various and not consistent with each other, we are fortunate in that the Court of Appeal has on two occasions despaired of extracting the ratio decidendi from all the speeches and has adopted Lord Wilberforce's speech as containing that ratio: *Church of Scientology of California* v *Commissioner of the Metropolitan Police* (1976) 120 SJ 680 and *Coupland* v *Arabian Gulf Petroleum Co* [1983] 3 All ER 226. Henceforth Lord Wilberforce will be treated as authoritative.

The cited dictum immediately reveals the difficulty faced by Simon in this case: because Algarvian law does not recognise the liability of employers for the torts of their employees, there is no civil liability under the law of Algarvia between Simon and Holiday Homes plc. It thus appears that the double actionability rule is not satisfied and Simon's action against Holiday Homes plc is bound to fail and that Simon is left with the altogether more problematical claim against Tom (in respect of which the English court may not have jurisdiction).

However, there is more to Lord Wilberforce's speech than the cited dictum suggests, for he went on to say that there should be some flexibility in the application of the basic rule 'in the interests of individual justice'. This was illustrated by the facts of *Boys* v *Chaplin* itself. Here two British servicemen had been involved in a motor accident in Malta (where they were stationed). The injured serviceman brought action against the other serviceman in England but what could he recover? Under the law of Malta he could recover only his damages for loss of earnings and his expenses, while under the law of England he could recover, in addition, damages for pain and suffering. If the rule of double actionability was applied strictly, then all that the plaintiff could recover would be his loss of earnings and expenses for there was no civil liability under the law of Malta between him and the defendant in regard to the damages for pain and suffering. Fortunately, all the law lords held that the damages for pain and suffering were recoverable; and that must be right for the non-availability of damages for pain and suffering under the law of Malta seems quite irrelevant to the actions between these particular two parties.

In Simon's case it may be that the judge would be persuaded to adopt a similar flexible approach to overcome the absence of a law of vicarious liability in Algarvia. However, it would be up to Simon to show 'clear and satisfying grounds' why the flexibility should be exercised. This is not an easy task: essentially what is undertaken by the court in deciding whether to apply flexibility is a study of the policy of the rule of the foreign law that denies recovery. If that policy was intended to apply to cases such as the present then the rule would not be flexibly applied. Perhaps it may be possible to argue that the policy of the Algarvian rule was restrictive because ample provision was made in Algarvia for third parties who had suffered damage under an accident compensation scheme or some compulsory insurance scheme. Then, if Simon did not fall within that scheme, there would be strong grounds for applying the double actionability rule flexibly.

Should Simon fail against Holiday Homes plc because the rule is not flexibly applied he may still succeed against Tom provided the English court granted leave to serve the writ outside the jurisdiction.

Robert's executor

As far as the conflict of laws is concerned Robert's executor seems to be in the same situation as Simon. The only novel point is that should Robert's executor succeed against Tom (and one supposes against Holiday Homes plc too) he will be entitled to triple damages. Triple damages, however, are likely to be irrecoverable through the English courts as such damages will be considered penal rather than compensatory. And this is so whether or not the damages would be considered penal under the law of Algarvia: see *Huntingdon* v *Atrill* [1893] AC 150 Note that in terms of s5(3) of the Protection of Trading Interests Act 1980 a judgment for multiple damages is unenforceable in England; it is hard to imagine that, if such a judgment could not be enforced in England, the same result could be reached in an English action.

Again, the position is different under the Private International Law (Miscellaneous Provisions) Act 1995. The general rule which is now in force will require the application of the law of Algarvia and there are few factual circumstances arising from the case which would allow for the displacement of this rule under s12 of the 1995 Act.

QUESTION TWO

Last year a car driven negligently by John, a British serviceman stationed in West Germany, was in collision with another car, driven by Tom, an American serviceman also stationed in West Germany. Tom was severely injured in the crash and so were Jean, an English tourist, whom Tom met at a night-club the night before, and Mirella, an Italian hitch-hiker picked up by Tom half an hour earlier.

Tom, Jean and Mirella all wish to sue John in England where he is now stationed. Assume that damages for pain and suffering are not recoverable by the law of West Germany. They are by English and Italian law, and also by the law of Ohio, Tom's home state. Will the plaintiffs be able to recover damages for such loss in the English courts?

Address the question from the contrasting positions of (a) the common law and (b) the Private International Law (Miscellaneous Provisions) Act 1995.

Adapted from University of London LLB Examination
(for External Students) Conflict of Laws June 1990 Q4(ii)

General Comment

Once again this question has been addressed from the common law position, mainly due to the minimal case law that has, to date, developed under the Private International Law (Miscellaneous Provisions) Act 1995.

Skeleton Solution

Boys v *Chaplin* – flexibility; should it be applied? – differences between the plaintiffs discussed.

Suggested Solution

The facts postulated here are somewhat similar but more complicated than those in the leading case of choice of law in tort in English law: *Boys* v *Chaplin* [1971] AC 356. That complexity may well mean that an English court faced with our case might well decide it differently to *Boys* v *Chaplin*, but we will consider that below.

In *Boys* v *Chaplin* all five members of the House of Lords who heard the case gave judgment, but unfortunately their different speeches are based on a range of grounds. Thus the ratio decidendi is difficult, if not impossible, to extract. However, in recent years a consensus has emerged amongst the judges that the ratio dedicendi of the decision is to be found in Lord Wilberforce's speech. This, at any rate, is what the Court of Appeal has held on two occasions: *Church of Scientology of California* v *Commissioner of the Metropolitan Police* (1976) 120 SJ 690 and *Coupland* v *Arabian Gulf Petroleum Co* [1983] 3 All ER 226. Thus, henceforth, we too will take Lord Wilberforce's speech as authoritative.

As is well known, Lord Wilberforce in *Boys* v *Chaplin*, although critical of the state of the law as 'unprincipled', approved a modern version of the rule first laid down in *Philips* v *Eyre* (1870) LR 6 QB 1. That rule is a rule of 'double actionability', namely, as Lord Wilberforce said, before there could be recovery in England for a tort committed abroad the wrong had to be 'actionable as a tort according to English law, subject to the condition that civil liability in respect of the relevant claim exists between the actual parties under the law of the foreign country where the act was done', ie there had to be actionability under both the lex fori and the lex loci delicti commissi before there could be recovery in England. This rule is much criticised as leading to arbitrary results and injustice.

Applying this rule to the facts of the present case, it is plain that because damages for pain and suffering are not recoverable under the law of West Germany the requirement of civil liability in respect of that head of damage is not satisfied; and thus, prima facie, Tom, Jean and Mirella would not be able to recover such damages in the English courts. This would be consistent with earlier decisions in British courts such as *M'Elroy* v *M'Allister* 1949 SC 110 (a Scottish case).

However, although the rule of 'double actionability' was approved in *Boys* v *Chaplin* Lord Wilberforce also injected a measure of flexibility into that rule 'in the interest of individual justice'. He said that

> '... the necessary flexibility can be obtained from that principle which represents a common denominator of the United States decisions [where a much more flexible approach is generally adopted, usually called the approach of the proper law of the tort], namely, through segregation of the relevant issue and consideration whether, in relation to that rule, the relevant foreign rule ought, as a matter of policy ... to be applied. For this purpose it is necessary to identify the policy of the rule, to inquire into what situations, with what contacts it was intended to apply; [and] whether or not to apply it, in the circumstances of the instant case, would serve an interest that the rule was devised to meet ... [But] the general rule must apply unless clear and satisfying grounds are shown why it should be departed from.'

Applying this approach to the facts of the instant case, it is clear that Jean has a strong case for the operation of flexibility. After all, if Jean's case is seen in isolation it is very similar to *Boys* v *Chaplin* itself where two British servicemen had been involved in a motor accident in Malta (where they were stationed). The injured serviceman brought action against the other serviceman in England but what could he recover? Under the law of Malta he could recover only his damages for loss of earnings and expenses, while under the law of England he could recover, in addition, damages for pain and suffering. If the rule of double actionability was applied strictly, then all that the plaintiff could recover would be his loss of earnings and expenses for there was no civil liability under the law of Malta between him and the defendant in regard to the damages for pain and suffering. Fortunately, all the law lords held that the damages of pain and suffering were recoverable; and that must be right for the non-availability of damages for pain and suffering under the law of Malta seems quite irrelevant to the actions between these particular two parties. This is essentially the position that Jean is in, save that she is not a servicewoman but a tourist.

However, if it is plain that the German rule denying recovery for pain and suffering has no interest in applying to the dispute between two English persons, what interest does it have in applying to a dispute between an American and an Englishman or an Italian woman and an Englishman? Plainly in the cases of Tom and Mirella German law has no great interest in applying; it is simply that English law has a weaker interest in applying. The argument that might persuade the English court to apply its rule flexibly is this one: in Tom's and Mirella's cases the policy of both Ohio law and Italian law was the same as English law, and the German law had no significant claim to apply.

A different result will arise under the principles introduced by the Private International Law (Miscellaneous Provisions) Act 1995. The lex loci delicti is quite clearly West Germany and this will be the country from which the applicable law is selected, unless this choice can be displaced by the special rule set out in s12(1). It is not clear whether the facts of this particular case would give rise to the existence of special circumstances to prevent the application of the general rule. The nationalities of the plaintiffs and that of the defendant may be factors which a court may take into account in balancing the significant factors. The fact that John was a British serviceman serving abroad may also be a counterbalancing factor against the application of the general rule.

QUESTION THREE

i) How is it decided where a tort has been committed?

ii) John, a British citizen domiciled in England, signs in England a contract with Superoil, a Utopian-registered oil company, to work for them in exploratory drilling operations in Illyria. His salary is £15,000 a year. One clause of his contract states: 'This contract is governed by the law of Utopia. The District Court of Utopia City shall have exclusive jurisdiction over any dispute arising out of it.' Another clause provides that the company is not liable for any injury suffered by John in the course of his employment, even if caused by the negligence of another employee of Superoil. This provision is valid under Utopian law, but invalid under the law of both England and Illyria. John suffers serious injuries in an accident which takes place in Illyria and which is caused by the negligence of another employee of Superoil.

Advise John how best to obtain compensation in an English court.

University of London LLB Examination
(for External Students) Conflict of Laws June 1988 Q7

General Comment

As with any two-part question, the student must ensure that sufficient time is devoted to each section. In this particular instance the temptation is to spend too long on part (i). Time management is essential.

Skeleton Solution

i) CPR r6.20 – *Distillers Co* v *Thompson* applied – other approaches considered.

ii) Jurisdiction of the English court – submission to the Utopian jurisdiction – *Sayers* v *International Drilling* applied – criticism of *Sayers* – s27(2) of the Unfair Contract Terms Act 1977.

Suggested Solution

i) It may be vital to know where a tort is actually committed since upon that fact depends the rules applicable to the actions arising out of that wrong. Although this will often be straightforward, there are cases of difficulty. For instance, if an archer standing in France shoots an arrow over the border into Switzerland where it injures an innocent party, is the wrong committed in France or Switzerland?

One point is clear. In determining the place of a tort we are determining a connecting factor; and it is fundamental, one or two exceptions aside, that the lex fori issued to determine connecting factors. (See, for instance, *Re Martin* [1900] P 211 on the law to be used in determining the connecting factor of domicile.)

Now, secondly, there are no English cases dealing with the determination of the locus of the tort where choice of law is in issue but there are several dealing with the interpretation of the old version of RSC O.11 r1(1)) which provided that leave could be granted to serve outside the jurisdiction in respect of a tort committed 'within the jurisdiction' ie in England. (This question no longer arose under the amended version of the RSC O.11 r1(1) (now CPR r6.20) as it was much broader and provides that leave may be granted where 'the claim is founded upon a tort and the damage was sustained, or result from an act committed, within the jurisdiction'.) Although these decisions will doubtless be referred to should the question of the locus of the tort simplicter arise before an English court, they might not be an entirely reliable guide for the decisions are sometimes contradictory and, moreover, the decision whether to grant leave is, as we know, a discretionary one, so discretion may taint some of these cases.

Although a decision of the Court of Appeal, *George Monro Ltd* v *American Cyanamid Corporation* [1944] KB 432, appears to favour a test of the place where the defendant acted (in our example, France), it must be considered suspect today. It has frequently been distinguished by English courts and must be considered too restrictive.

On the other hand, a test of the place of harm has been relied upon in several cases (ie in our example, Switzerland). Thus in *Bata* v *Bata* [1948] WN 366 a defamatory letter, written and posted in Switzerland, was read in England; it was held that the tort of libel was committed in England for that was where the plaintiff lived and where his reputation suffered.

However, the test of the place of the harm is being subsumed into a test of the 'substance of the tort'. This at any rate is the substance of the decision of the Privy Council in *Distillers Co (Biochemicals) Ltd* v *Thompson* [1971] AC 458. The case concerned the marketing of a drug containing thalidomide in New South Wales, the drug having been manufactured in England. The Privy Council held that the cause of action had arisen in New South Wales. Lord Pearson said that the correct approach was 'to look back over the series of events constituting [the tort] and ask the question, where in substance did the cause of action arise?' This approach has since been followed on several occasions in Commonwealth jurisdiction including in England. Thus in *Castree v ER Squibb* [1980] 1 WLR 1248 the Court of Appeal in a case of machinery negligently manufactured in Germany but marketed in England held that the substance of the tort occurred in England because that was where the plaintiff was injured.

With bills of lading that contain misrepresentations as to the quality of the goods, the tort is committed where the bills are delivered (even if not read), not where the defective goods are delivered: *Cordova Land Co v Victor Bros Inc* [1966] 1 WLR 793. But where the misrepresentation is made in a telex, it is made where the telex is received: *Diamond v Bank of London and Montreal Ltd* [1979] 1 All ER 561.

ii) It is difficult to advise John. As we shall see, although it is possible that John will be able to rely upon s27 of the Unfair Contract Terms Act 1977, there remain difficulties over the jurisdiction of the English court.

First of all, there are serious problems with establishing the jurisdiction of the English court. Superoil apparently will have to be served with a claimform in Utopia, thus the leave of the English courts will have to be obtained to do so. At first sight this appears possible in terms of CPR r6.20(5)(a) which provides that leave may be granted in respect of various contractual matters where the contract 'was made within the jurisdiction' (as is the case here). However, the immediate difficulty is the jurisdiction clause granting exclusive jurisdiction to the Utopia City court. English courts are reluctant to exercise their own jurisdiction when the parties have agreed that another court is to have jurisdiction: *Trendtex Trading Corporation v Credit Suisse* [1982] AC 679 (a stay case); *Mackender v Feldia AG* [1967] 2 QB 590 (in a CPR r6.20 case, like this one, the jurisdiction clause will only be disregarded if the contract is void). The English courts do retain a discretion to exercise jurisdiction contrary to the terms of such clauses, but they are reluctant to do so: *The Eleftheria* [1970] P 94. A strong case would need to be shown by the plaintiff (John) (on whom the burden rests). One of the factors that the court will take into consideration will be whether the matter is governed by a foreign law (as is the case here) that is different from English law (as is the case here). These factors suggest that the English court is likely to decide that Utopia is the proper forum and refuse to grant leave to serve outside the jurisdiction.

Should John, contrary to the view expressed above, persuade the English court to grant leave then the question of the validity of the exemption clause will arise before the English courts. In the leading, although unsatisfactory, case on this issue, *Sayers v International Drilling* [1971] 1 WLR 1176, a majority of the Court of Appeal assumed that the question was simply contractual; and thus if the exemption clause was valid under the proper law of the contract then it was effective to prevent recovery notwithstanding the existence of s1(3) of the Law Reform (Personal Injuries) Act 1948 which provides that a clause which exempts the employer from liability for personal injuries caused by persons in common employment with him shall be void.

In *Sayers'* case what happened was that an English domiciled workman, employed by a Dutch company on an oil rig in Nigerian waters, was injured through the negligence of his fellow workmen. He sued his employers in England (the contract was made in England) but they relied on Dutch law under which the exemption clause was valid. The majority of the Court of Appeal (Salmon and Stamp LJJ) held that the proper law of the contract was Dutch law; and thus, treating the matter as a purely contractual one, reliance could not be placed on s1(3). This decision has been much criticised. For instance, it may be argued that before an exemption clause is effective it needs to be established both that it is valid under the proper law of the contract and that such clauses are valid under the law governing the tort.

If the court were persuaded not to follow *Sayers* on such grounds, the position might appear more helpful to John. Given the predominance of the lex fori in the English choice of law rules for tort (subject, of course, to civil liability under the law of the place where the wrong was committed: see *Boys* v *Chaplin* [1971] AC 356) John might think that he would not be able to rely upon s1(3). But this is probably not the case for the most sensible interpretation of the later Scottish case of *Brodin* v *A/R Seljan* 1973 SLT 198 (where s1(3) (which also forms part of the law of Scotland) did deny effectiveness to an exemption clause) is that that was because the accident took place in Scottish waters, even though the injured man's contract of employment had a Norwegian proper law under which the exemption clause was valid.

So the position looks bleak for John at common law. However, there is one ray of hope that one can hold out to him which is the Unfair Contract Terms Act 1977. This Act which, broadly speaking, subjects exemption clauses to a test of reasonableness and provides that a person cannot exclude his liability for death or personal injury by a contractual term, also provides in s27(2) that

> 'This Act has effect notwithstanding any contract term which applies ... the law of some country outside the United Kingdom, where ...
> (a) the term appears to the court ... to have been imposed wholly or mainly for the purpose of enabling the party imposing it to evade the operation of this Act'.

If John can show that that was Superoil's purpose in imposing the exemption clause he may yet succeed but the evidence of this seems very thin.

QUESTION FOUR

A train operated by Chuffa Ltd, a Blueland company, becomes derailed as it crosses the border with Orangeland owing to the negligence of the driver. Some of the carriages land on each side of the border. Panic, who is in the Blueland part of the train, and Faint, who is in the Orangeland part of the train, are killed instantly. Panic and Faint are both domiciled and resident in Blueland.

Grab, who is domiciled and resident in Orangeland, and Rush, who is domiciled and resident in Blueland, start fighting in an effort to get through the emergency exit in the Blueland part of the train. Grab knocks Rush unconscious and then jumps out landing on the Orangeland side of the border. Grab and Rush both suffer extensive injuries.

The contract between the passengers and Chuffa Ltd contains a term exempting Chuffa Ltd from liability. This term is valid by Blueland law, but invalid by Orangeland law and English law.

Under Orangeland law, but no other relevant law, contributory negligence is an absolute defence to actions for personal injury. Under English law, but not other relevant law, a cause of action survives for the benefit of the estate of a deceased victim. Also, under English law, but no other relevant law, damages for pain and suffering are available.

Advise the executors of Panic and Faint, and Grab, who all wish to sue Chuffa in England, and Rush, who wishes to sue Grab in England. Chuffa and Grab have both agreed to submit to the jurisdiction of the English courts.

How, if at all, would your answer differ if Grab and Rush were both resident and domiciled in England?

University of London LLB Examination
(for External Students) Conflict of Laws June 1993 Q5

General Comment

Quite a straightforward question which demands the application of the rule of double actionability together with exclusion clauses. As with any problem question application as opposed to description of the appropriate rules is required.

Skeleton Solution

Apply the *Boys* v *Chaplin* rule of double actionability to each of the plaintiffs in turn – effectiveness or otherwise of the exclusion clause – introduction of flexibility into the double actionability rule in the interests of individual justice.

Suggested Solution

The issues under consideration in this problem relate, principally, to the English choice of law rule in tort. There is no jurisdictional problem: Chuffa and Grab have agreed to submit to the jurisdiction of the English courts. That the English court has jurisdiction to hear actions based on torts committed abroad was decided by Lord Mansfield in *Mostyn* v *Fabrigas* (1774) 1 Cowp 161.

In relation to the issue of the locus of a tort, the general rule is that where all the elements of the tort (with the exception of the bringing of the action) occur in one country, then that is the locus delicti. However, if D's tortious act takes place in one country, whereas the harm inflicted on P is suffered by P in another country, then the approach of English law is to determine where in substance the cause of action arose

(*Castree* v *ER Squibb* [1980] 1 WLR 1248), a test confirmed in a jurisdictional context in *Metall und Rohstoff AG* v *Donaldson Lufkin & Jenrette Inc* [1990] 1 QB 391. It is submitted that, from the facts of the problem, the executors of Panic and Faint will be pursuing actions on behalf of injuries sustained in one country. The same applies to Rush. With regard to Grab, the position is not so clear.

The current English choice of law rule in *Boys* v *Chaplin* [1971] AC 356 has evolved from *Phillips* v *Eyre* (1870) LR 6 QB 1, where Willes J said:

'As a general rule, in order to found a suit in England for a wrong alleged to have been committed abroad, two conditions must be fulfilled. First, the wrong must be of such a character that it would have been actionable if committed in England ... Secondly, the act must not have been justifiable by the law of the place where it was done.'

The first arm of this double-actionability rule was based on the decision in *The Halley* (1868) LR 2 PC 193. Here a defence to an action in negligence succeeded on the basis that, under the then prevailing English law, a collision caused by the negligent pilotage of a British steamship in Belgian territorial waters imposed no liability on the persons from whom damages were claimed. Although the dictum of Selwyn LJ to the effect that an English court would not enforce a foreign domestic law and award damages for an act which, according to English law, could be invoked as a defence has been criticised as inaccurate, parochial and making a plaintiff surmount a double hurdle if he is to succeed in his action, it is still good law following its unanimous approval in *Boys* v *Chaplin*.

In the second arm of the double-actionability rule, the requirement for the act to be 'not justifiable' has been interpreted in at least three different ways, viz: it must be a tort under the lex loci (*The Mary Moxham* (1876) 1 PD 107); it is sufficient if criminal liability attaches (*Machado* v *Fontes* [1897] 2 QB 231); and it must be susceptible to civil action as between the actual parties to the action: *M'Elroy* v *M'Allister* 1949 SC 110. It is the last interpretation which has been favoured by the decision in *Boys* v *Chaplin*. The ratio of *Boys* was identified in *Church of Scientology of California* v *Commissioner of the Metropolitan Police* (1976) 120 SJ 690 and in *Coupland* v *Arabian Gulf Petroleum Co* [1983] 3 All ER 226 as being that part of Lord Wilberforce's speech where he said for a plaintiff to succeed in an action for a tort committed abroad the alleged act must be:

'... actionable as a tort according to English law, subject to the condition that civil liability in respect of the relevant claim exists as between the actual parties under the law of the foreign country where the act was done'.

However, this second arm (requiring 'civil liability ... under the law of the foreign country') is to be tempered by a degree of flexibility to allow, for example, the English court to disregard limitations or exclusion of damages for personal injuries provided for under the lex loci, provided that this can be achieved 'on clear and satisfactory grounds'.

The claims of the plaintiffs in the given problem are now analysed in the light of this modified double-actionability rule.

Executors of Panic and Faint

There is no doubt that a claim in respect of a fatal accident is actionable as a tort in English law: Law Reform (Miscellaneous Provisions) Act 1934; Fatal Accidents Act 1976. Accordingly, the executors of Panic and Faint will succeed on the first arm on the ratio in *Boys* v *Chaplin*. A number of issues arise under the second arm, however.

First, whereas the exclusion clause, if it is formally valid by Blueland law, may exclude civil liability in respect of Panic's fatal accident as he was in the Blueland part of the train when he was killed, it may be ineffective with respect to Faint as he received his fatal injuries in Orangeland where it was invalid. *Sayers* v *International Drilling* [1971] 1 WLR 1176 illustrated that an exclusion clause may be effective in excluding liability where it is valid by the proper law of the contract, whereas, with respect to Faint, *Brodin* v *A/R Seljan* 1973 SLT 198 illustrated that such a clause may be ineffective in the country of the forum.

Second, neither Blueland law nor Orangeland law permits a cause of action to survive for the benefit of the estate of a deceased victim. In *Boys* v *Chaplin,* Lord Wilberforce said that a cause of action must vest in the same person and be against the same person in both legal systems. Accordingly, this would appear to prevent the executors from succeeding in an action in the same way that the widow, as executrix, was defeated in her claim in *M'Elroy* v *M'Allister* 1949 SC 110.

Third, there is no 'clear and satisfactory ground' for flexibility and displacing the lex loci in Panic's case: Lord Wilberforce specifically stated that it would be inappropriate to oust the lex loci delicti where one or both of the parties hailed from the locus. Here, Chuffa is a Blueland company and Panic is domiciled and resident in Blueland. Although Faint was killed in Orangeland, again it would appear that application of the flexibility exception is inapplicable.

It would appear, then, that the executors of Panic and Faint would not succeed in their actions in the English courts.

Grab

Grab can succeed on the first arm of *Boys* v *Chaplin*: a claim for personal injuries following a transport accident is actionable. With regard to civil liability under the locus delicti, whereas a claim for pain and suffering is not recognised under either Blueland law or Orangeland law, and any injury he may have sustained in jumping off the train in Orangeland may be met with the absolute defence of contributory negligence, the first problem to confront as to his extensive physical injuries, is where, in substance, did the harmful event occur?: *Castree* v *ER Squibb*. It is possible that harm may be inflicted in one jurisdiction but suffered in another: *Distillers Co (Biochemicals) Ltd* v *Thompson* [1971] AC 458. It might not be detrimental to Grab that he was in the Blueland part of the train at the time of the accident since he escaped from it in Orangeland and the exclusion clause would be regarded as invalid in Orangeland where he is domiciled and resident. Furthermore, even if some of Grab's injuries were sustained when he jumped from the train, if it was deemed that he had acted in an emergency then he may not be guilty of contributory negligence. However, whereas it may appear that Grab has a good arguable claim, it must be remembered that if he is to succeed then he must discharge the burden of proof on a balance of probabilities.

Rush

Clearly, Rush will not succeed on the second arm of the ratio in *Boys* v *Chaplin* in a claim against Grab for damages for pain and suffering: civil liability for pain and suffering does not exist in Blueland.

If Rush and Grab were resident and domiciled in England, there would be a case for replacing the second arm of the ratio in *Boys* v *Chaplin* with an element of flexibility *'in the interest of individual justice'*, per Lord Wilberforce. As in *Boys*, the issue of a claim for damages in respect of pain and suffering would be classified as substantive and, to put another comment of Lord Wilberforce into the current context: 'Nothing suggests that the [Blueland] state has any interest in applying [its] rule to persons resident outside it, or in denying the application of the English rule to these parties.' Accordingly, the law of the state which, with respect to the issue of Rush's claim for damages for pain and suffering, has the most significant relationship with the occurrence and the parties may be applied. Thus, English law should be applied and Rush should be able successfully to pursue his claim for damages. A recent case which confirmed that English law was able to displace the lex loci delicti was *Johnson* v *Coventry Churchill* [1992] 3 All ER 14. Here an English employee of an English company was working in Germany under a contract of employment governed by English law. When he was injured during the course of his employment it was held that the country with which the occurrence and the parties had the most significant relationship was England.

QUESTION FIVE

Last summer Mr Jones set off on a motoring holiday from his home in London to Costabravadia. He was accompanied by his wife, by a neighbour Dawn and by their student lodger, Juan, who was from Costabravadia and was studying at the University of London for three years. Juan paid £50 towards the cost of the journey. Shortly after their arrival in Costabravadia, having misjudged the potency of the local wine, Mr Jones crashed the car into a ravine. He escaped with minor cuts and bruises but his wife was seriously injured and Dawn was killed. Juan was unconscious as a result of the accident for a month at which point his life support machine was switched off by his mother unlawfully. She was prosecuted for manslaughter in Costabravadia but acquitted.

You are asked to advise Mrs Jones, Dawn's executor and Juan's parents, under the common law, all of whom wish to sue Mr Jones in England. Comment on how your advice may differ under s11 of the Private International Law (Miscellaneous Provisions) Act 1995.

You are told that in Costabravadia:

i) a driver cannot be sued unless he is first successfully prosecuted in a criminal court. The state prosecutor took the view that Mr Jones had already suffered enough;

ii) a wife cannot sue a husband in tort;

iii) gratuitous passengers cannot sue;

iv) damages are only payable for pain and suffering which continues for more than three months after a tort has been committed;

v) and Juan's death is regarded as directly attributable to Mr Jones's tortious act. English law would regard Juan's mother's action as a novus actus interveniens.

> Adapted from University of London LLB Examination
> (for External Students) Conflict of Laws June 1994 Q4

General Comment

This is a straightforward problem question relating to tort actions. The problem is broken up into a number of parts which makes it easier for the candidate to build up a store of marks. However, as with any multi-issue question, the student must ensure that all parts are dealt with effectively.

Skeleton Solution

The rule in *Boys* v *Chaplin* – consider each of the factual elements in turn – s11 Private International Law (Miscellaneous Provisions) Act 1995.

Suggested Solution

The question requires considering the cases of Mrs Jones, Dawn's executor and Juan's parents in bringing actions against Mr Jones. I shall deal with each of these plaintiffs in turn.

The central issue is as to the appropriate system of law in each case. All the potential actions are in tort, and in each case the tort occurred outside the United Kingdom, in Costabravadia. Therefore, the foreign tort rule in *Boys* v *Chaplin* [1971] AC 356 applies. If there had been any doubt as to the place of the tort it would have been necessary to apply the rule in *Metall und Rohstoff AG* v *Donald Lufkin & Jenrette Inc* [1990] 1 QB 391, but the place of the tort is clear on these facts.

The requirements in *Boys* v *Chaplin* are twofold (the so-called double actionability rule), namely there must be an actionable tort had the actions taken place in England and, second, the action must be civilly actionable (not necessarily as a tort) between the parties in the place of the commission of the tort.

As a further general principle, Lord Wilberforce found that there is an inherent idea of flexibility in the test. That is to say, the test must not be applied so strictly as to exclude actions. This principle is unclear in its theoretical application but may be more clear on the facts.

There is a general question as to whether Mr Jones can be sued under the second head in *Boys* v *Chaplin*, where it would be required that under Costabravadian law Mr Jones had been convicted of a crime. The notion of flexibility would suggest that this procedural rule (especially given that it has not been enforced as a result of a non-legal decision) should be ignored in this instance. It would be repugnant, it is submitted, for the potential plaintiffs to be refused their right to sue in tort on this ground.

Mrs Jones

Mrs Jones was injured in the crash and therefore, under English law, would have an action under the tort of negligence against Mr Jones for his driving. In Costabravadia, a wife is refused the ability to sue her husband in tort. It is submitted that an English court would not necessarily consider itself to be bound by this rule of foreign public policy if, for example, it would rob Mrs Jones of the ability to recover money to pay for medical expenses.

Dawn's executor

Under English law, the executor would be able to sue in place of Dawn for the duty of care owed to her by Mr Jones. Therefore, there would be an English cause of action and the first limb of the test in *Boys* v *Chaplin* is satisfied. However, it would be impossible for Dawn to sue under Costabravadian law on the basis that she is a gratuitous volunteer. This, it is submitted, is a substantial restriction on the cause of action rather than a matter of general public policy. Therefore, Dawn's executor would not be able to bring an action under *Boys* v *Chaplin*.

Juan's parents

Juan's parents would be entitled to sue under English law on the basis of the cause of action disclosed in *McLoughlin* v *O'Brian* [1983] 1 AC 410. This deals with the situation where the immediate relatives of a person injured as a result of another's negligence can claim in tort for their own suffering. The second issue is whether or not the prohibition under Costabravadian law against actions for pain and suffering lasting more than three months after the accident would put a cap on the level of damages which could be obtained by the parents. It is therefore submitted that this would restrict the size of the claim which the parents could obtain.

English law might restrict the ability of the parents to sue Mr Jones on the basis that Juan's mother caused his death by switching off the life support system. This would transfer tortious liability to Juan's mother and away from Mr Jones. However, English law would still allow recovery for the pain and suffering which Juan suffered. Therefore, under principles of English tort law there would still be a partial action in tort on behalf of the parents acting for the estate of Juan, against Mr Jones. The action considered against Mr Jones under Costabravadian law would be somewhat different in that it would permit of an action for the death caused by Mr Jones (with attendant loss of earnings claims resulting from death). The issue here would be whether or not it is possible to bring the extended action for damages caused by the death.

It is submitted that, because the first leg of the *Boys* v *Chaplin* test is only satisfied with reference to an action for pain and suffering before Juan's mother's intervention, there cannot be a claim in relation to the extended form of action. To argue to the contrary would be to say that both limbs of the *Boys* v *Chaplin* test do not need to be satisfied – this is not position of any of their Lordships in their judgments.

Therefore, the action brought by the parents would be restricted.

Reform of the rule in Boys *v* Chaplin

The law in this area has altered now that the Private International Law (Miscellaneous Provisions) Act 1995 is in force. The Act contains a provision which introduces the rule that the law of the country where the tort occurred is the applicable law in such cases. This general rule, contained in s11(1) of the Act, applies in all circumstances unless special circumstances are deemed by a court to exist. In order to find the existence of special circumstances, a court must examine: (a) the significance of the factors which connect a tort with the country whose law would be the applicable law under the general rule; and (b) the significance of any factors connecting the tort with another country. Only if this latter set of factors displaces the factors occurring in the place the tort occurred can a court displace the general rule.

QUESTION SIX

'Is the new statutory choice of law rule in tort in Part III of the Private International Law (Miscellaneous Provisions) Act 1995 an improvement on that which was developed by the common law?'

University of London LLB Examination
(for External Students) Conflict of Laws June 1999 Q2

General Comment

In order to produce an effective answer the student must not only be able to evaluate the common law rules in terms of approach, flexibility and the solutions produced but also the way in which the Private International Law (Miscellaneous Provisions) Act 1995 differs from this. In addition, given the sparse case law to date under the 1995 Act, the student should make use of academic opinion in order to highlight its strengths and potential weaknesses.

Skeleton Solution

Consideration of the main provisions in Part III – ss9–12 – abolishes double actionability rule (*Phillips* v *Eyre*, *Boys* v *Chaplin*) – common law exceptions (*Red Sea*

Insurance) – statutory rules: where the events occur – exception: proper law of the tort – fairer solutions? – preferable to common law?

Suggested Solution

The common law choice of law rules in tort were the subject of criticism due in no small part to its complex nature and the belief that it frequently favoured the wrongdoer. In response to this Part III of the Private International Law (Miscellaneous Provisions) Act (PIL(MP)A) 1995, which implemented the Law Commission's 1990 draft Bill, attempts to simplify the choice of law question. It establishes a general rule in relation to the determination of the applicable law to torts and then follows this with a series of exceptions to the rule. The new statutory regime is applicable to all tortious issues except defamation. Consequently, the common law still remains applicable in this area.

As noted above, s10 of the 1995 Act abolishes the common law rule of double actionability (*Phillips* v *Eyre* (1870) LR 6 QB 1) as modified in *Boys* v *Chaplin* [1971] AC 356. This is replaced by the lex loci delicti commissi (the law of the country in which the events constituting the tort occurred). Consequently, under the common law the plaintiff was obliged to satisfy two conditions, namely: (a) that the wrongful act must be actionable in the law of the lex fori; and (b) must be actionable in the law of the lex loci. Whilst this test was tempered by the introduction of a third element – 'flexibility' – it nevertheless placed a demanding burden upon the potential plaintiff. In many respects, it is this aspect of the common law approach which was seen as being in need of reform and simplification.

Section 11(1) states that the general rule in relation to the applicable law is that 'of the country in which the events constituting the tort in question occur.' Consequently, where all of the events giving rise to culpability take place in a single country, the law of that country is to be the applicable law. In order to identify the lex loci delicti commissi when significant elements take place in different countries, s11(2) specifies specific rules in relation to:

a) personal injury – 'the law of the country where the individual was when he sustained the injury';

b) damage to property – 'the law of the country where the property was when it was damaged; and

c) other torts – 'the law of the country in which the most significant element of those events occurred.'

It should be noted that the application of the lex loci delicti commissi is in line with most other countries. It is felt that the most important effect of the approach is the discouragement of forum shopping, as most countries will apply the same law. In addition, it is frequently suggested that this is the law which most plaintiffs and defendants expect to be applied to the case and as such responds to the reasonable expectations of the parties.

However, as noted earlier, the general rule contained in s11 may be displaced and the law of another country may be applied if a more significant connection is established. In such circumstances, s12 instructs the courts to consider two elements: (a) the significance of the factors which connect a tort with the country whose law would be the applicable law under the general rules; and (b) the significance of any factors connecting the tort with another country. If as a result of this comparison it appears that (b) is more substantially appropriate than the prima facie applicable law under (a) then the court will apply the law of that country. Whilst an exhaustive list of factors which may be taken into account during this process is not provided, s12 nevertheless does specify a selection of factors.

Whilst this provision has been criticised as maintaining the 'common law' exceptions (*Red Sea Insurance Co Ltd* v *Bouygues SA and Others* [1994] 3 WLR 926) via the backdoor as well as introducing certain interpretative problems, it may be argued that the proper law exception is an important inclusion. The provision ensures that a certain degree of flexibility is maintained in order to deal effectively with multi-state torts where problems may be experienced when attempting to connect parties, acts and damage to specific states. Equally, it also provides the courts with the necessary discretion to apply the law of another country where it may prove substantially more appropriate to apply that law than that of the lex loci delicti (where all significant factors point towards one law).

One restriction is contained in s9(1) of the 1995 Act, which provides that the characterisation of issues relating to a tort is to be determined by the forum. In addition, the 1995 Act states that the law determined via the above series of rules and exceptions will be disregarded if it is contrary to English public policy, if it is penal in character or relates to foreign revenue laws. Significantly, the Act expressly rejects renvoi under s9(3), which will inevitably ensure the simplicity of the statutory process.

Consequently, it may be suggested that the PIL(MP)A 1995 represents an improvement on the common law. However, it is by no means a perfect system. If one refers to the work of Briggs – 'Choice of Law in Tort and Delict' [1996] Lloyds MCLQ 519 – he describes the 1995 Act as 'user-hostile' and 'intellectually weak'. First of all, it has been criticised as giving no more certainty than the old common law rules and that in places it tends to be both vague and ill-defined. Second, it is stated that the term 'where the events occurred' remains unclear. However, it should be noted that commentators such as Morse – 'Torts in Private International Law: A New Statutory Framework' [1996] ICLQ 888 – takes a rather more positive view of the Act, stating that 'it as a sensible statutory framework within which courts will have a creative role to play in the development of the law.'

There are certainly a number of contradictions and confusions within Part III of the Act. However, it should be noted that it cannot be perfect as it is impossible to find an ideal formula in this area of the law. It can simply aim to achieve a balance between the certainty and flexibility that are necessary characteristics for dealing with the choice of law in tort. The general rule is clear. Perhaps the real area of contention is that of the exceptions to this rule. However, as with any exception to a general rule, there must be an in-built flexibility to the exception, which in turn leads to uncertainty. However, as Morse indicates, this is an area where the courts may play a positive role in developing the law. Nevertheless, when compared to the common law and the rule of double actionability, the 1995 Act should be preferred in so much as the plaintiff and defendant are treated equally and aims to eliminate the unjust solutions generated by the common law.

Chapter 8

Property

8.1 Introduction

8.2 Key points

8.3 Key cases and statutes

8.4 Questions and suggested solutions

8.1 Introduction

This chapter will deal both with the choice of law aspects of individual transfers of property (as when A sells his car to B) as opposed to universal transfers as when A by his will leaves all his estate to B which will be dealt with in Chapter 10. As you ought already to know, different rules govern these two different kinds of transfer.

The rules involved are generally not difficult, although there are several points of uncertainty or areas in which the law is unjust, particularly where the transfer of intangible property is concerned.

8.2 Key points

The distinction between movable and immovable property

In the conflict rules for property a critical distinction is made between movable property (which broadly speaking corresponds to personalty in English legal terminology) and immovable property (which broadly corresponds to realty).

Different conflicts rules, particularly concerning choice of law, are applied depending on whether property is classified as movable or immovable. The classification of property into one or other of these categories is the first step towards identifying the law which will apply to the resolution of an issue involving property.

Immediately, one significant difficulty arises. Not all legal systems classify forms of property into the same groups. Take for example, a mortgagee's interest in land. The mortgagee has loaned money and the loan is secured over land entitling the mortgagee to repossess the land in the event of default by the borrower. In English law, the mortgagee's interest in the land is classed as immovable: *Re Hoyles* [1911] 1 Ch 179. However, in other legal systems, such as New Zealand and Australian law, such an interest is considered movable since it is viewed as a loan of money.

Naturally, where the property in question is clearly immovable (eg land) or movable (eg a motor vehicle), the problem of classification is not difficult. It is when this distinction is not clear-cut that problems arise.

The classification of the property as movable or immovable is a matter for the lex situs. In other words, if an English court has to decide the character of property located in a foreign jurisdiction, it must decide the issue by applying the laws of that legal system.

Immovable property and the exercise of jurisdiction by the English courts

The basic rule is that English courts will not exercise jurisdiction over disputes concerning title to immovable property located in a foreign country. This rule was definitively stated in *British South Africa Company* v *Companhia de Mocambique* [1893] AC 602, where it was held that an English court:

'... has no jurisdiction to entertain an action for (1) the determination of title to, or the right to possession of, any immovable situated out of England; or (2) the recovery of damages for trespass to such immovables.'

This rationale for this rule is simply the impracticability of attempting to exercise authority in another country. Ultimately, only a court of the lex situs of immovable property can enforce a judgment. As Lord Cottenham observed in *Re Courtney* (1840) Mont & Ch 239:

'If the law of the country where the land is situated should not permit or not enable the defendant to do what the court might think it right to decree, it would be useless and unjust to direct him to do the act.'

Article 22 of Council Regulation 44/2001/EC has also adopted this rule by providing that, as far as the member states of the European Union are concerned, the courts of the lex situs have exclusive jurisdiction in proceedings which have as their object rights in rem in, or tenancies of, immovable property: see *Webb* v *Webb* [1994] ILPr 389.

As is the case with most rules, the rule limiting the jurisdiction of the English courts over property situated in foreign countries is subject to certain exceptions:

a) Where a court has jurisdiction in personam over a defendant, then that court has jurisdiction to hear an action in respect of a contract or equity affecting the foreign land: see *Penn* v *Baltimore* (1750) 1 Ves Sen 444. This exception is permitted because of the existence of personal obligations between the plaintiff and the defendant from which the plaintiff can derive rights.

b) If an English court has jurisdiction to administer an estate or a trust and some of the assets in that estate or trust consists of foreign land, the court may exercise jurisdiction in respect of the foreign land: see *Re Duke of Wellington* [1948] Ch 118.

c) When an English court exercises its admiralty jurisdiction in rem, it may exercise jurisdiction over foreign immovable property: see *The Tolten* [1946] P 135.

Immovable property and choice of law

Questions concerning immovables are governed by the lex situs which in this case is deemed to include the conflict of laws of the lex situs. The reason for the application of the whole gambit of the laws of the lex situs is simply that, in order to have any prospect of being enforceable, a decree from an English court relative to foreign property must be absolutely consistent with the rules of that legal system: see *Re Ross* [1930] 1 Ch 377.

In practical terms, the lex situs governs each of the following matters:

a) the formal validity of the transfer of immovable property;

b) the essential validity of the transfer of immovable property; and

c) the capacity to transfer immovable property.

Formal validity of the transfer

The validity of the formal requirements necessary for the transfer of immovable property is regulated by the lex situs. For example, in *Adams* v *Clutterbuck* (1883) 10 QB 403, a transfer in writing was made of shooting rights over land in Scotland between two Englishmen both domiciled in England. English law required such a conveyance to be under seal but Scots law permitted such conveyances to be in writing. The formal validity of the transfer was upheld since it complied with the formalities of the lex situs.

Essential validity of the transfer

The essential validity of a transfer of immovables is also decided under the lex situs. There are a number of cases holding that the lex situs governs issues such as the types of estates which can be created in foreign land, whether gifts of land to charities are subject to statutory rules and whether the rules against perpetuities and accumulations are infringed by transfers of land: see *Freke* v *Carbury* (1873) LR 16 Eq 461 and *Row* v *Jugg* [1911] 1 Ch 179.

Capacity to transfer

There is some authority for the proposition that capacity to transfer land is regulated by the lex situs. In *Bank of Africa* v *Cohen* [1909] 2 Ch 129, the court held that a married woman domiciled in England who refused to give a mortgage over her land in South Africa in respect of loans made to her husband, after agreeing to do so, could rely on a South African law which provided that married women could not give security over land for their husbands' debts.

Nevertheless, it is not certain how much reliance can be placed on this rule in modern conflict of laws. Surprisingly very few cases on this point have in fact come before the courts for consideration.

Movable property and choice of law

For the purposes of discussing the general rules relating to the choice of law in cases involving the transfer of property in movable property, it should be emphasised that we are concerned with individual and particular transfers of movables and not general transfers such as those which take place in the event of bankruptcy or succession on death. The transfers which are considered here concern contractual arrangements, gifts or other voluntary processes.

In common with immovables, the basic rule is that the validity of a transfer of property in movables is governed by the lex situs. This rule was well stated by Diplock LJ in *Hardwick Game Farm* v *Suffolk Agricultural Poultry Producers' Association* [1966] 1 WLR 287 in the following terms:

> 'The proper law governing the transfer of corporeal movable property is the lex situs. A contract made in England and governed by English law for the sale of specific goods situated in Germany, although it would be effective to pass the property in the goods at the moment the contract was made if the goods were situate in England, would not have that effect if under German law ... delivery of the goods was required in order to transfer the property in them.'

This is the position where the goods are not moved from a particular country. The situation becomes more complicated when the goods change their physical location. For example, in *Winkworth* v *Christie Manson and Woods Ltd* [1980] 2 WLR 937, works of art were stolen from the plaintiff in England and taken to Italy where they were sold to the second defendant in circumstances which gave him a valid title to the works under Italian law. The second defendant gave the works to the first defendants for auction in England. The plaintiff sought a declaration from the court that the works belonged to him.

In rendering judgment, Slade J declared that proprietary rights to movables must be generally determined by the lex situs to which they are subject at the particular time at which the property was transferred. If any other rule was adopted, a purchaser would be required to examine all the laws of the countries through which the goods have passed in order to ascertain whether a valid title could be effected. Clearly this would be unreasonable.

Hence, the general rule regarding the choice of law applicable to the transfer of property in movables is that if property is validly transferred according to its lex situs at the time of its transfer, the transaction will be recognised as a valid conveyance in English law: see also *Cammell* v *Sewell* (1860) 5 H & N 728.

This general rule is subject to three minor exceptions:

a) cases involving reservation of title;

b) goods in transit; and

c) public policy considerations.

Reservation of title

If a seller reserves title in property transferred to a purchaser until a certain event, ie full payment of the purchase price, and the property is subsequently transferred by the purchaser to a third party in another country, a question arises as to the effect of the private rights between the first two parties on the subsequent transaction.

There is no authoritative English case on this point but there is American and Canadian authority to suggest that the lex situs would apply and if that law enforced reservation of title rights, these would apply: see *Goetschius* v *Brightman* (1927) 245 NY 186: and *Century Credit Corp* v *Richard* (1962) 34 DLR (2d) 291. Naturally, the converse will also apply and if the lex situs does not recognise the application of reservation of title clauses, even if valid in a country where the goods were previously located, the term will not be enforced.

Goods in transit

Especially in international sales contracts, goods may be transported through one or more country to the ultimate purchaser. When goods are in transit, their situs at any particular time may be quite fortuitous. According to Dicey & Morris (*The Conflict of Laws* (1993), 12th ed at p969), although no legal authority is cited, if a tangible movable is in transit, and its situs is casual, a transfer which is valid and effective by its proper law will be considered valid and effective in England.

Public policy exceptions

In *Winkworth* v *Christie Manson and Woods Ltd*, above, Slade J made reference to five exceptions to the lex situs rule based on public policy. These included the public policy exclusionary rule, the overriding effect of statutes of the lex fori, and special rules relating to the general transfer of movables, eg succession on death. These five rules may provide grounds for deviating from the general lex situs rule.

Assignment of intangible movables

Where an assignment of intangible movables (choses in action) falls within the terms of the Rome Convention 1980 by virtue of the Contracts (Applicable Law) Act 1990, the matter will be regulated by art 12 of that Convention.

The Convention stipulates that the mutual obligations of an assignor and an assignee under a voluntary assignment of a right against another person are governed by the law which applies to the contract between the assignor and assignee. For the purposes of convenience, we shall term this the proper law of the assignment.

The proper law of the assignment is deemed, by virtue of art 12(2) of the Convention, to regulate the following matters:

a) the assignability of the right;

b) the relationship between the assignee and the person against whom the right is to be enforced;

c) the conditions under which the assignment can be invoked against the person owing the obligation; and

d) any questions concerning whether or not the obligations of the person owing the obligation have been discharged.

In the event of the non-application of the Convention, the assignment of intangible movables falls to be determined by the common law rules. The common law rules regulating assignment and the formal validity of the assignment are outlined below.

The competency of assignment of an intangible right

Before deciding whether or not an assignment is formally valid, it must be determined is the intangible right itself is capable of competent assignment. Some legal systems do not permit the assignment of certain types of debt (eg future wages, pensions, insurance policies). The competency of an assignment is ascertained by reference to the proper law of the contract of assignment: see *Re Fry* [1946] Ch 312 and *Campbell Connelly & Co Ltd* v *Noble* [1963] 1 WLR 252.

Formal and essential validity of an assignment

Again, both these matters are governed by the proper law of the assignment. The validity of the assignment concerns matters such the capacity of the assignee and assignor and the formalities required to affect the assignment.

In *Lee* v *Abdy* (1886) 17 QBD 309, a husband domiciled in the Cape Colony assigned in the Cape Colony a life insurance policy issued by an English company to his wife. This assignment was void under the law of the Cape Colony but valid under English law. The court held that the law of the Cape Colony governed and therefore the assignment was void.

Assignments of debt

The most common form of intangible right is a simple debt. Debts may be assigned if the formalities for doing so are complied with and the assignment is valid in all other respects. There are two rules of conflicts which should be noted at this point in connection with assignment of a debt.

The question of priority of debts

It is perfectly feasible for there to be two or more valid assignment of the same debt. In these circumstances, it is important to prioritise these in order to determine which claim will succeed. Questions of priorities are governed by the proper law of the debt.

Garnishment

Garnishment, which is a form of involuntary assignment, is governed by the lex situs of the debt. When a conflict of laws is involved, the problem caused by garnishment is that unless the garnishee orders are recognised by foreign courts, the garnishee, having paid a creditor in England, may find himself forced to pay again by a foreign court.

The former rule was that an English court would make a garnishee order if England was the situs of the debt: see *Swiss Bank Corporation v Boehmische Bank* [1923] 1 KB 673. However, the rule has been modified slightly in a more recent case, namely *Deutsche Schachtbau und Tiefbohrgessellschaft mbH v R'As al-Khaimah National Oil Co* [1987] 3 WLR 1023, where the House of Lords made it clear that where there was a serious risk that a debtor might be forced to pay the same debt twice, the English courts would not make a garnishee order absolute.

Expropriation of property by governments

Certain governments have in the past expropriated property from both nationals and non-nationals for public purposes often without adequate compensation. It is possible for some of this type of property to find its way to England and, on occasion, the original owners have sought to recover their property through litigation.

The English courts have then had to face the question of how to resolve the competing claims between the expropriating authorities or a purchaser who has bought the property from the expropriating government and the original private owner.

The rule which has been developed by the courts is that if the lex situs considers that the property has been validly expropriated, its expropriation will be recognised by the English courts.

Conversely, if the lex situs considers the expropriation to be invalid then it will not be recognised as valid in English law: *Luther v Sagor* [1921] 3 KB 532. These principles have been applied in a relatively recent case, namely *Williams & Humbert Ltd v W & H Trade Marks (Jersey) Ltd* [1986] 1 All ER 129.

8.3 Key cases and statutes

- *Berschtold, Re, Berchtold v Capron* [1923] 1 Ch 192
  Doctrine of conversion does not operate in field of conflict of laws

- *British South Africa Co v Companhia de Mocambique* [1893] AC 602
  English courts have no jurisdiction to try title to immovable property situated outside England

- *Hardwick Game Farm v Suffolk Agricultural Poultry Producers' Association* [1966] 1 WLR 287
  Proper law governing transfer of movables is the lex situs

- *Hesperides Hotels Ltd* v *Muftizade* [1978] 3 WLR 378 House of Lords
  English courts have no jurisidction to try trespass to foreign land – common law

- *Hoyles, Re, Row* v *Jugg* [1911] 1 Ch 179
  Division of property into movables and immovables

- *Kwok Chi Leung Karl* v *Commissioner of Estate Duty* [1988] 1 WLR 1035
  Debt is situated where it is recoverable

- *Macmillan Inc* v *Bishopsgate Investment Trust plc and Others (No 3)* [1996] 1 WLR 387
  Choses in action – title to shares governed by lex situs

- *Penn* v *Baltimore* (1750) 1 Ves Sen 444
  Where court has jurisidction in personam over defendant then it has jurisdiction to entertain an action against defendant in respect of a contract or equity affecting foreign land

- *The Tolten* [1946] P 135
  Admiralty action – under admiralty law a maritime lien could be enforced anywhere in the world

- *Tyburn Productions Ltd* v *Conan Doyle* [1990] 3 WLR 167
  Matters of copyright are for the local sovereign to order

- *Winkworth* v *Christie Manson and Woods Ltd* [1980] 2 WLR 937
  Change of title under lex situs – change will be recognised and enforced

- Civil Jurisdiction and Judgments Act 1982, s30 – jurisdiction to entertain proceedings for trespass to, or any other tort affecting, immovable property shall extend to property situated outside England

- Council Regulation 44/2001/EC, art 22 (art 16 Brussels Convention) – courts of the lex situs have exclusive jurisdiction in matters of immovable property

- Rome Convention, art 12 – proper law of the assignment deemed to regulate: assignment of right; relationship between assignee and person against whom right is to be enforced; conditions under which assignment can be invoked

8.4 Questions and suggested solutions

QUESTION ONE

i) A lawfully sold his car to B in Redland on condition that until all instalments of the price were paid

   a) the title to the car should not vest in B but should remain in A;

   b) B should not remove the car from Redland.

   In breach of (b), B took the car to Blueland where he sold it to C, an innocent purchaser, in a manner which gave a good title to C, according to the law of

Blueland, but not according to the private international law of Redland. C has brought the car to England, where A wishes to sue him to recover the car. Advise A.

ii) Caroline, domiciled in Blueland, married David, domiciled in Whiteland, and went to live with him in that country. By the terms of her marriage settlement, Caroline purported to settle all her property upon her husband. This settlement is valid by the law of Whiteland, but under the law of Blueland a woman can neither settle her property on marriage, nor dispose of it during coverture, and on her death it is divided equally between the husband and her children. Some 20 years after the marriage Caroline and David acquired an English domicile, which they still retained when Caroline died in 1987. Consider David's claim to his wife's property.

University of London LLB Examination
(for External Students) Conflict of Laws June 1989 Q5

General Comment

A classic two-part solution is required here. The student must ensure that sufficient time and attention is devoted to each section, and that all appropriate points are covered.

Skeleton Solution

i) Reservation of title clause – predominance of the lex situs illustrated.

ii) Matrimonial property – capacity to enter a marriage settlement – domicile of parties governs – preservation of vested rights in movables – immovables governed by the matrimonial domicile.

Suggested Solution

i) This question poses in a straightforward way the effectiveness of a reservation of title clause in a contract of sale. Such clauses are commonplace in commerce and yet there is very little English authority on this point in the context of the conflict of laws. Morris (*The Conflict of Laws* (2000), 5th ed) has written extensively on this issue and his views should be considered with care as they may well guide the English courts should an appropriate case come before them.

We may begin with two fundamental points of principle. First, reservation of title (at any rate other than in the contractual context between buyer and seller) is a proprietary matter not a contractual matter. Thus, secondly, the lex situs will predominate as the appropriate law to use in determining whether the reservation of title is effective. What this means is that if title is acquired under the law of the lex situs, then that title will be effective but not otherwise. We may make this point concrete by looking at the leading American case *Goetschius v Brightman* (1927) 245 NY 186. What had happened here was that a car had been sold in California on terms that reserved title with the seller until it had been fully paid for. Before it was paid for, however, the car was taken to New York without the seller's consent where it was sold to a bona fide purchaser. Under the law of New York, the bona fide purchaser acquired good title because such reservation of title clauses were void against subsequent purchasers in good faith, unless the reservation of title was registered in a New York register of such matters (and the sale of the California car was not so registered).

Now, the New York court held that the New York rules about registration were intended to apply only to domestic (ie New York) transactions. Thus the reservation of title clause was not void as against the subsequent purchasers; the Californian seller's title was held good and the New York purchaser was limited to his contractual rights against the person who had sold the car to him.

Note that had the law of New York, the lex situs of the car at the time, held under the law of New York a valid title was obtained, then that would have overridden the California title. This is borne out by the Canadian case of *Century Credit Corp* v *Richard* (1962) 34 DLR (2d) 291. Here the slightly simplified facts were that M had sold a car to F under a contract that reserved title in M until the price was paid. All this took place in Quebec. The car was, however, taken by F to Ontario and sold to R. Under the law of Quebec a reservation of title clause was effective without registration, but under the law of Ontario it had to be registered. The Quebec title was not upheld by the Canadian courts; and this appears to be in conflict with *Goetschius* v *Brightman*. However, some reflection reveals that it is not: the relevant Ontario law provided in the circumstances of the case that F was to be treated as the agent of the owner; thus R acquired from the agent of the owner a good title. Thus under the lex situs a good title was obtained by R, and that title overrode the Quebec title.

(There are several other American cases discussed by Morris (*Marvin Safe Co* v *Norton* (1886) 48 NJIL 410; *Dougherty & Co* v *Krimke* (1929) 105 NJL 470) but they are all reconcilable with the propositions put forward above.)

How do these principles apply to our case? Since C acquired good title under the lex situs at the time, that title will be recognised in England in accordance with the above principles. It is irrelevant that this is not recognised under the private international law of Redland.

Thus A will not be able to recover the car from C. However, since B has plainly acted in breach of contract in taking the car to Blueland, A will have an action for the damages as a result. (If he can still find B!)

ii) The English choice of law rules applicable to matrimonial property are not yet particularly clear. However, where there is an antenuptial contract (or marriage settlement) the terms of that contract will be decisive provided that that contract is valid. The proper law of such a marriage contract is, if the parties have not expressly chosen another law, the law of the matrimonial domicile, ie the law of the husband's domicile: *Duke of Marlborough* v *Attorney-General* [1945] Ch 78. Thus, in our case the proper law of the marriage settlement is the law of Whiteland (under which the contract is valid).

However, that is not an end of the matter because before the contract can be valid the parties must have capacity to enter into such a contract. In principle, one expects that capacity to enter such a contract will be governed by the lex domicilii of the party whose capacity to contract is in question. Although Morris (*The Conflict of Laws*, pp421–422) suggests that the proper law of the contract should be used to test capacity in these circumstances, the general current of authority, although not devoid of doubt, suggests that the lex domicilii should be used: *Cooper* v *Cooper* (1888) 13 App Cas 88 and *Re Cooke's Trusts* (1887) 3 TLR 558. (The lex domicilii would not be used in the case of ordinary commercial contracts where the parties can hardly be expected to make enquiries as to each other's domiciles, but it is not unexpected in the context of marriage.)

And under the law of Blueland, Caroline's lex domicilii, 'a woman can neither settle her property on marriage, nor dispose of it during coverture [ie while she is under the legal protection of her husband, namely, while the marriage lasts], and on her death it is divided equally between the husband and her children.' Should this provision be held to relate to capacity (as well it might) then the marriage settlement will be void and Caroline will be able to escape its consequences.

Should this be held to be the case, will David be able to claim anything from Caroline? In the absence of a marriage settlement then the law of the matrimonial domicile continues to apply until such time as that domicile is changed; thereafter, at least as far as movables are concerned, the law of the new domicile applies (both to inter vivos transactions and in respect of succession) although vested rights acquired under the law of the earlier domicile are protected (Dicey and Morris, Rule 156). Immovables will probably still be governed by the matrimonial domicile; that seems implicit in *Chiwell* v *Carlyon* (1897) 14 SC (SA) 61 where a husband and wife domiciled in the Cape of Good Hope, where in the absence of an antenuptial agreement community of property applied, acquired a domicile in England. The English court held that the land which the husband had bought in Cornwall was still subject to the South African community of property. Thus in our case the law of Whiteland will govern the relationship between the parties as far as immovables are concerned.

Since Caroline and David are now domiciled in England the law of England will govern their proprietary relationship in regard to movables. Thus there is no restriction on Caroline disposing of property 'during coverture' as the law of Blueland requires, nor will David be entitled to a legitimo portio of one half on Caroline's death as the law of Blueland requires. Indeed, this latter restriction is plainly a matter of succession not matrimonial property and so in any event would never be governed by the law of the matrimonial domicile.

David may be able to claim some vested rights under the law of Whiteland that are protected by the proviso to Rule 156, but more details will be required to answer this. It may be said, however, that, assuming that the settlement was void, David never acquired any rights under the settlement; thus the only vested right that he would have would be in property acquired under the law of Whiteland while he was domiciled in Whiteland.

QUESTION TWO

a) Under the terms of a contract General Construction Limited, an American company, agreed to construct a factory in Palermo, in Sicily, for Goodfellas Limited, an English company. The contract contained a term incorporating the application of Italian law to the contract. The contractual price was £50 million and the contract stipulated that General Construction Limited was prohibited from assigning the benefits to that sum to any third party. This type of restriction is effective to prevent a valid assignment in English law but not under Italian law.

Despite this stipulation, General Construction Limited assigned its right to the sum to Wren Construction Limited, an English company, by an exchange of letters. In the exchange, both companies agreed that their agreement was to be governed by Italian law. Thus, the right to the £50 million was assigned to Wren Construction. The actual assignment itself is formally valid by English law but formally invalid under the laws of both the United States and Italy.

The construction project was duly completed and Wren Construction requested payment from Goodfellas Limited. Goodfellas Ltd claim that there is no valid obligation to pay any sums over to Wren Construction.

What is your view?

b) Grant is the owner of a brooch which he keeps in his house in Estonia. He enters into a contract, governed by Polish law, to sell the brooch to Lech. The brooch was duly delivered to Lech but Grant did not receive payment for the item. By Polish law, title to goods does not pass until the seller of the goods is adequately paid, but by Estonian law, property passes on delivery to the buyer.

Lech took the brooch to show to a jeweller in Latvia where it was stolen from his possession and sold to Eric in circumstances which, according to Latvian law, would give him a valid title, but no such title was conferred under Estonian, Polish or English law. Eric sent the brooch to an auction house in London for sale. However, both Grant and Lech claim that the brooch belongs to them.

Advise Eric.

Question prepared by the Editor

General Comment

In order to answer this question effectively, the student must have a sound understanding of the rules governing tangible/intangible movables (ie appropriate application of the Rome Convention 1980).

Skeleton Solution

a) Assignment of intangible movables – assignability – formal validity of assignment – Rome Convention 1980, arts 9 and 12.

b) Transfer of tangible movables – lex situs rule – divestiture of existing title by transaction having that effect under lex situs.

Suggested Solution

a) The issue of Goodfellas Limited's liability to Wren Construction depends on whether Goodfellas Limited's debt to General Construction Limited was assignable and whether it has been validly assigned to Wren Construction. By the Rome Convention 1980, art 12(2), in force in English law from 1 April 1991 under the Contracts (Applicable Law) Act 1990, 'The law governing the right to which the assignment relates shall determine its assignability.' The contract between General Construction Limited and Goodfellas Limited prohibited assignment, however this contract was governed by Italian law by express choice of the parties, thus Italian law is the applicable law of this contract: Rome Convention, art 3(1). By Italian law the contractual prohibition is not effective to prevent assignment, thus the right to the contract sum was assignable.

Given that it is assignable, has it actually been assigned to Wren Construction by General Construction Limited? By the Rome Convention, art 12(1), the mutual obligations of assignor (General Construction Limited) and assignee (Wren Construction) are governed by the law which under the Convention applies to the contract between assignor and assignee. That contract is the one made by exchange of letters between General Construction Limited and Wren Construction; the only problem which arises concerning it is its formal validity. Under the Convention, art 9(2), a contract concluded between persons who are in different countries (General Construction Limited in the United States and Wren Construction in England) 'is formally valid if it satisfies the formal requirements of the law which governs it under this Convention or of the law of one of those countries'.

The contract of assignment between General Construction Limited and Wren Construction is formally invalid by the law of Italy, which is the law governing it under the Convention (art 3(1)), and by the law of the United States, where General Construction Limited is; however this matters not, since it is formally valid by the law of England, where Wren Construction is at the time of making the contract, and thus is formally valid by art 9(2).

So, the contract between General Construction Limited and Wren Construction being formally valid (there is nothing to suggest that it is not materially valid or that there is any problem over capacity), is effective as between General Construction

Limited and Wren Construction to assign the contract debt, by art 12(1); and, since Italian law permits this assignment and by art 12(2) Italian law as the law applicable to the contract debt governs the conditions under which the assignment can be invoked against the debtor, it follows that Goodfellas Limited is obliged to pay the contract price to Wren Construction.

Note that these conclusions have been reached on the basis of the Convention as this now has statutory force: Contracts (Applicable Law) Act 1990, s2(1). However a similar result would probably have been arrived at on the basis of the common law in force before the Act: cf *Campbell Connelly & Co Ltd* v *Noble* [1963] 1 WLR 252 on assignability, and the difficult case of *Republica de Guatemala* v *Nunez* [1927] 1 KB 669 on assignments generally.

b) The problem here relates to a tangible movable, the brooch. The Rome Convention is not applicable, as art 12 is concerned solely with assignments of 'rights', ie intangibles.

At the beginning of the story the brooch is in Estonia. Under the Polish law applicable to the contract between Grant and Lech, title would not have passed until payment, but this is immaterial, as the passage of title is governed by the lex situs, Estonian law (*Cammell* v *Sewell* (1860) 5 H & N 728), and thus title passed to Lech on delivery even though he had not paid. Accordingly, when Lech took the brooch over the frontier into Latvia it was Lech's property.

I take it that the thief could not acquire good title by stealing the brooch from Lech and no civilised law would make theft a ground of title in the thief, and if Latvian law were so to provide it may be doubted whether English law would follow its normal approach of giving effect to the lex situs, or would rather treat such a provision as contrary to public policy: cf *Winkworth* v *Christie Manson and Woods Ltd* [1980] 2 WLR 937.

However, the brooch now comes into the possession of Eric in circumstances which give Eric title by the lex situs, Latvian law. It is immaterial that Polish, Estonian and English law would not recognise the transfer of title under these circumstances. The conclusion that Eric has obtained good title – even though his vendor, the thief, had no title to give – is irresistible, in principle and on the authorities, if Eric was in good faith, see *Winkworth* v *Christie*. If Eric was not in good faith: then Slade J's judgment in *Winkworth* admits an exception, apparently in favour of the relevant provisions of English law, so that Lech would remain the owner, but this passage in the *Winkworth* judgment is obiter and has been powerfully criticised.

It is submitted that it is for Latvian law as the lex situs of the movable to determine whether good faith is relevant and to define it, subject to any overriding considerations of English public policy. The conclusion is that Eric has good title as he had title in Latvia, and no transaction has occurred either in Latvia or, subsequent to the brooch's removal to England, in England, to defeat his title.

QUESTION THREE

When on a hiking holiday in Athenia two years ago, Jim, an English domiciliary from London, uncovered an ancient vase, and also bought a painting in the local market. He knew the painting looked like an El Greco, but assumed it was a reproduction. In fact it was a genuine El Greco, which had been stolen from a church in Athenia. On his way back to England, whilst in Berlinnia, he sold the vase to Enrico, a collector of antiquities, whom he met in Berlinnia. Enrico paid half the agreed sum in cash and agreed to transfer royalties in a book of his in lieu of the remainder of the price. By the law of Berlinnia a transfer of royalties must be witnessed by a notary and this was not done. By the law of Pomplonia (Enrico's domicile and his national law) it is illegal to transfer any future income.

Jim now seeks advice on the following matters.

i) Can he recover the sum owing to him from Enrico? He wishes to sue Enrico in England where he has substantial assets, though he fears these may soon be removed to Pomplonia.

ii) Does he own and can he retain the El Greco painting? The church in Athenia is threatening to sue him in the English courts to recover it.

University of London LLB Examination
(for External Students) Conflict of Laws June 1994 Q8

General Comment

While students often fight shy of questions to do with property, this is a relatively straightforward problem question. Care must, however, be taken in applying the awkward principles to the facts.

Skeleton Solution

The appropriate principles with reference to the law of movable property – the appropriate principles with reference to intangible property and its assignment – the action brought against Enrico – the action brought by the church.

Suggested Solution

Conflict of laws recognises the continental distinction between movable and immovable property. This question relates to movable property. The choice of law rule with reference to movable property was stated by Diplock LJ in *Hardwick Game Farm* v *Suffolk Agricultural Poultry Producers' Association Ltd* [1969] 2 AC 31 where it was held that 'The proper law governing the transfer of corporeal movable property is the lex situs'. This rule applies even in circumstances where the situs of the movable property changes: *Cammell* v *Sewell* (1858) 3 H & N 617. In that case a cargo of timber was purchased by a person domiciled in England in Russia. The timber was being shipped to England when it was wrecked off the coast of Norway. Such of the cargo as remained after the wreck was sold by the ship's master in Norway. Norwegian law gave the new owner of the timber good title to the timber – even though the purchaser had not consented to the sale. The timber was then transported to England and sold to another party. The court found that good title passed because the lex situs, Norway, enabled good title to be conveyed when the ship's master sold the timber in Norway.

The principle in *Cammell* v *Sewell* applies even in circumstances where the new situs of the property follows a theft of the property from its original location. This rule was set out in *Winkworth* v *Christie Manson and Woods Ltd* [1980] 2 WLR 937. In that case works of art were stolen from the plaintiff's house in England and taken to Italy. The artworks were sold in Italy to a person who sold them back to a third party in England. The original owner sought to apply to the court for a declaration as to ownership of the property. Slade J decided on the basis that, on the grounds of commercial convenience, the rule established by the court must be to preserve certainty in commercial transactions. Accordingly, the rule in *Cammell* v *Sewell* was affirmed.

The question whether a debt can be assigned is decided by the proper law of the debt: *Campbell Connolly & Co Ltd* v *Noble* [1963] 1 WLR 252. The intrinsic validity of any assignment of a debt is governed by the proper law of the assignment (rather than the debt): *Republica de Guatemala* v *Nunez* [1927] 1 KB 669. There is, however, a distinction between formal validity in a transfer (which is governed by the law of the place where the assignment is made: per Lawrence and Scrutton LJJ in *Republica Guatemala*); capacity to transfer (which is governed by the lex domicilii, per Lawrence LJ); and essential validity (the law of the place of the action).

i) The question with the assignment of the royalties from Enrico is (a) whether the assignment is formally valid, and (b) whether Enrico has capacity to transfer the rights.

    a) Under the law of Berlinnia, the assignment must be witnessed by a notary, which was not done. Therefore the transfer of the rights is formally invalid.

    b) Enrico does not have capacity to transfer according to the law of his domicile and therefore the transfer is doubly invalid.

    The result is that Jim will not be able to enforce his rights to the royalties before an English court. Therefore, he would need to bring an action in contract against Enrico for failure to provide consideration as necessary under the contract.

    With reference to the removal of assets from the jurisdiction, Jim would be required to seek a freezing injunction, which is likely to be granted in circumstances where he is waiting for the matter to come before the English courts. An English court will accept jurisdiction in the circumstances where the matter concerns a contract and assets are required in England to meet any obligations.

ii) The rule in *Winkworth* establishes that theft of an artwork will not prevent an innocent purchaser from retaining good title. As in the case of *Winkworth*, Jim purchases the painting as an innocent purchaser. It is the lex situs which is applied to decide the choice of law issue. Therefore, Athenian law governed the purchase of the painting and it is English law which is applied to decide Jim's ability to act with the painting. Therefore, the church in Athenia must sue under English law if the matter comes to an English court. Following the approach of Scarman J in *Winkworth*, to preserve freedom of commercial activity, the church will not be able to obtain title to the painting again.

QUESTION FOUR

Bill bought a car from Ann in Berglandia under conditional sale agreement. This provided that ownership of the car remained vested in Ann until all instalments of the price had been paid. Bill drove the car to Montania, before he had paid all the instalments, and sold it there to Karl, who took it in good faith, knowing nothing of Ann's rights.

Karl has been sent by his employers to work in their London office and brought the car to England. Under the law of Berglandia, no title can pass by a transfer of the car unless the terms of the conditional sale agreement regarding payment of the price have been complied with.

Ann is now seeking the return of the car. Advise Karl on each of the following alternative assumptions:

i)   By the law of Montania, a sale by the person in possession of goods will pass a good title to a buyer in good faith without notice of the owner's rights.

ii) The law of Montania requires conditional sales of cars to be registered and makes unregistered agreements void against a bona fide purchaser without notice. Ann has not registered the agreement with Bill.

University of London LLB Examination
(for External Students) Conflict of Laws June 1996 Q6

General Comment

A fairly standard two-part question, which deals with tangible, movable property and the problems faced by a bona fide purchaser with regard to title.

Skeleton Solution

The general rule, governing the transfer of corporeal movable property – reservation of title clauses – facts and analysis of *Goetschius* v *Brightman* and *Century Credit Corporation* v *Richard*: whether valid transfer of title is limited to domestic transactions.

Suggested Solution

Before examining the alternative assumptions, certain general propositions need explanation and clarification. In *Cammell* v *Sewell* (1860) 5 H & N 728, Pollock CB stated:

'if personal property is disposed of in a manner binding according to the law of the country where it is, that disposition is binding everywhere'. More recently in *Hardwick Game Farm* v *Suffolk Agricultural Poultry Producers' Association* [1969] 2 AC 31 Diplock LJ stated that: 'The proper law governing the transfer of corporeal movable property is the lex situs'.

The issue here is whether the general principles noted above apply and there has been a valid transfer of title under the lex situs at the time of the transfer; and if so, whether such a transfer will be recognised in English law: Cammell v Sewell.

The long-established principles were followed in *Winkworth* v *Christie Manson and Woods Ltd* [1980] 2 WLR 937 where Slade J said:

> 'Security of title is as important to an innocent purchaser as it is to an innocent owner whose goods have been stolen from him. Commercial convenience may be said imperatively to demand that proprietary rights to movables shall generally be determined by the lex situs under the rules of private international law. Were the position otherwise, it would not suffice for the protection of a purchaser of any valuable movables to ascertain that he was acquiring title to them under the law of the country where the goods were situated at the time of the purchase; he would have to try to effect further investigations as to the past title, with a view to ensuring, so far as possible, that there was no person who might successfully claim a title to the movables by reference to some other system of law.'

Accordingly, the authorities are consistent and they expound and reinforce the rule that if property is validly transferred according to its lex situs at the time of its transfer, then the transaction will be recognised as a valid transfer by English law.

The case involving Karl relates to a reservation of title clause and whether Ann may reclaim the car, relying on the relevant law of Montania. That the question poses alternative assumptions suggests that there could be different consequences for Karl. Addressing the assumptions in sequence, it is noted that:

i) At present, the lex situs of the car is London, England. In order for English law to recognise Karl's title, there must have been a valid transfer from Bill to Karl according to the lex situs, which was Montania. According to Montanian law, Karl has acquired a good title and thus English law will recognise his title to the car: Cammell v Sewell.

ii) Is a little less straightforward. Lack of English authority on the issues in question necessitates analysis of two cases of persuasive authority in order to establish whether Karl may successfully fend off Ann's claim. First, the American (New York) case of *Goetschius* v *Brightman* (1927) 245 NY 186. Here a car was sold in California on terms that reserved title until it had been fully paid for. Until then it was not to be removed from California. Before it was paid for, it was taken to New York without the owner's consent and there it was sold to a bona fide purchaser. By the law of New York, the bona fide purchaser acquired good title because such reservation of title clauses were void against subsequent purchasers in good faith, unless the contract was registered in a New York register. By contrast, the law of California provided that the original seller's title was good against even innocent, subsequent purchasers. It was held that since the New York statute which required registration was limited to domestic transactions, ie, New York transactions, the New York law did not prevent the recognition of the reservation of title in a Californian sale. Thus, the Californian seller's title prevailed.

Accordingly, if the principle in Goetschius v Brightman applies in Montania, that is, the law of Montania applies only to domestic transactions, then the fact that the agreement was unregistered would not render Ann's title void.

The second case of persuasive authority, is the Canadian (Ontario) case of *Century Credit Corporation* v *Richard* (1962) 34 DLR (2d) 291. Here, A sold a car to B in Quebec, under a conditional sales agreement, which provided that the car should remain the property of A until the price was fully paid. The car was then taken by B to Ontario without the knowledge or consent of A and sold it to C (a resident of Ontario), who had no knowledge of A's interest in the car. The law of Ontario required conditional sales agreements to be registered, the law of Quebec did not. It was held by the Ontario Court of Appeal that C's title prevailed, basing the decision on a statute which treated B as the agent of A, because he was in possession of the car with the consent of the seller, and thus C acquired good title under the Ontario Sale of Goods Act. Accordingly, Karl would hope that the principle enshrined in this case – that of overriding a prior title without giving extraterritorial effect to the statute – will prevail under Montanian law, and that the title of the car will validly be transferred to him.

In conclusion, Karl will succeed in (i) as the general rule is clear that where the lex situs regards the transfer as valid, the English courts will do likewise. Ann will therefore fail in her claim for the return of her car. In (ii), however, the outcome will be dependent on the philosophy adopted under Montanian law: if transactions involving registration are confined to domestic transactions, so acknowledging the title of the initial owner, he will not acquire good title; conversely, if Montanian law overrides prior titles – or simply ignores the validity of transactions in the previous forum – then he will succeed in acquiring good title to the car.

Chapter 9

Family Law

9.1   **Introduction**

9.2   **Key points**

9.3   **Key cases and statutes**

9.4   **Questions and suggested solutions**

9.1 Introduction

The choice of law issues that arise in the context of family law are potentially quite complex in nature. For instance, persons domiciled in different countries can marry in a third and divorce in a fourth. In addition, issues concerning the recognition of foreign divorce decrees and the like, may arise. This position is sometimes made more 'interesting' as a result of public policy considerations. Generally English law is, on public policy grounds, resistant to concepts such as polygamous marriages or extra-judicial divorce, quite apart from issues such as child marriages or marriages that are considered in English law to be incestuous.

This area has also been affected by the growing role of statutes. In response both to international conventions agreeing the rules between a number of states and other considerations, much of the common law has been replaced with statute in this area.

Note finally that, although a range of family law issues are presented here, the subject is so wide ranging that it is quite possible for a problem to be set that is not touched upon here. It is suggested that there is no substitute for a good textbook, casebook and a thorough study of both. However, the most important issues are, it is believed, set out in this chapter.

9.2 Key points

The conflict rules for family law – preliminary considerations

Family law in this context refers to the relationships between husband and wife, and between parents and their children. There can be little doubt that the conflict rules regulating family law are complicated. This may be attributed to the fact that the conflict rules have not only been developed over a considerable period but many of the rules have been developed by the courts in such a way that they are frequently subject to the criticism that insufficient attention has been paid to consistency in terms of jurisprudential development.

There are two principal reasons why the law in this area is not quite as clear and satisfactory as it should be:

a) There is no universally accepted concept of marriage. Even at the most basic level, while monogamy is at the heart of the concept in many legal systems, other legal systems recognise that marriages can be polygamous or polyandrous. In a similar vein, in some legal systems death is the only event which will terminate marriage, whereas other systems approve of other methods of termination such as divorce.

b) The nature of marriage and family relationships are core concepts at the heart of each society. Thus, many of the rules to regulate family relationships within each legal system are the creatures of public policy.

The validity of marriage

Formal validity

The original rule prescribing the law regulating the formal aspects of marriage was that the formalities must conform with the lex loci celebrationis – the law of the place of the celebration of the marriage: see *Scrimshire* v *Schrimshire* (1792) 2 Hagg Con 395. This rule was, however, open to abuse. The formalities for marriage in England could be circumvented by couples prevented by law from marrying in England travelling abroad to countries with less restrictive rules concerning marriage formalities.

For example, in *Brook* v *Brook* (1861) 9 HLC 193, an Englishman wished to marry his deceased wife's sister. At the time, such a marriage was prohibited in England but not in Denmark. So the couple went to Denmark to evade the restrictions on prohibited relationships.

In fact, this case marked the eclipse of the old liberal rule permitting the formal validity of a marriage to be regulated by the lex loci celebrationis. Instead, the House of Lords ruled that virtually all legal matters of substance relating to marriage were to be regulated by the lex domicilii of the parties.

Following from this case, the present rule is now that restrictions and formalities of any true significance are to be regulated by the lex domicilii of the parties whereas matters of pure form, such as the ceremony and periods of notice, are left to the lex loci celebrationis: see *Berthiaume* v *Dastous* [1930] AC 79.

Exceptions to the regulation of formalities by the lex loci celebrationis include the following:

a) Consular marriages – the Foreign Marriage Act 1892 provides that where one of the parties intending marriage is a British subject, their marriage may be solemnised outside the United Kingdom by a British ambassador, High Commissioner and consuls if they have been duly authorised by warrant.

The Act stipulates the formalities which must be observed which may differ from those prevailing in the place the marriage is solemnised.

b) Marriages between service personnel serving abroad – the 1892 Act also provides that a marriage celebrated in foreign territory by a chaplain in the forces with at least one of the parties being in the forces is valid as if celebrated in the United Kingdom. It is not an essential prerequisite that either of the parties must be a British national.

c) Marriages celebrated in conditions in which compliance with local formalities is impossible – in these circumstances, the courts have been prepared to accept that it is sufficient if the marriage complies with the formal requirement of the common law which essentially is that the parties should agree in each other's presence to take each other as man and wife: see *Isaac Penhas* v *Tan Soo Eng* [1953] AC 304.

Essential validity

Matters of essential validity must be distinguished from those of purely formal validity. Some matters are obviously of formal validity (eg the number of witnesses required) and others obviously matters of essential validity (eg the relationship of the parties in terms of prohibited degrees). At other times this distinction is not so obvious.

For example, in *Ogden* v *Ogden* [1908] P 46, a domiciled Frenchman married a domiciled Englishwoman in England without the consent of his surviving parent which was a requirement of the French Civil Code. If the consent was a matter of formal validity, it was irrelevant but if it related to essential validity the marriage would be void or at least voidable. In the final event, the court found the consent to be a formal matter and the marriage was held valid. See also *Apt* v *Apt* [1948] P 83.

Once a requirement has been classified as a matter of essential validity, the applicable law must be selected to regulate these matters. It should be noted that there is still some uncertainty as to the rule which applies so as to determine the applicable law to be used to determine whether a marriage is valid in essential respects. To date it appears that the 'dual domicile' test and the 'intended matrimonial home' test are the two leading contenders and support for these will vary depending upon the textbook that you choose to read.

a) Dual domicile test

The dual domicile test can be illustrated by reference to a previous case. In *Sottomayor* v *De Barros (No 1)* (1877) 3 PD 1 (CA) two cousins with strong Portuguese connections married in England and lived there together for six years.

Under Portuguese law, a marriage between cousins was not valid unless Papal consent had been granted which was not the case. The question was whether the marriage was valid.

The court found that the essential validity of the marriage depended on the lex domicilii of both parties. In light of the facts, the court found the domicile of both parties to be Portugal, although their intended matrimonial home was presumably England. Hence the marriage was void because it was prohibited by the lex domicilii of both parties: see also *Shaw v Gould* (1868) LR 3 HL 55.

A slight modification to the dual domicile test was instituted in *Sottomayor v De Barros (No 2)* (1879) 5 PD 94. Although the dual domicile rule was applied at first instance, at a second hearing the court adopted a more flexible approach. In upholding the validity of the marriage, Sir James Hannan P held that where a marriage is celebrated in England between persons, one of whom is domiciled in England, capacity is tested by English law.

However, this principle has not been adopted in any subsequent cases in which it has a bearing.

Other cases, which are taken as supporting the dual domicile approach include: *Padolecchia v Padolecchia* [1968] P 314; *R v Brentwood Superintendent Registrar of Marriages, ex parte Arias* [1968] 2 QB 956; *Szechter v Szechter* [1970] 3 All ER 905.

b) Intended matrimonial home test

It may be suggested that in recent times, the courts have been gradually developing a doctrine akin to a proper law of the marriage but which is best described as the intended matrimonial home test.

This test was alluded to in both *Perrini v Perrini* [1979] Fam 84 and *Lawrence v Lawrence* [1985] Fam 106. The intended matrimonial test was also adopted in *Radwan v Radwan (No 2)* [1973] Fam 35, but the test was expressly limited to questions of capacity to contract a polygamous marriage.

A number of arguments have been forwarded as to why the dual domicile test should be favoured over the intended matrimonial home approach:

a) Practically, the intended matrimonial test cannot work. The parties need to know in advance which law governs their capacity to marry. Equally, it may be argued that the capacity to enter a marriage depends on the present circumstances of the parties and not the future.

b) The use of the intended matrimonial home test has the potential to permit the evasion of other laws which should properly apply. There is an argument that it should be the law of the person's domicile (the person's society/community) that should decides if the person has the capacity to marry.

c) Finally, there is the issue of certainty. Given the increasingly mobile nature of society, then can the intended matrimonial home be determined in advance and, even if it can, then for how long?

By contrast, the major objection to the dual domicile test is that it makes the process of determining the validity of a marriage more complex and time consuming to determine. In other words, the court must not only consider the lex loci celebrationis (for the formalities of the marriage), but also the domicile of the individuals in order to determine whether they have the capacity to enter into the marriage – potentially three legal systems.

At present, the scales continue to tip in favour of the dual domicile test, although this may be an area which will develop in favour of a more flexible principle.

One final point should be made in relation to this debate. If one considers the cases of *Brook* v *Brook* (1859) 1 Sw & Tr 416, *Re Paine* [1940] Ch 46 and *Pugh* v *Pugh* [1951] P 482, then the results would have been the same whichever test the courts had applied.

The treatment of polygamy by the English courts

Traditionally, the English courts have approached the concept of polygamy in a somewhat guarded and less than enthusiastic fashion with the general approach being to deny such marriages any legal effect even if the marriage is both formally and essentially valid: see *Hyde* v *Hyde* (1866) LR 1 P & D 130.

However, in recent times, the courts have adopted a more flexible approach to the issue because of the hardships which might be caused if polygamous marriages were denied recognition. The following examples demonstrate the more flexible approach of the courts:

a) Children of a valid polygamous marriage are legitimate: see *Bamgbose* v *Daniel* [1955] AC 107.

b) A validly polygamous marriage prevents a second marriage: see *R* v *Sagoo* [1975] QB 885.

Modification of this strict approach has also come by way of statute. Thus, s47(1) of the Matrimonial Causes Act 1973 provides that a court is not precluded from granting matrimonial relief or making a declaration concerning the validity of a marriage by reason only that the marriage was entered into under a law that permits polygamy. Matrimonial relief includes making divorce, nullity decrees and maintenance orders.

Part II of the Private International Law (Miscellaneous Provisions) Act 1995 also alleviates the strictness of the approach adopted by English courts to the issue of the validity of polygamous marriages. The relevant sections of the Act are designed to ensure that English domiciliaries, irrespective of sex, are only prevented from entering into marriages abroad which are, in reality, actually polygamous. Section 5(1) of the Act provides that a marriage contracted abroad:

> '... between parties neither of whom is already married is not void under the law of England and Wales on the ground that it is entered into under a law which permits polygamy and that either party is domiciled in England and Wales.'

This means that English domiciliaries who are not already married can marry abroad under legal systems that allow polygamy. Such marriages will be valid but they will be monogamous and will always remain so under English law.

Although this provision is intended to be retrospective (s6(1)), it does not apply to persons who have remarried in the belief that their first marriage was void, and does not affect rights under a will or settlement or entitlement to benefits, allowances or pensions: s6(6).

Divorce and recognition of foreign divorce decrees

The common law rules concerning divorce have been largely superseded by a statutory system of rules. Previously, at common law, the court of the matrimonial domicile (which was deemed to be the domicile of the husband) and only the court of the matrimonial domicile had jurisdiction to grant a divorce. It followed from this that only a divorce decree granted by the court of a matrimonial domicile would be recognised in England: *Le Mesurier* v *Le Mesurier* [1895] AC 517.

This rule had unfair implications. First, if a husband deserted his wife and settled in another country and acquired a domicile there, his wife would have to sue for divorce in the courts of the foreign country which would obviously be very inconvenient. Second, a deserted wife may be unable to locate her husband's whereabouts and would therefore be prevented from suing for divorce. (The rule was modified in *Armitage* v *Attorney-General* [1906] P 135, which provided that if the divorce decree of a non-domicilary court was recognised by the domiciliary court, then it would be recognised in England.)

Part II of the Family Law Act 1986 now regulates the issue of divorce in English law where there is a conflict of laws problem. It deals with the following matters.

Divorces and annulments granted within the British Isles

Divorces granted by courts of civil jurisdiction in the British Isles (England, Wales, Scotland and Northern Ireland) are entitled to special recognition by the other courts in the United Kingdom. Section 44(2) of the Family Law Act 1986 provides that 'the validity of any divorce, annulment or judicial separation granted by a court of civil jurisdiction in any part of the British Isles shall be recognised throughout the United Kingdom.' In addition, s44(1) makes it clear that only judicial divorces can be obtained in the British Isles.

Recognition of foreign divorces

Section 46(1) of the 1986 Act deals with recognition of divorces obtained 'by means of proceedings', while s46(2) regulates the recognition of divorces obtained 'otherwise than by means of proceedings'. This distinction revolves around having some form of formal legal process for divorce as against a non-judicial informal procedure. An example of proceeding by means of an informal non-judicial process is the 'bare talaq' form of divorce allowed in Islamic countries whereby a man can divorce his wife simply by addressing the talaq statement to her three times: see *Chaudhary* v *Chaudhary* [1985] Fam 19.

On the other hand, other Islamic countries such as Pakistan require compliance with a more formal procedure as laid down in the Muslim Family Law Ordinance 1961: see *Quazi v Quazi* [1980] AC 744. Such a procedure was held to constitute 'proceedings' under the old legislation. In the case of divorces obtained by means of proceedings, s46(l) provides:

> 'The validity of an overseas divorce, annulment or legal separation obtained by means of proceedings shall be recognised if –
> (a) the divorce, annulment or legal separation is effective under the law of the country in which it was obtained; and
> (b) at the relevant date either party to the marriage –
> (i) was habitually resident in the country in which the divorce, annulment or legal separation was obtained; or
> (ii) was domiciled in that country; or
> (iii) was a national of that country.'

Satisfaction of the requirements of domicile is determined in accordance with the law of the country from where the divorce decree was obtained. Hence, so-called 'quickie divorces' may be recognised in English law if the law of the country issuing the divorce decree has lax rules regarding the period of residence required to establish domicile.

The next section of the Act regulates divorces obtained by means other than proceedings. By s46(2):

> 'The validity of an overseas divorce, annulment or legal separation obtained otherwise than by means of proceedings shall be recognised if –
> (a) the divorce, annulment or legal separation is effective under the law of the country in which it was obtained;
> (b) at the relevant date –
> (i) each party to the marriage was domiciled in that country; or
> (ii) either party was domiciled in that country and the other party was domiciled in a country under whose law the divorce, annulment or legal separation is recognised as valid; and
> (c) neither party to the marriage was habitually resident in the United Kingdom throughout the period of one year immediately preceding that date.'

Consequently, the conditions that must be satisfied for a 'bare talaq' to be recognised are more onerous than those set down in s46(1). It should also be noted that 'the relevant date' means something different in s46(2) to that of s46(1). Refer to s46(3) for further details.

Proof of facts relevant to recognition of divorces obtained by means of proceedings

Section 48 of the Family Act 1986 provides that any finding of fact on the basis of which jurisdiction was assumed in the proceedings shall be 'conclusive evidence of the facts found' provided both parties took part in the proceedings.

In the event that both parties did not participate, the finding is simply 'sufficient proof of the facts unless the contrary is shown'.

Refusal of recognition

Divorces which would otherwise be recognised under the 1986 Act may be refused recognition in certain situations. Section 52 of the Act specifies the occasions on which divorces obtained before the commencement of the Act should be denied recognition.

Section 51, on the other hand, provides additional grounds for refusing recognition to divorces obtained after the statute entered force. These include the following:

a) Recognition of a divorce may be refused if the divorce was granted or obtained at a time when it was irreconcilable with a decision determining the question of the substance or validity of the marriage of the parties previously given by a United Kingdom court or by a decision of a court elsewhere and recognised in that part of the United Kingdom.

b) A divorce need not be recognised if the divorce or separation was granted or obtained at a time when, according to the law of that part of the United Kingdom, there is no subsisting marriage between the parties.

c) A divorce obtained by proceedings may be refused recognition if either party was not given reasonable notice of the proceedings and was denied a reasonable opportunity to participate in them.

d) Where a divorce is not obtained by proceedings, recognition may be refused unless there is an official document certifying that the divorce is effective under the law of the place where it was obtained.

e) Recognition of an overseas divorce may be refused where such recognition would be 'manifestly contrary to public policy'.

Non-recognition of divorce in other jurisdictions as a bar to remarriage

As a general principle, if a foreign divorce is not recognised within a particular country, the parties are considered to be still married and are therefore effectively prevented from remarrying under the law of that country: see *Lawrence* v *Lawrence* [1985] Fam 106.

This situation is now regulated by s50 of the 1986 Act which states that the fact that a divorce or annulment would not be recognised in another country shall not necessarily preclude either party to the marriage from remarrying in the United Kingdom or cause the remarriage of either party to be treated as invalid.

Jurisdiction of the English courts to grant divorce and choice of law in divorce cases

In the above, we have been principally concerned with the recognition of foreign divorce decrees before the English court. It is now time to turn to the subject of the grounds on which the English courts will exercise jurisdiction to grant divorce.

Under s5(2) of the Domicile and Matrimonial Proceedings Act 1973, if either spouse is domiciled in England at the time of commencing divorce proceedings, or if either party had been habitually resident in England for a period of a year before the commencement of proceedings, the English courts will have jurisdiction. Similar rules govern the jurisdiction of the English courts to grant nullity decrees: s5(3).

As regards the issue of choice of law in English divorce proceedings, there is only one single rule. The lex fori applies as the applicable law in divorce cases and therefore, in England, divorce proceedings are exclusively regulated by English law.

The recognition and enforcement of foreign maintenance orders

Maintenance orders issued in other European Community states are enforceable in England by virtue of the Civil Jurisdiction and Judgments Act 1982. Special provisions have also been put in place under the Maintenance Orders (Facilities for Enforcement) Act 1920 and the Maintenance Orders (Reciprocal Enforcement) Act 1972. The first of these deals with the enforcement of orders made by those Commonwealth countries to which the Act 1982 extends by Order in Council and the second applies to the enforcement of the orders of other countries for which arrangements for reciprocal enforcement have been made.

Legitimacy, legitimation and adoption

There are no less than three conflicting theories as to which law is to be used to determine whether a particular person is legitimate or not:

a) A child is legitimate if and only if he or she is born or conceived in a marriage recognised as valid in accordance with the English choice of law rules: *Shaw* v *Gould* (1868) LR 3 HL 55.

b) A child is legitimate if it is legitimate under its domicile of origin.

c) The matter is not a question for the conflict of laws to resolve. It is simply a question of the interpretation of words such as 'child' or 'issue' appearing in documents such as wills.

Originally, the decision of the House of Lords in *Shaw* v *Gould* appeared to have shaped the law in this area. However, doubts have been raised in a number of cases as to the usefulness of this theory: see *Re Bischoffsheim* [1948] Ch 79.

In fact, in the most recent case, *Motala and Others* v *Attorney-General and Others* [1990] 2 FLR 261, the decision was based in a determination of the law of the domicile of the children. On the facts of this case, the domicile of origin of the children was found to be India and since according to Indian law they were legitimate, then the children were legitimate under English law. However, in this case both parents had the same domicile. If the domiciles of the parents are different, the domicile of origin of their child varies according to whether it is legitimate or illegitimate. Hence, this formulation can never be used when the parents are deemed to have different domiciles.

The position is no clearer as regards legitimation. The common law rule was that if a child's father was domiciled at the time of birth and at the time of the subsequent marriage with the child's mother in a country whose law recognised legitimation, then the legitimation would be recognised in English law: *Re Goodman's Trusts* (1881) 17 Ch D 266.

The Legitimacy Act 1976 now provides in s3 for the recognition of foreign legitimations in English law provided at the time of the subsequent marriage the father was domiciled in a country by whose law the child is legitimated by subsequent marriage.

Statutory provisions have been made for the recognition of foreign adoption orders under s4(3) of the Adoption Act 1968. The procedure requires the Secretary of State to specify the countries whose adoption orders will be recognised.

Custody and guardianship

The rule governing the jurisdiction of the English courts over this matter are contained in Part I of the Family Law Act 1986.

Recognition and enforcement of foreign orders relating to custody and guardianship are governed by different principles. The overriding principle in the recognition of foreign orders is the need to protect the best interests of the child. So, a custody order will not be enforced if it appears contrary to the court's view of the best interests of the child: see *McKee* v *McKee* [1951] AC 352.

One statute which should also be mentioned at this stage is the Child Abduction and Custody Act 1985 which implements the Hague Convention on the Civil Aspects of International Child Abduction 1980. This Act sets up machinery designed to facilitate the return of abducted children: see *Re G (A Minor)* [1990] 2 FLR 325.

The effect of marriage on property

It will come as no surprise that in this field, in common with other areas of family law, the rules applicable to matrimonial property are not yet particularly clear. With hesitation, the following rules may be identified.

Where there is an antenuptial contract (or marriage settlement) the terms of the contract will be decisive provided that the contract is valid. The proper law of such a marriage contract is, in the absence of an express choice, the law of the matrimonial domicile, ie the law of the husband's domicile at marriage: see *Duke of Marlborough* v *Attorney-General* [1945] Ch 78.

In the absence of a marriage settlement, the law of the matrimonial domicile continues to apply until such time as that domicile is changed. In the event of change, as far as movables are concerned, the law of the new domicile applies although vested rights acquired under the law of the earlier domicile are protected. Immovable property will probably continue to be governed by the law of the matrimonial domicile if this is the lex situs: see *Chiwell* v *Carlyon* (1897) 14 SC (SA) 61.

9.3 Key cases and statutes

- *A and Others, Re* [1996] 1 All ER 24
  Article 4 Hague Convention – Convention applies to any child who was habitually resident in a contracting state immediately before the breach of custody rights – residence in a military base overseas could not be a continuation of residence in the country which the father served

- *Apt v Apt* [1948] P 83
  Validity of proxy marriage – matter of formal validity

- *Baindail v Baindail* [1946] 1 All ER 342
  Polygamous marriage will be recognised in England unless there is strong reason to the contrary

- *Berthiaume v Dastous* [1930] AC 79
  Formalities of marriage are governed in general by the lex loci celebrationis

- *Brook v Brook* (1861) 9 HL Cas 193
  Capacity to marry is governed in general by the lex domicilii of each party immediately before the marriage

- *C (Abduction: Consent), Re* [1996] 1 FLR 414
  Article 13 Hague Convention – onus of proof with respect to consent is on the person opposing the return of the children – consent in writing not required – neither is it necessary for it to be in a positive form

- *Hyde v Hyde* (1866) LR 1 P&D 130
  Definition of marriage – voluntary union for life

- *Kochanski v Kochanska* [1958] P 147
  Marriage – where the parties do not subject themselves to the law of the lex loci celebrationis

- *Lawrence v Lawrence* [1985] 3 WLR 125
  Validity of foreign divorce – capacity to remarry

- *Ogden v Ogden* [1908] P 46
  Characterisation as formal or essential validity

- *Penhas (Isaac) v Tan Soo Eng* [1953] AC 304
  Marriage and the common law

- *Pugh v Pugh* [1951] P 482
  Validity of marriage – either party domiciled in England and one party is under the age of 16

- *R v Immigration Appeal Tribunal, ex parte Asfar Jan* [1995] Imm 440
  Recognition of talaq divorce pronounced in the United Kingdom – validity of subsequent marriage

- *Sottomayor* v *De Barros (No 1)* (1877) 3 PD 1
  Essential validity of marriage

- Family Law Act 1986, Part II – recognition of divorces – s46 and impact on talaqs

- Private International Law (Miscellaneous Provisions) Act 1995, s5 – a marriage entered into outside England and Wales is not void on the ground that it is entered into under a law which permits polygamy and that either party is domiciled in England and Wales

- Private International Law (Miscellaneous Provisions) Act 1995, s6(6) – nothing in s5 of the Act gives or affects any entitlement to an interest under the will or on the intestacy of a person who died before commencement

9.4 Questions and suggested solutions

QUESTION ONE

Are the following marriages valid?

a) Ann went through a ceremony of marriage by proxy in Nirvana in 1988. She is domiciled in England: her husband, Carlos, is a Nirvanian domiciliary. By the law of Nirvana in 1988 proxy marriages were allowed but in 1993 Nirvana passed a law retrospectively invalidating all proxy marriages celebrated in the country in the previous 20 years.

b) Betty who is 21 and who has always been domiciled in England recently married Pierre, a domiciliary of Gallia, in England. Pierre is 17 and by the law of Gallia requires the consent of his parents to marry. He did not obtain this. Betty herself had previously married Robert, a Gallian domiciliary in Gallia four years ago. She left him shortly afterwards and when she married Pierre believed that her marriage to Robert was void because she did not have her parents' consent to the first marriage.

c) Carol, whilst on voluntary service overseas, married Asif, a national and domiciliary of Arabia. Asif already had two wives and was entitled by his personal law to four. The ceremony of marriage with Carol was in polygamous form. At the time of the marriage Carol had decided that her future life was to be spent in Arabia and that she would only return to England if an Islamic revolution occurred in Arabia. At the time, 1988, this was thought unlikely. But the existing regime has just been overthrown and Carol has fled to England.

> University of London LLB Examination
> (for External Students) Conflict of Laws June 1995 Q3

General Comment

The individual elements of this question are set at an appropriate standard for a first degree paper. However, it would be preferable for the question to ask 'Which, if any, of the following marriages are valid?' rather than being 'closed' (ie permitting a 'yes' or 'no' answer). Aside from that the successful student should display a sound knowledge of the case law and ability to apply it to the scenarios posed.

Skeleton Solution

General introduction to the question; then:

a) law on validity of proxy marriages and attitude of courts to purported retroactive invalidity of such a marriage;

b) age as formal or essential validity;

c) validity, or otherwise, of polygamous marriage.

Suggested Solution

A valid marriage is one in which the formalities are complied with; the parties have the legal capacity to marry each other; each party voluntarily consents to marry the other; and the marriage is consummated.

That the formal requirements of a marriage are regulated by the lex loci celebrationis there is no doubt. This old rule was reaffirmed in the leading modern Privy Council case of *Berthiaume* v *Dastous* [1930] AC 79 where Lord Dunedin said:

> 'If there is one question better settled than any other in international law, it is that as regards marriage – putting aside the question of capacity – locus regit actum. If a marriage is good by the laws of the country where it is effected, it is good all the world over ...'

a) In *Apt* v *Apt* [1948] P 83, the Court of Appeal decided that formalities included the method of giving consent, which they distinguished from the fact of consent, and upheld a marriage that had been celebrated by proxy in Argentina between a man domiciled and resident there and a woman domiciled and resident in England on the basis that proxy marriages were valid in Argentina, though not in England. That retrospective legislation can validate a marriage which was formally invalid at the time it was celebrated was decided in *Starkowski* v *Attorney-General* [1954] AC 155. Given that this decision has been welcomed by many on the basis that it upheld a marriage, it is submitted that retrospective legislation having the opposite effect, ie invalidating a marriage, may not be recognised in England, particularly since the Nirvanan law purports to invalidate all proxy marriages celebrated over such a long period as the past 20 years.

b) The issue of parental consent to marriage has been treated by the English courts as a matter of formal validity and not capacity to marry: *Simonin* v *Mallac* (1860) 2 Sw Tr 67. This means that whereas a marriage celebrated in the absence of parental consent might, at best, be voidable, it is not void. Consequently, there appears to be no basis for Betty's belief that her marriage to Robert was void. That Betty then undergoes a ceremony of marriage with Pierre in England gives rise to a set of facts analogous with *Ogden* v *Ogden* [1908] P 46 where parties to a marriage in England later separated and the Frenchman, who was a minor, obtained a decree of nullity in France for lack of parental consent to the marriage. However, notwithstanding that the Frenchman and his English wife from his first marriage had both remarried on the strength of the French nullity decree, the English courts regarded their original marriage as subsisting! If English law has recognised Betty's first marriage as valid by Gallian law, the lex loci celebrationis, then she does not have the capacity to marry Pierre and the latter's apparent lack of capacity is immaterial.

c) There is a statutory bar to a party who is domiciled in England and Wales from entering a valid polygamous marriage outside England and Wales: s11(d) Matrimonial Causes Act (MCA) 1973. Section 11(b) renders void a purported marriage where the man is already married.

Carol will be unable to rely on the decision in *Radwan* v *Radwan (No 2)* [1973] Fam 35, that the capacities of the parties to enter into a valid polygamous marriage were governed by the law of the intended matrimonial home where the parties were domiciled in different countries prior to the marriage. The decision was so heavily criticised that it led to the passing of s11(d) MCA 1973. Moreover, the decision in *Hussain* v *Hussain* [1983] Fam 26, a purported interpretation of s11(d), is of no benefit to Carol: what was a valid monogamous marriage in that case would be void where the woman is domiciled in England and Wales and the man is domiciled in a country, Arabia in this case, which permits polygamy.

Section 5(1) Private International Law (Miscellaneous Provisions) Act 1995 now confines incapacity to actually polygamous marriages and does not prevent potentially polygamous marriages. Accordingly, just as Carol's 1988 marriage would be void, so it would be again if she were to go through another ceremony in the same circumstances in 1995.

QUESTION TWO

Doreen, whose domicile of origin is in England, married Sadiq in England in 1986. Sadiq is a Muslim who was born in Pakistan but has spent his working life in Saudi Arabia. After their marriage Doreen went to live in Saudi Arabia. The marriage was not successful. She returned to England in 1988. In 1989 Sadiq came to England to try to persuade her to come back with him. She agreed when he said that they would spend the next year in the USA. In January of this year he purported to divorce her in New York by pronouncing a triple repudiation before witnesses. Doreen immediately returned to England. Sadiq was advised last month that an English court might not recognise this divorce and so last week he divorced her by talaq in Saudi Arabia. Once again this involved a triple repudiation before witnesses who confirmed Sadiq's action in writing. Doreen wants to know if she is married or not.

University of London LLB Examination
(for External Students) Conflict of Laws June 1990 Q8(ii)

General Comment

A classic question which requires the student to discuss the issue of extra-judicial divorces (talaqs) and whether or not they will be recognised. It requires knowledge of case law and the Family Law Act 1986.

Skeleton Solution

Recognition of extra-judicial divorces – obtained by proceedings or not? – s46(1) and (2) of the Family Law Act 1986 – requirements for recognition – criticism of the law.

Suggested Solution

We shall assume, as seems reasonable, that Doreen's marriage in England to Sadiq is valid. Then the question of her marital status in English law depends upon whether either of the extra-judicial divorces pronounced by Sadiq would be effective to end that marriage.

The first talaq pronounced in New York is plainly not obtained by 'proceedings' for the purposes of the Family Law Act 1986 since it was held by the Court of Appeal in *Chaudhary* v *Chaudhary* [1985] Fam 19 that an oral pronouncement whether before witnesses or not did not amount to 'proceedings' for the purpose of the legislation then in force governing the recognition of extra-judicial divorces. Consequently, for the New York talaq to be effective in England it must comply with the terms of s46(2) of the 1986 Act (which deals with the recognition of divorces not obtained by 'proceedings'). Section 46(2) requires:

a) that the divorce is effective under the law of the country in which it was obtained, namely, New York. This is unlikely to be the case given the history and predominent culture in New York;

b) that at the time that the divorce was obtained, namely, 1990, either:

   i) both parties were domiciled in the country in which the divorce was obtained. Doreen and Sadiq are plainly not domiciled in New York in the English sense for they envisage leaving New York after a year. However, s46(5) provides that it is sufficient if the parties in question are domiciled there in accordance with the law of that country. They may be domiciled in New York according to the law of New York and so the requirement is fulfilled in that way, so the talaq would be recognised in England, but the information presently available does not permit one to say; or

   ii) either party to the marriage was domiciled in that country, namely, New York, and the other party was domiciled in a country under whose law the talaq was valid. Now it is possible that Doreen had acquired a domicile in New York in terms of the law of New York and Sadiq was domiciled in Saudi Arabia and the law of that country recognised the talaq. If this were the case, then, once more, the talaq would be recognised in England.

All this is rather uncertain but some certainty is brought to the matter by s46(2)(c) which requires in addition that neither party should have been habitually resident in the United Kingdom through the year preceding the date of the talaq. Since the year in the USA had not elapsed before Sadiq pronounces talaq at some stage in that previous year Doreen must have been habitually resident in England. Thus s46(2)(c) is not complied with and the talaq will not be recognised.

Does the second talaq fare any better? The Saudi Arabian talaq is slightly more formal since the witnesses confirmed that talaq in writing and this may persuade the court that it is a talaq obtained by 'proceedings'. I doubt whether this is so; although some remarks by Lord Scarman in *Quazi* v *Quazi* [1980] AC 744 were more liberal, the approach of the Court of Appeal in *Chaudhary* v *Chaudhary* requires something more than writing to transmute the divorce into one obtained by 'proceedings'. In that case Oliver LJ said that the proceedings must 'impart a degree of formality and … the involvement of some agency, whether legal or religious, of or recognised by the state having a function that is more than merely probative'. This does not seem to be the case here. Thus once more the more onerous s46(2) must be used; and plainly the talaq will not be recognised whatever the domicile of the parties because of a failure to comply with s46(2)(c).

However, should I be wrong and the court finds that the written witnessing of the talaq does transmute the nature of the talaq into one obtained by proceedings, then s46(1) applies to the Saudi Arabian talaq.

Section 46(1) also requires that the talaq should be effective under the law of the country in which it was obtained. The talaq is probably effective under the law of Saudi Arabia, so this requirement is fulfilled. Then at the date of commencement of the proceedings either party must be habitually resident there (this seems not to be the case since Sadiq's visit to Saudi Arabia seems to have been temporary and perhaps just for the pronouncement of the talaq and Doreen is certainly not habitually resident in Saudi Arabia) or domiciled there (Sadiq may well be domiciled in Saudi Arabia (either under the law of England or under the law of Saudi Arabia) since he has spent his working life there; in which case the requirement would be met and the talaq would be recognised) or a national of that country (this is not fulfilled since neither Sadiq nor Doreen is a national of Saudi Arabia). It seems from this that should it be the case that s46(1) rather than s46(2) applies, so the Saudi Arabian talaq may well be recognised in England.

Two final points may be made: first, that since Sadiq is a Pakistani national it is possible for him to divorce Doreen by talaq. He must pronounce talaq in Pakistan, inform the appropriate Union Council there, give written notice to Doreen and wait the necessary 90 days. This procedure will ensure that the talaq is obtained by 'proceedings'. Section 46(1) will apply and Sadiq can fulfil all the requirements of s46(1); the talaq is effective in Pakistan and he is a national of Pakistan.

Second, the distinction between 'bare' talaqs and talaqs obtained by 'proceedings' although it dominates the law in this area seems quite artificial. With both forms of talaq the man is able to rid himself of his wife by unilateral act. English law should decide whether that is so offensive to its ideas of public policy that it cannot be tolerated (at least where either party is resident or domiciled in England or a United Kingdom national) or it should decide that for whatever reasons of social peace or community relations talaqs, bare or otherwise, should be recognised even where the parties have strong links with this country, and should legislate accordingly.

QUESTION THREE

Ronald and Nancy, a married couple, are at all material times US citizens domiciled in New York and habitually resident in England. Ronald flies to Nevada, stays there for six weeks, and then obtains a divorce from Nancy, the Nevada court taking jurisdiction on the basis that six weeks' residence constitutes domicile under the law of Nevada. Nancy is served with notice of the proceedings in England but takes no part in them. The divorce is not recognised by New York law. Will it be recognised in England?

University of London LLB Examination
(for External Students) Conflict of Laws June 1988 Q3(ii)

General Comment

This question focuses on the issue of divorces granted in other states and as such requires the student to discuss recognition under the appropriate section of the Family Law Act 1986.

Skeleton Solution

Recognition of a judicial divorce – s46(1) of the Family Law Act 1986 – s49(2): divorce obtained in a 'country' consisting of more than one state – grounds upon which divorce may be granted – public policy grounds for the refusal of recognition.

Suggested Solution

This is a straightforward question. Since the divorce is obtained in a court the divorce is obtained by 'proceedings' and recognition will be governed by s46(1) of the Family Law Act 1986. This requires firstly that the divorce should be 'effective under the law of the country in which it was obtained'. Section 49(2) makes clear that it does not matter that the Nevada divorce is not recognised in New York; for the purposes of the relevant subsections of s46 'country' means the relevant State of the USA and it seems reasonable to presume that the divorce is effective under the law of Nevada.

The s46(1) requires, secondly, that at the time that the proceedings were commenced either party was habitually resident (this seems not to be satisfied) or domiciled in the country in question. Domiciled here means domiciled there under either the law of England or under the local law: s46(5). So this seems satisfied in the case of Ronald; and the divorce should now in principle be recognised in England.

However, Ronald is fortunate that the Nevada court exercised its jurisdiction on the ground of his domicile in Nevada. The reason for this rather cryptic remark is the following: s46(1)(b)(iii) provides an alternative ground of recognition based upon nationality. However, Ronald is a USA national and the USA consists of 49 states in addition to Nevada. Thus he would have difficulty relying on this, for s49(3) lays down that in these circumstances the divorce must be recognised throughout that country, namely the entire USA, and after all the Nevada divorce is not recognised in New York.

One final point: Nancy has been served with notice of the Nevada proceedings but has taken no notice of them. Does this provide her with the basis of a defence? Section 51(3)(a) provides that a divorce obtained by 'proceedings' may be refused recognition if a party to the marriage had not been given 'reasonable' notice of the proceedings or a 'reasonable' opportunity to take part in the proceedings. It may be that Nancy will be able to show either or both of these but as at present advised there is little evidence that she was denied reasonable notice or opportunity to participate. Recognition may also be refused if it is 'manifestly contrary to public policy' (s51(3)(c)) but no foundation for such a defence has been laid.

Thus the divorce will be recognised in England.

QUESTION FOUR

'The Family Law Act 1986, Part II, not only entrenches the mistakes made in the name of public policy in the past, but adds new layers of restrictions to the already suspicious treatment of informal divorces.'

Discuss.

University of London LLB Examination
(for External Students) Conflict of Laws June 1993 Q6

General Comment

The essay question is frequently a favourite of students; viewed as more straightforward than problem scenarios. It should be noted that whilst a 'pass mark' may be easier to achieve, the examiner will only award higher range marks if the student can demonstrate a sound critical analysis of the relevant principles.

Skeleton Solution

Brief review of common law provisions in order to establish transition to statutory provisions – focus on Part II Family Law Act 1986, ie ss44–54 – analysis of the principal provisions.

Suggested Solution

With regard to the recognition of divorces, annulments and legal separations, Part II of the Family Law Act (FLA) 1986 represents the culmination of the evolution of this area of the law from one which has been governed by common law provisions to one which is now governed exclusively by statutory provisions. However, the theme of one of the assertions in the question to be addressed suggests that the statutory provisions are not entirely new or beneficial. Indeed, the implication is that there is now statutory enactment of 'mistakes made in the name of public policy in the past'.

The aim of this essay is to review the principal stages in this evolution, with particular emphasis being placed on the current law under Part II FLA 1986, and critically to assess the accuracy or otherwise of the assertions.

At common law, the only court which could grant a divorce was that of the husband's domicile. From this it could be deduced that this was also the only court which would have a divorce decree recognised in England, a principle established in *Harvey* v *Farnie* (1882) 8 App Cas 43, in relation to a divorce granted in another country within the British Isles (Scotland in this case), and *Le Mesurier* v *Le Mesurier* [1895] AC 517, where the divorce had been obtained outside the British Isles.

The inequity in this rule is immediately apparent. If a married woman who lived in England and who had an English domicile of dependence was deserted by her husband who acquired a new domicile of choice, she could only petition for a divorce in the courts of the country of her husband's new domicile – wherever that was. The practicalities and cost involved in pursuing such an action, even assuming the new country in which the husband was now domiciled was known, could combine effectively to render the deserted wife remediless.

A degree of liberalisation throughout the Commonwealth was achieved during the first half of this century, although conditions attached to the grant of a divorce were not uniform. One example may have been that if a woman was domiciled within a particular country and, perhaps, she had been deserted there, then she could petition for divorce. This in essence was an extension of the principle in *Harvey* v *Farnie* where it was held by the House of Lords that a Scottish divorce would be recognised in England if both parties were domiciled in Scotland at the date of the institution of the proceedings.

However, it is within the last 25 years that judicial activity in divorces, etc, has been replaced by statutory provisions. In *Travers* v *Holley* [1953] P 256, Hodgson LJ recognised a foreign divorce obtained by a wife on the basis that the English court would, mutatis mutandis, have had jurisdiction to grant her a divorce (under what is now the Matrimonial Causes Act 1973). He said that 'it would be contrary to principle and inconsistent with comity if the courts were to refuse to recognise a jurisdiction which mutatis mutandis they claim for themselves.'

Following the vague, and much maligned, test in *Indyka* v *Indyka* [1969] 1 AC 33, in which a foreign divorce was recognised if there was a 'real and substantial connection' between the petitioner or the respondent and the foreign country where the divorce was obtained, the Hague Convention on the Recognition of Divorces and Legal Separations 1970 became enacted by the provisions of the Recognition of Divorces and Legal Separations Act 1971. Whereas the Act applied to all divorces and legal separations obtained in any country outside the British Isles and abandoned connecting factors such as habitual residence and nationality, it did not extend to foreign annulments. In 1984, the Law Commission recommended that essentially the same statutory rules should apply to all three matrimonial causes – divorces, annulments and legal separations – and that they should be based on the 1971 Act subject to some amendments. Most of their recommendations have now been enacted in Part II FLA 1986.

Part II FLA 1986 consists of ss44–54, inclusive. Section 44 provides for recognition in the United Kingdom of divorces, annulments and judicial separations granted in the British Islands, and s44(1) provides that as from 1 January 1974 only divorces and annulments obtained in a court of civil jurisdiction are to be recognised. Thus a unilateral non-judicial divorce will now only merit recognition if it was granted before 1 January 1974 and the husband's personal law at that time allowed him to divorce his wife by those means: *Qureshi* v *Qureshi* [1971] 2 WLR 518. However, it also means that this section does not accommodate a transnational unilateral divorce such as a talaq, for example a talaq pronounced in England and communicated to a local official in Pakistan will not come within the ambit of s44 and so will not be recognised.

That s45 provides for overseas divorces, annulments or legal separations to be recognised in the United Kingdom if, and only if, they are entitled to recognition under the 1986 Act or some other statutory provisions means that the common law rules in, inter alia, *Travers* v *Holley* and *Indyka* v *Indyka* have been abolished. Furthermore, it means that the scope for development of judge-made rules of recognition is precluded. Whereas the wording of this section is sufficient to overturn the House of Lords decision in *Fatima's Case* [1986] AC 527 that a 'transnational divorce' could not be an 'overseas' divorce within the 1971 Act, the issue of whether a transnational divorce would be recognised under this section is very much a moot point. If a wife who is resident in England is presented with a copy of (say) a divorce obtained by talaq by her husband in Pakistan who has complied with the necessary proviso of communicating it to a local official there, (i) does notification equate with service, in which case it is an overseas divorce; or (ii) is it to be regarded as a procedural necessity and thus categorised as a divorce partly obtained abroad and partly obtained in the UK? If the latter, it is likely to be denied recognition by s44.

Section 46 contains one of the most controversial provisions in Part II of the Act in that it distinguishes between the recognition of divorce 'obtained by means of proceedings' (s46(1)) and the recognition of those 'obtained otherwise than by means of proceedings' (s46(2)), ie it distinguishes between categories of extra-judicial divorce.

The clear aim of s46 is to make it harder to comply with the requirements for recognition of 'non-proceedings divorces' than with those for divorces 'obtained by means of proceedings'. Thus the 1986 Act has a change of emphasis in comparison with the 1971 Act (and the Matrimonial Causes Act 1973) in which the distinction was between judicial divorces and non-judicial divorces.

That s54(1) defines proceedings as 'judicial or other proceedings' means that case law interpretation of this phrase post-1971 continues to have relevance. In *Quazi* v *Quazi* [1980] AC 744 the House of Lords held that a 'full' talaq came within 'other proceedings' on the basis that it constituted an act which was officially recognised by the law of Pakistan as leading to an effective divorce. In contrast, in *Chaudhary* v *Chaudhary* [1985] Fam 19 the Court of Appeal held that a 'bare' talaq pronounced in Kashmir was not an 'overseas divorce' because it had not been obtained by 'other proceedings'. There was a unanimous view that while the mere pronouncement of the talaq may have constituted a 'procedure' it did not constitute 'proceedings'. '"Proceedings" would require a degree of formality and at least the involvement of some agency': per Oliver LJ.

Irrespective of whether a talaq is 'bare' or 'full', the wife is placed in a relatively very weak position. Nevertheless, and offensive to public policy or not, the distinction between 'full' talaq and 'bare' talaq is preserved in the 1986 Act, with the former only having to comply with the less onerous requirements for recognition in s46(1), whereas the latter have to satisfy the more onerous requirements of s46(2). Indeed, it is now more difficult to satisfy the requirements for 'non-proceedings divorces' under s46(2) than it was before the passing of the Act.

Section 51 provides a judge with discretionary grounds on which to refuse to recognise a divorce, with s51(3) specifically providing for refusal where there is no official document certifying that the divorce is effective under the law of the country in which it was obtained, or, when either party is domiciled in another country at the relevant time, there is no official document certifying that the divorce is recognised as valid under the law of that other country. The significance of this restriction is noted by Pearl who says: 'Given the difficulty in obtaining documentation from countries such as India and Kashmir, this provision may form a considerable stumbling block.'

The conclusion to be drawn from the enactment of Part II FLA 1986 is dependent on one's perspective. It may be regarded as a success in that minor problems with earlier legislation have been eradicated and that essentially the same statutory rules apply to each of the three forms of matrimonial causes – divorces, annulments and legal separations. However, if the Act is seen as an attempt to codify the law, then, it is submitted, there is a good argument for claiming that: 'The Family Law Act 1986, Part II, [has] entrench[ed] the mistakes made in the name of public policy in the past [and it] adds new layers of restrictions to the already suspicious treatment of informal divorces.'

QUESTION FIVE

'By what laws are:

i)   capacity to enter into marriage;

ii) capacity to make a commercial contract

governed? Can the differences be justified?'

University of London LLB Examination
(for External Students) Conflict of Laws June 2000 Q9

General Comment

This is actually quite a demanding question given the fact that the student is required to comment on two separate areas (family and contract) as well as make relevant comment on the rules in these areas.

Skeleton Solution

Validity of marriage – formal validity and essential validity – two possible approaches: dual domicile test; intended matrimonial home test – common law rules on capacity to contract – three possible approaches: (a) lex domicilii; (b) objective proper law; (c) lex loci contractus – art 11 Rome Convention.

Suggested Solution

i)   For many years the law of the place of celebration of the marriage (lex loci celebrationis) determined whether a particular marriage was valid: see *Scrimshire* v *Scrimshire* (1792) 2 Hagg Con 395. However, this simple rule was too easily evaded and had the possibility of leading to undesirable results: *Brook* v *Brook* (1861) 9 HL Cas 193. Consequently, this basic rule was restricted to matters of form whilst 'the essentials of the contract depend upon the lex domicilii ... and [the law of the place] in which the matrimonial residence is contemplated.' The modern authority for the law of the lex loci celebrationis is *Berthiaume* v *Dastous* [1930] AC 79; this makes it clear that the application of this law only applies to matters of form as opposed to matters of essential validity – the latter includes the capacity to marry.

Consequently, once a requirement has been classified as a matter of essential validity, the applicable law must be selected to regulate these matters. However it should be noted that there is still considerable uncertainty as to the rule which applies to determine the applicable law. To date the two main possibilities are the 'dual domicile' test and the 'intended matrimonial home' test.

Dual domicile test

The dual domicile test is illustrated in *Sottomayor* v *De Barros (No 1)* (1877) 3 PD 1, where the court found that the essential validity of the marriage depended on the lex domicilii of both parties. See also *Shaw* v *Gould* (1868) LR 3 HL 55. A slight modification to the dual domicile test was instituted in *Sottomayor* v *De Barros (No 2)* (1879) 5 PD 94 when the court adopted a more flexible approach. Sir James Hannan P held that where a marriage is celebrated in England between persons, one of whom is domiciled in England, capacity is tested by English law. However, this principle has had limited application by the courts. Other cases, which support the dual domicile approach include: *Padolecchia* v *Padolecchia* [1968] P 314 and *Szechter* v *Szechter* [1970] 3 All ER 905.

Intended matrimonial home test

It may be suggested that in recent times, the courts have been gradually developing a doctrine akin to a proper law of the marriage but which is best described as the intended matrimonial home test. This test was alluded to in both *Perrini* v *Perrini* [1979] Fam 84 and *Lawrence* v *Lawrence* [1985] Fam 106. The test was also adopted in *Radwan* v *Radwan (No 2)* [1973] Fam 35, but was expressly limited to questions of capacity to contract a polygamous marriage.

In terms of which is the most appropriate test to be applied, a number of arguments have been forwarded as to why the dual domicile test should be favoured over the intended matrimonial home approach. First of all, the intended matrimonial test would be difficult to apply in practice as the parties would need to know in advance which law governs their capacity to marry. Equally, it may be argued that the capacity to enter a marriage depends on the present circumstances of the parties and not the future.

Second, the use of the intended matrimonial home test has the potential to permit the evasion of other laws which should properly apply. There is an argument that it should be the law of the person's domicile that should decide if the person has the capacity to marry.

By contrast, the major objection to the dual domicile test is that it makes the process of determining the validity of a marriage more complex and time-consuming to determine. In other words, the court must not only consider the lex loci celebrationis (for the formalities of the marriage), but also the domicile of the individuals in order to determine whether they have the capacity to enter into the marriage – potentially three legal systems. However, it is worth noting that if one considers the cases of *Brook* v *Brook* (1859) 1 Sw & Tr 416, *Re Paine* [1940] Ch 46 and *Pugh* v *Pugh* [1951] P 482, then the results would have been the same whichever test the courts had applied.

At present, the scales continue to tip in favour of the dual domicile test although this may be an area which will develop in favour of a more flexible principle.

ii) Under the common law there is no established definitive view on the law applicable to the determination of capacity to contract. In principle a person's capacity to contract is a matter of personal law or status and as such governed by their lex domicilii. However, this approach is inconvenient within commercial contexts. There are a few cases which support the application of the lex domicilii, but the majority of these cases concern capacity to marry – *Sottomayor* v *de Barros (No 1)* (1877) 3 PD 1 – where different considerations apply to those relevant in a commercial contract.

The alternative and most recent view that has been put forward is that capacity is a matter of the validity of a contract and as such governed by the proper law. However, this approach cannot be applied as it would enable the parties to a contract to choose an appropriate law to govern their contract that would also confer the necessary capacity upon them. in *Cooper* v *Cooper* (1888) 13 App Cas 88 Lord Macnaghten rejected the proposition that a party to a contract could confer capacity upon himself 'by contemplating a different country as the place where the contract was to be fulfilled.' Consequently, commentators in the area agree that in this context the term 'proper law' actually means 'the objective proper law'. In other words, the law that would be the proper law of the contract had there been no choice of law by the parties. See also *Bodley Head Ltd* v *Flegon* [1972] 1 WLR 680.

A further possibility is to allow the lex loci contractus to determine capacity to contract: see *Male* v *Roberts* (1800) 3 Esp 163. However, whilst this approach certainly appears both simple to apply and certain in terms of being able to identify the law, it may nevertheless be entirely fortuitous.

Consequently, as Morris notes (*The Conflict of Laws* (2000), 5th ed at p346), the actual law that would be applied under the common law in a matter of capacity to contract is 'anyone's guess'. From a practical perspective, it may be suggested that application of the objective proper law may be regarded as offering the most logical choice. However, perhaps the ideal rule should vary depending upon which party is seeking to rely upon the incapacity (ie should a person who has capacity under his lex domicilii be permitted to establish incapacity under the proper law of the contract?). In many respects, it may be suggested that the situation that exists at present reflects this flexible approach, given the fact that no one is able to identify one definitive view.

By contrast, the Rome Convention 1980 contains only one provision – art 11 – that addresses this issue. This is due to the fact that questions of capacity are excluded from the scope of the Convention and are therefore still governed by the common law rules (see above). Article 11 provides that where the parties are in the same country, then a natural person (as opposed to a corporation) who would have capacity under the law of that country may only invoke an incapacity arising out of another law if the other party to the contract knew of the incapacity or was unaware of it through his negligence.

The implications of this provision are that a person only has the right to invoke his own incapacity. As Morris notes (p346), if the other party was to raise the issue of capacity then the common law rules outlined above would apply, unaffected by the Convention.

QUESTION SIX

Mrs Jones seeks your advice about her daughters, Angela, Barbara and Claire, all of whom have domiciles of origin in England.

i)   Angela, when she was 18, went on voluntary service overseas to Muslimia. Within six months of arriving there she went through a ceremony of marriage with Wasim. The marriage was polygamous in form and was valid by the law of the Muslimia. Last month Wasim took a second wife and Angela, now 22, left him in disgust and has returned to England. Wasim's response was to write out a document of divorce and get a friend of his to deliver it to Angela in London. By the law of Muslimia a marriage may be dissolved in this way, the divorce being complete when formally delivered to the recipient wife. Mrs Jones wants to know whether Angela was married and, if so, whether she is now divorced.

ii) Barbara, when she was 18, went as a nurse to assist in Balkania during its civil war. She went through a ceremony of marriage with Leos in a Balkanian orthodox church. This marriage met the requirements of Balkanian law. Last month, however, legislation in Balkania retrospectively annulled all church marriages which took place during the civil war. Barbara and Leos are now living in London but Leos will not support Barbara because he says she is not his wife. Mrs Jones wants to know whether Leos can justifiably claim this.

iii) Claire, when she was 16, went through a proxy marriage with Juan, a pen-friend of hers. The marriage took place in Santa Margerita and was valid accordingly to the law of that country. Claire did not have the consent of one of her parents to marry (which English law requires): there is no such requirement in Santa Margerita. Claire has just discovered, as she was about to join Juan in Santa Margerita, that Juan is seeking to have the marriage annulled on the ground known to Santa Margeritian law that Claire was not a virgin at the time of the ceremony. She wasn't. Mrs Jones is trying to stop Claire, now 18, going to Santa Margerita and has told her that she is not married or soon will not be so.

University of London LLB Examination
(for External Students) Conflict of Laws June 1996 Q5

General Comment

Another three-part, 'family law' question. Why 'the mother' is to be advised instead of each of the autonomous women is unclear and, perhaps, unrealistic: her legal position is unaffected whatever the marital status of each of her daughters.

Skeleton Solution

i)   Validity of polygamous marriage entered into outside England and Wales – subsequent 'divorce' obtained otherwise than by proceedings.

ii) Domicile of, and maintenance from, ex(?) husband.

iii) Validity of proxy marriage – recognition of divorce on ground unknown to English law.

Suggested Solution

i) Prior to enactment of Part II of the Private International Law (Miscellaneous Provisions) Act 1995, where a polygamous marriage was entered into outside England and Wales and 'either party [to the marriage] was at the time of the marriage domiciled in England and Wales', that marriage was void under s11(d) Matrimonial Causes Act (MCA) 1973.

In particular, a man who was domiciled in England and Wales did not have the capacity to enter into a polygamous marriage by virtue of s11(b) MCA 1973. Accordingly, if he married a woman, the law of whose domicile did not permit her to have more than one husband, their marriage would not be polygamous so as to come within the scope of s11(d). Conversely, where a woman who was domiciled in England and Wales purported to marry a foreign domiciled man whose personal law permitted him to have more than one wife, she would be a party to a void marriage: the effect was clearly discriminatory in that the marriage of the woman domiciled in England and Wales was void, whereas, as noted, the marriage of the man in similar circumstances was valid. That the dual domicile test applies to capacity for polygamy was decided by the Court of Appeal in *Hussain* v *Hussain* [1983] Fam 26.

However, s5(1) Private International Law (Miscellaneous Provisions) Act (PIL(MP)A) 1995 has introduced a significant change in relation to the capacity of persons domiciled in England and Wales to marry under a law which permits polygamy. It provides that:

> 'A marriage entered into outside England and Wales between parties neither of whom is already married is not void under the law of England and Wales on the ground that it is entered into under a law which permits polygamy and that either party is domiciled in England and Wales.'

Whilst Angela's marriage took place prior to the 1995 Act coming into force, s6 gives s5 retrospective effect in that s5 'shall be deemed to apply, and always to have applied, to any marriage entered into before commencement [of these provisions]'. Moreover, the circumstances of the parties to the marriage in this question, Angela and Wasim, appear to be such that they have been the parties to a valid marriage. However, s5(1) is silent on the effect of Wasim's subsequent marriage on his marriage to Angela.

Wasim's marriage to Angela is almost certainly going to be recognised under the general rule in *Baindail* v *Baindail* [1946] P 122 on the recognition of polygamous marriages and under Rule 76 of Dicey and Morris which provides that a polygamous marriage will be recognised in England unless there is some strong reason to the contrary.

As to the purported divorce, this is governed by Part II (ss44–54) of the Family Law Act 1986. The relevant section is s46(1) or (2) which provides for an overseas divorce obtained by proceedings and otherwise than by proceedings, respectively. The absence of a statutory definition of proceedings means that the Act is likely to import the meaning given in *Chaudhary* v *Chaudhary* [1985] Fam 19 that there is an absence of proceedings when the divorce results from the private act of one or both of the parties to the marriage. Accordingly, if Wasim's document of divorce is to be recognised in England, and Angela is to be regarded as divorced, then, to satisfy the provisions of subs(2), Wasim must be domiciled in Muslimia and the English courts must recognise the divorce. Domicile is the connecting factor that must be satisfied for the operation of s46(2): no other connecting factor satisfies the statutory requirements. Angela's domicile of origin has revived, but Wasim's domicile is uncertain, though, in the absence of evidence to the contrary, is probably Muslimian, given that he has the factum and, it would appear, the coincidental animus. Mrs Jones would be advised accordingly.

ii) Barbara had the capacity to contract a valid marriage and Balkanian law as the lex loci celebrationis provided the formal validity. Nothing suggests the marriage was other than valid. However, the effect of retrospective legislation must be considered in the light of s45 Family Law Act (FLA) 1986 which provides that Barbara's divorce will be recognised in the UK if, and only if, it is entitled to recognition by virtue of the relevant part of the Act. Section 51(3) FLA 1986 provides a couple of grounds on which the English courts may refuse to recognise her divorce, viz: failure to give 'notice of the proceedings to a party to the marriage as, having regard to the nature of the proceedings and all the circumstances, should reasonably have been taken (s51(3)(a)(i))'; or 'without a party to the marriage having been given ... such opportunity to take part in the proceedings as, having regard to those matters, (s)he [Barbara] should reasonably have been given (s51(3)(a)(ii))'. But even if these provisions did not provide the grounds for refusing to recognise Barbara's divorce, the offence to public policy, as provided for in s51(3)(c), provides for the non-recognition of a divorce which is manifestly contrary to public policy.

However, the statutory provisions have to be read in the light of the subsequent change in the lex causae. That a retrospective change in the law affecting marital status can be recognised in England was confirmed in *Starkowski* v *Attorney-General* [1954] AC 155. Here, a marriage void under Austrian law at the time of the ceremony was subsequently validated by a later Austrian law, thus making the second marriage of one of the parties in England bigamous and void. The later Austrian law was recognised because, as Lord Reid opined: 'There is no compelling reason why the reference should not be to that law as it is when the problem arises for decision.'

Of course, the major difference between Starkowski's case and Barbara's case is that the former 'preserved' or upheld a marriage, whereas the retrospective legislation in Barbara's case purports to invalidate her marriage. This may be manifestly contrary to English public policy and her divorce might not be recognised.

Even if Barbara and Leos are divorced, Leos does not have a justifiable claim for not maintaining Barbara. However, as to what statutory provisions will apply to the making of a maintenance order will depend on where Leos is domiciled. If he is domiciled in Balkania, the English courts have jurisdiction under s6(1) Domicile and Matrimonial Proceedings Act 1973. If, however, he is domiciled in England, the courts have jurisdiction under art 5(2) of EC Council Regultion 44/2001/EC: *De Cavel* v *De Cavel (No 2)* [1980] ECR 731. This is the case, even if maintenance is treated as an ancillary matter in proceedings primarily concerned with divorce. Mrs Jones would be advised accordingly.

iii) That Santa Margeritan law formally validates a proxy marriage is, per se, sufficient for the English courts to recognise it: *Apt* v *Apt* [1948] P 83. Claire's lack of parental consent does not, per se, invalidate the essential validity of her marriage according to English law and, more importantly, for the purposes of the question, it does not invalidate the formal validity which is governed by the lex loci celebrationis, Santa Margeritan Law: *Simonin* v *Mallac* (1860) 2 Sw & Tr 67 and *Ogden* v *Ogden* [1908] P 46. The marriage would be valid unless the English courts decide that public policy should regard Claire and Juan as not being husband and wife in England.

That Juan is seeking an annulment on a ground unknown to English law is, again, per se, no bar to the English courts recognising such a decree. If the annulment is obtained by proceedings in Santa Margerita then, as above, s45 FLA 1986 provides that it may be recognised under s46(1), subject to the non-recognition provisions of s51.

Chapter 10

Succession

10.1   Introduction

10.2   Key points

10.3   Key cases and statutes

10.4   Questions and suggested solutions

10.1 Introduction

Succession is often treated as an aspect of property law in conflict of laws, but this may lead to confusion insofar as many of the principles relating to succession are only remotely linked to the issue of the distribution of property on death. For example, the rules relating to the validity of wills have no obvious link with the rules governing the distribution of the estate of a deceased. Hence, this subject will be treated separately in this, rather brief, chapter.

It should be mentioned that this subject has in the past been a favourite hunting ground for examiners which makes it an attractive area for study. In addition, the principles regulating succession are not nearly as complicated as those in other areas of the conflict of laws syllabus.

10.2 Key points

Intestate succession

Intestate succession is the term used when a person dies without leaving a valid testamentary instrument. Where this is the case, the law can be summarised in the following rule: after the debts of the deceased have been paid, the remaining movable property will be distributed according to the law of that person's last domicile, while the immovable property will be distributed according to its lex situs.

The application of this rule is best illustrated by an example. In the case *Re Collens, Royal Bank of Canada (London) Ltd* v *Krogh and Others* [1986] 1 All ER 577, the deceased died intestate domiciled in Trinidad and Tobago leaving immovable and movable property in this location as well as in Barbados and the United Kingdom. His widow had accepted a large sum in full settlement of all her rights to the property situated in Trinidad and Tobago. She then claimed her entitlement to a statutory legacy from the immovable property situated in England in reliance on s46 of the Administration of Estates Act 1925.

The court held that regardless of the settlement of the estate in Trinidad and Tobago, the immovable assets in England were subject to English law which creates a charge on the proceeds in a widow's favour in accordance with the 1925 Act. In other words, English law was the lex situs of the immovable property and so succession to these assets was governed by English law.

The main criticism of this rule is that in the internal laws of most countries, no important distinction is drawn between movable and immovable property for the purposes of intestate succession. Why then should such a distinction be made in conflict of laws?

This point is not purely academic. If the conflict of laws rules require the property to be separated according to whether it is movable or not, only the internal legal rules of that state can be used for this purpose. Again, each separate country has different rules for identifying whether property is movable or immovable.

Testate succession

The distribution of the assets of a deceased will generally be executed in accordance with the testator's wishes as expressed in the terms of his or her will. The validity of the will is therefore critical. If the will is invalid, distribution will occur in accordance with a different series of conflict rules, namely those for intestate succession.

Once the formal and essential validity has been established, the dispersion of assets can be accomplished in accordance with the terms of the will.

The starting point for applying the conflict of laws rules to matters of testate succession is therefore to ascertain the existence of a valid will and to interpret and apply the terms of that document. This requires an examination of the following legal matters.

Formal validity of wills

This is regulated by the Wills Act 1963 which gives effect to the Hague Convention on the Formal Validity of Wills 1961. Section 1 of the Act provides that a will shall be treated as properly executed if it is executed in accordance with any one of four legal systems:

a) the law of the country where the will was executed;

b) the law of the testator's domicile at the time of execution or the testator's death;

c) the law of the place where the testator had his or her habitual residence at the time of execution or of the testator's death; or

d) the law of the country of which the testator was a national at the time of execution or his or her death.

If the will is invalid under all of these legal systems, s2 of the Act goes on to provide some more grounds for validity:

a) where a will is made on board an aircraft or ship, the internal law of the place of registration of the ship or aircraft or the law with which the ship or aircraft is most closely connected;

b) where a will disposes of immovable property, the internal law of the territory where the property is situated;

c) where a will revokes another will then any law which under the Act would uphold the validity of the revoked will can be used to test whether the revoking will effectively revoke the earlier will; and

d) the formal validity of the exercise of a power of appointment can be tested by the law governing the essential validity of the power.

Capacity to make a will/capacity to take under a will

Capacity to make a will of movable property is regulated by the law of the testator's domicile: *Re Fuld* [1968] P 675. Capacity to make a will of immovables is probably governed by the lex situs.

Two points should be noted:

a) Where capacity is regulated by domicile, is this a reference to the domicile of the testator at the time of execution of the will or the time of death? Authority favours the former option, namely the time of execution.

b) It is often difficult to characterise certain principles as being rules relating to capacity or to formalities.

Capacity to take under a will is governed by the lex domicilii of the recipient: see *Re Hellman* (1886) LR 2 Eq 363.

Essential validity of a will

The essential validity of a will of movable property is governed by the law of the testator's domicile: *Re Levick's Will Trusts* [1963] 1 All ER 311. The essential validity of a will of immovable property is regulated by the lex situs: *Re Ross* [1930] 1 Ch 377.

Issues of essential validity have in the past included the following: entitlement of relatives to a portion of the estate, whether beneficiaries can witness the will and whether gifts to charities are valid.

Interpretation of a will

The construction of a will is governed by the law which the testator intended, and in the absence of contrary indications, this will be taken to be the law of the testator's domicile: see *Re Cunnington* [1924] 1 Ch 68.

In the event that a testator changes his domicile between execution and death, the lex domicilii at the time of execution prevails: *Philipson-Stow* v *IRC* [1961] AC 727.

Revocation

If a will is revoked by express intention in a subsequent will or codicil, the effectiveness of the revocation depends on the validity of the will in which the revocation is contained and the usual rules for determining formal validity, essential validity and capacity are applicable.

Alternatively, if there is only an implicit revocation of the earlier will, this is considered to be a question of interpretation and is governed by the law of the testator's domicile at the time of execution.

A will may also be revoked by operation of law. For example, in English law a marriage revokes the earlier wills of the spouses. This issue is governed by the testator's domicile at the time of marriage and hence an existing will can only be revoked by operation of law if that law is part of the lex domicilii.

Trusts

This area of the law has been subject to statutory regulation since the Recognition of Trusts Act 1987 was enacted which implemented the Hague Convention on the Law Applicable to Trusts and on Their Recognition 1986.

The Convention defines a trust as 'the legal relationship created – inter vivos or on death – by a person, the settlor, when assets have been placed under the control of a trustee for the benefit of a beneficiary or for a specified purpose': art 2. However, in addition, in order to fall within the scope of the Convention the trust must also be created voluntarily and must be evidenced in writing: art 3.

The operative provisions of the Convention are found in arts 6 and 7. These provide that the settlor may, either expressly or impliedly, choose the law that governs the trust but if no law is chosen the trust will be governed by the law with which it is most closely connected.

There are rules for ascertaining the legal system which is most closely connected to the trust. In this connection, the place of administration indicated by the settlor, the situs of the trust assets, the residence and place of business of the trustee and the objects of the trust are all to be taken into account.

Article 11 of the Convention provides that, in the event that a trust is recognised as being validly created under the legal system specified in arts 6 and 7, then it will be recognised in every country which is a party to the Convention.

The administration of estates

On the death of a testator or an intestate, the question of the appointment of an administrator to distribute the assets in accordance with the will or the applicable rules of intestate succession arises. This task is usually undertaken by a personal representative of the deceased. In England, such a person must be appointed by the court.

This raises the question of the powers of the court to appoint representatives. This power is wide. The English courts have, in the past, considered themselves able to appoint representatives even when the deceased leaves no assets within the jurisdiction and the grant may extend to all the property of the deceased wherever situated.

10.3 Key cases and statutes

- *Collens, Re, Royal Bank of Canada (London) Ltd v Krogh and Others* [1986] Ch 505
  Confirmed that intestate succession to immovables is governed by the lex situs

- *Cunnington, Re* [1924] 1 Ch 68
  Construction of a will governed by the lex domicilii of the testator

- *Fuld, Re* [1968] P 675
  Capacity to make a will of immovables governed by the lex situs

- *Hellman, Re* (1886) LR 2 Eq 363
  Capacity to take under a will governed by the lex domicilii of recipient

- *Levick's Will Trusts, Re* [1963] 1 All ER 311
  Essential validity of will of movables governed by the lex domicilii of the testator

- Recognition of Trusts Act 1987 – implemented the Hague Convention on the Law Applicable to Trusts and on Their Recognition 1986

- Wills Act 1963 – gives effect to the Hague Convention on the Formal Validity of Wills 1961

10.4 Questions and suggested solutions

QUESTION ONE

Alan, a domiciled Ruritanian national, was executed in Saevitia for espionage. The day before his death he was visited in his cell by his mistress, Eugenie, an English domiciliary. He told her he wished to make the following gifts on his death:

i) his land in England to his son, Jake, a domiciled Ruritanian national;

ii) his art collection in the Ruritanian National Gallery to his daughter, Blanche, a Moronian domiciliary;

iii) shares in a Moronian company to his wife, Mary, a Ruritanian domiciliary;

iv) the residue of his movable estate to Eugenie.

Eugenie wrote down these instructions on a piece of paper. By Saevitian law, but no other relevant law, such writing constitutes a formally valid will. By Ruritanian law, but no other relevant law, Ruritanian nationals may not own foreign land, and a testator may not leave any of his property to his mistress. By Moronian law, but no other relevant law, a foreign national may not own shares in a Moronian company.

Soon after Alan's death, Ruritania passed legislation which stated that all works of art situated in Ruritania shall, after the death of the owner, vest in the Ruritanian state as 'universal successor'. The legislation was expressed to be retrospective to a date before Alan's death.

Will the instrument written by Eugenie be admitted to probate in England? Will the gifts contained therein be upheld?

University of London LLB Examination
(for External Students) Conflict of Laws June 1991 Q4

General Comment

Whilst the legal principles involved in this problem scenario are pretty straightforward, this question nevertheless demands that the successful student demonstrates a sound knowledge of a significant amount of this area of the law.

Skeleton Solution

Validity of Alan's will – essential and formal validity – the gift of movables – capacity to take under a will – the validity of the gift of immovables – retrospective legislation – government expropriation of property.

Suggested Solution

The first issue to be addressed is whether the will made by Alan is valid, for if it is invalid, there can be no question of it being admitted to probate.

Is the will formally valid?

The formal validity of the will presents few problems. Section 1 of the Wills Act 1963 provides a wide range of laws by which the formal validity of a will may be tested and in particular provides that 'a will shall be treated as properly executed if its execution conformed to the internal law of force in the territory where it was executed'. (Section 6 tells us that 'internal law' means the law that would apply in a case where no question of the conflict of laws arose.) Since the Saevitian law provides that a will written by someone else but on the instructions of the testator is valid and it was in Saevitia where Eugenie wrote the will for Alan, it follows that the will is formally valid.

The essential validity of the will

Whether the will is essentially valid or not is a slightly more complicated question.

The essential validity of a will of movables is governed by the law of the testator's domicile: see, for instance, *Re Levick's Will Trusts* [1963] 1 All ER 311. (*Re Goss* [1915] Ch 572 suggests that this means the testator's domicile at the time of death rather than at the time of the execution of the will, but nothing turns on this in this question.) The essential validity of a will of immovables is governed by the lex situs: *Nelson v Bridport* (1846) 8 Beav 547.

a) The validity of the gifts of movables

Thus we determine the essential validity of the gifts of the movables (namely, the art collection in Ruritania, the shares in the Moronian company and the residue of his movable estate) by the law of Alan's domicile, ie Ruritanian law.

Here there is plainly a problem with the gift to Eugenie for Ruritanian law denies the validity of gifts to mistresses. However, this difficulty may be able to be overcome in the following way: the provision of Ruritanian law denying succession rights to mistresses may be viewed as relating to the capacity of mistresses to take under a will rather than the essential validity of the will. If this is so, then, although authority is sparse, capacity to take is in principle governed by the law of the recipient's domicile (not the domicile of the testator). If this view were accepted, the Ruritanian law would not be applied to deny Eugenie's rights to the residue, since as an English domiciliary she, as a mistress, is not precluded from benefiting. This would mean, of course, that a Ruritanian mistress could not benefit but that an English mistress could!

There seems to be no difficulty with the works of art (other than the possible application of the retrospective Ruritanian law which will be discussed below); Blanche should be able to enjoy them. With the Moronian shares there is no difficulty under the applicable law (Ruritanian law). And even if the Moronian restriction is seen as relating to capacity to take this presents no problems for the beneficiary, Mary, is domiciled in Ruritania. (There may, however, be practical difficulties over the provision of Moronian law that foreign domiciliaries cannot own shares in a Moronian company for a change of ownership may need to be registered in Moronia; but I do not believe that this difficulty was intended to be addressed in this answer.)

b) The validity of the gift of immovables

Since the land is situated in England, English law applies and the gift is plainly valid under English law. There is, however, the difficulty over Jake's Ruritanian domicile, since Ruritanian domiciliaries cannot own foreign land. If this provision is considered as relating to capacity to take under the will and, if that issue, as discussed above, is governed by the recipient's domicile, namely, Ruritanian law, Jake will not be able to take under the will. There is no authority on this point, but the lex situs is so predominant in matters touching immovables that it is likely that even matters of capacity to take will be held governed by the lex situs; in which case the gift to Jake would be upheld.

The retrospective Ruritanian legislation

We now need to consider whether the Ruritanian legislation vesting the ownership of the works of art in the Ruritanian state will be applied by the English court. As we have seen Ruritanian law governs the gift of the works of art and the general rule is that the lex causae as it changes continues to apply. However, in *Lynch* v *Provisional Government of Paraguay* (1871) LR 2 P & D 268 where the facts were similar (the Paraguayan government had passed a retrospective law denying validity to the will of the previous dictator who had left his movable property (in a London bank) to his mistress) Lord Penzance held that the foreign law 'as it stands at the time of the death applies'.

Although *Lynch* was followed in *Re Aganoor's Trusts* (1895) 64 LJ Ch 521 its reasoning, if not its result, is open to criticism. There are sound public policy reasons why the English courts should be cautious about applying retrospective legislation (especially when it is penal as it was in *Lynch*) but it is not necessary in order to achieve that end to create as Lord Penzance does an exception to the general rule that the lex causae as it changes applies. In our case, however, *Lynch* is likely to be followed; and the gift of the works of art to Blanche will be held valid.

It is vital, however, to bear the practicalities in mind. The works of art are in Ruritania; and whatever the English courts may say the crucial question will be whether the English representative of Alan's estate will be allowed by the Ruritanian courts to gather in the works of art and hand them over to Blanche. That seems unlikely, and even if the works of art are removed from Ruritania (on tour or on loan) the Ruritanian title acquired under the lex situs will be recognised elsewhere: *Williams & Humbert* v *W & H Trade Marks (Jersey) Ltd* [1986] 1 All ER 129. So Blanche's case is strong in law but weak in fact.

QUESTION TWO

Cindy is a British national. She owned an estate in South Africa and, in her bank account in London, she had £10,000 to her credit. She emigrated to Australia and acquired a domicile there. During her residence there, she decided to draw up a will in favour of her boyfriend, Richard, which entitled him to succeed to her land in South Africa. No other provision was made in the will to distribute any other property. She later met Hans and left Richard to live with Hans permanently in Germany.

Cindy's will was invalid under English, Australian, South African and German law. However, it was validated by a change in Australian law after she died.

According to German law, there is no-one entitled to succeed to Cindy's estate on her intestacy and therefore the money in her bank account would go to the German government by way of the German equivalent of bona vacantia. Under English law, Harry, a cousin, is eligible to receive the money.

Cindy's personal representatives have sought your advice as regards the distribution of both the land and the money in the bank account. What would you advise?

Question prepared by the Editor

General Comment

In many respects another straightforward series of events. Students may find this demanding due to the number of issues rather than the nature of the problems. Focus on organisation and time management.

Skeleton Solution

Succession – testate succession – formal validity of will – Wills Act 1963 – meaning of law of testator's nationality – retrospective validation of will.

Intestate succession – foreign state claiming property in England as bona vacantia – failure of both English and foreign law to dispose of movables – ultimate lapse to the Crown.

Suggested Solution

We need to consider separately the succession to Cindy's South African land and to her English bank account.

Taking the land first, she has left it to Richard by her will. The question is, is this a valid will? If seized of this point (see below), the English court will determine the formal validity of the will in accordance with the Wills Act 1963. That Act provides, s1, that a will shall be formally valid if it satisfies the formalities requirements of any of a number of legal systems. Thus a will might be valid as meeting the requirements of the law of the place where the land is situated (lex situs) – here, South Africa – of the country of domicile or residence at the time of making the will (Australia) or of the country of residence or domicile at the time of the testator's death (Germany). By all these laws – with a possible exception to be discussed in the case of Australia – the will was invalid.

It is also invalid by English law, and Cindy was a British citizen. An alternative validating law provided by the statute is the law of the testator's nationality, at making the will or at death (it is assumed that Cindy remained a British citizen at death), but what is the law of Cindy's nationality? While no problem arises in the case of unitary states with a single legal system, the United Kingdom contains several 'law districts' eg England and Scotland, with differing systems of private law, and we must not assume that a 'British citizen' is English rather than, say, Scottish (this may well be significant in relation to formalities: a Scottish will is valid without witnesses, if written entirely in the testator's handwriting, while an English will requires two witnesses in any case).

How is it to be decided which United Kingdom 'law district' is indicated by Cindy's British citizenship? Section 6(2) of the Act requires the application firstly of any choice of law rule in force throughout the State in question on this point, but this is unhelpful since the United Kingdom does not have such a rule, and secondly of the system of internal law with which the testator was 'not closely connected' at the relevant time. The effect of this latter provision is obscure, but in the absence of case law or further information presumably (bearing in mind that Cindy's only known connection is a bank account in England) English law is indicated. Thus the nationality provision of the Act will not validate Cindy's will either.

Thus the only way in which the will can be valid is if it is validated by the change in Australian law. Notice that Cindy was not domiciled or resident in Australia at the time of her death – if she had been, the will would straightforwardly have been validated by s1 of the 1963 Act. However, s6(3) of the Act prescribes that regard shall be had to the formal requirements of a particular law at the time of execution of the will, but that this shall not prevent account being taken of an alteration of the law if the alteration permits the will to be treated as properly executed, thus the effect of the change in Australian law is that the will is valid and the land goes to Richard. This assumes that Cindy had capacity to make the will and Richard has capacity to take the land. There is no English authority as to capacity to make a will of immovables, but probably the lex situs, South African law, would govern the former question. Richard's capacity to take and the essential validity of the gift would seem to be regulated by the lex situs also: cf *Nelson* v *Bridport* (1846) 8 Beav 547.

Turning to the bank account, Cindy died intestate as regards this movable property. The movable property of an intestate passes to the person(s) entitled upon intestacy under the law of the deceased's domicile at death: Dicey and Morris, Rule 137. Accordingly it should pass under German law, and Harry, whose claim arises under English law, is not thereby entitled. However, German law would give the property to the German state as bona vacantia.

This however is not a claim by way of succession but a claim in default of succession, under ius regale, and such a claim by a foreign Treasury cannot be admitted in respect of movables in England (it would be otherwise if the foreign claim was a genuine claim as ultimus haeres but this seems precluded by the wording of the question). Thus the English bank account is in truth ownerless property in England and the British Crown will take as bona vacantia under English law: cf *Re Musurus* [1936] 2 All ER 1666 and *Re Maldonado* [1954] P 223. (Note that in practice the Crown may well entertain in discretion an application from Harry for some of the property, but this is a matter of administrative discretion not of law.)

Note finally as regards the jurisdiction of the English courts that they will decide the succession to the property of any person if, but only if, there is a properly constituted representative of the estate before the court – thus the English personal representatives could take out a summons. As regards the land, which is in South Africa, any determination of succession by the South African courts would be followed by the English courts: Dicey and Morris, Rules 134 and 136.

QUESTION THREE

Clarissa, whose domicile of origin was in England, married Pierre, a wealthy Frogian property developer with a domicile in Frogia in 1960. By the law of Frogia, unless parties agree to the contrary, there is community of property between married couples. The matrimonial home was set up in Frogia where they lived until 1970. In 1970, when Pierre had accumulated 10 million dollars, they moved to England. Pierre's property development continued to prosper and when he died earlier this year he was worth 20 million dollars. By the law of Frogia, Clarissa is entitled to half of this. She wants to know whether she can claim half of his assets. Pierre's brother is likely to contest her claim.

Advise Clarissa.

University of London LLB Examination
(for External Students) Conflict of Laws June 1990 Q8(i)

General Comment

On face value this appears to be a simple scenario. However, the successful student should note immediately that it involves the issue of characterisation. This in turn dictates the direction of advice offered. The unwary student could go amiss with this question.

Skeleton Solution

Characterisation: succession or matrimonial property – matrimonial property – *De Nicols* v *Curlier* – *Chiwell* v *Carlyon*.

Suggested Solution

It is difficult to advise Clarissa in this problem since in Collier's words 'the effect of a change of the matrimonial domicile in [cases of matrimonial property] is one of the unanswered questions of the English conflict of laws'. There are several difficulties:

First, we have to decide a characterisation issue; are we concerned with a matter of succession (in which case the relatively clear choice of law rules relating to succession would apply) or are we dealing with a case of matrimonial property (in which case we have to set out to deal with the more uncertain rules relating to matrimonial property)? Although Clarissa's claim arises from Pierre's death, it seems clear that she is not claiming a legitimo portio (or portion of a husband's estate that must be left to the wife) but she claims that she was owner of one half of Pierre's estate throughout their marriage together (although it seems that Pierre was in charge of the administration of their joint estate). Thus Clarissa's claim is based upon her marriage, not upon succession to a share of Pierre's estate.

Thus, second, we need to decide what the English choice of law rules are in regard to matrimonial property. Dicey and Morris say in Rule 153 that where there is a marriage contract then the terms of that contract govern the rights of the husband and the wife in the matrimonial property (whether possessed at the time of the marriage or acquired afterwards) and notwithstanding any change of domicile. In our case there is, as far as we can tell, no express contract between them but there may be an implied contract between them. Indeed, the terms of the question suggest under the law of Frogia the parties are taken to have impliedly agreed to community of property since that is the rule 'unless they agree to the contrary'.

The leading case in this area is still *De Nicols v Curlier* [1900] AC 21. Two persons domiciled in France had married in France without making an antenuptial contract. However, in these circumstances, French law imposed an implied contract upon them containing the provisions of the Code Napoleon which provided for community of property. They afterwards acquired a domicile in England but the House of Lords held that the contract implied by French law continued to bind the parties even after they were domiciled in England. Thus the wife was entitled to half of all their movable property. Although in the House of Lords *De Nicols v Curlier* was limited to movables it appears from other cases (for example, *Chiwell v Carlyon* (1897) 14 SC (SA) 61) that the same principle applies to immovables. The proper law of any such implied marriage contract would be that of the husband at the time of the marriage: Dicey and Morris Rule 154; *Duke of Marlborough v Attorney-General* [1945] Ch 78. In our case this would plainly be the law of Frogia under which there is community of property. It may seem unjust that in these days of sexual equality that Clarissa's domicile in England should be ignored but the reforms to the law of domicile have not changed these rules in regard to the matrimonial domicile.

For Clarissa it would be most beneficial to establish that the law of Frogia is analogous to the French law applied in *De Nichols v Curlier*. She would then be entitled to one half of the $20 million. However, if this cannot be established then presumably (for authority is sparse) Dicey and Morris Rule 156 would apply. This rule provides that, as far as movables are concerned, where there is no marriage contract the proprietary regime of the marriage is mutable, namely, it is governed by the changed domiciliary law 'except insofar as vested rights have been acquired under the law of the former domicile'.

With immovables, however, it appears that the immutability principle continues to govern; that at any rate seems implicit in *Chiwell v Carylon* where a husband and wife domiciled in the Cape of Good Hope, where in the absence of an antenuptial agreement community of property applied, acquired a domicile in England. The English court held that the land which the husband had bought in Cornwall was still subject to the South African community of property.

In these circumstances, the precise outcome for Clarissa would depend upon whether Pierre's property is movable or immovable. The fact that he has made the money by property development is not decisive for his assets might in fact be shares in property development companies which would be movables. For the ease of exposition, let us assume that the entire estate consisted of movables. In this case Clarissa would only be entitled to the half share of the $10 million that Pierre was worth at the time he acquired a domicile in England.

QUESTION FOUR

Tom is a national of Cartoonland. After a serious accident caused by Jerry, he died intestate in England, domiciled in Disneyland. He left a huge estate in Cartoonland together with cash and company securities in Hanna-Barbara Productions Ltd in England. His wife predeceased him and he was survived by a son, Tom Jr, and three daughters the youngest of whom is 16.

Under the law of Cartoonland, the whole estate devolves to a surviving son to the exclusion of all surviving daughters. Under the law of Disneyland, a child under 17 cannot inherit and Tom Jr and the two eldest daughters would inherit the estate in equal shares. In terms of English law, all four children are entitled to share the estate equally.

Also under Cartoonland law, intestate succession to all forms of property is governed by the law of the country in which the deceased died. By Disneyland law, the property is governed by the law of the deceased's nationality.

Advise Tom's administrator as to how the estate should be distributed.

Question prepared by the Editor

General Comment

Another question focusing on movable/immovable property coupled with the area of renvoi. It is perhaps the latter point which may pose problems for the unprepared student (ie it reinforces the importance of a wide appreciation of the area, as opposed to simply focusing on 'question spotting').

Skeleton Solution

Rules for intestate succession – distinction between movable and immovable property – problems of renvoi – analogy to the English rules to resolve the problem of renvoi – need to obtain guidance from the courts.

Suggested Solution

By English conflicts law, different rules determine the destination of an intestate's movables and his immovables. The disposition of the immovables (Tom's land in Cartoonland) will be governed by the lex situs, here the law of Cartoonland. In this context that means the law which the Cartoonland court would apply in the instant case, ie total renvoi will be applied: *Re Ross* [1930] 1 Ch 377 (in this case testate succession – to both movables and immovables – was in issue, but the rationale of the decision is that it makes no sense for the English court to attempt to apply rules which will not be applied by the court which actually has power over the land, and this reasoning applies equally to intestate succession).

The Cartoonland court would apply the law of the country in which the deceased died, here England; thus the English court will 'accept the renvoi' and apply English domestic law, so that the four children will take the Cartoonland estate in equal shares. Note that this assumes (realistically) that Cartoonland courts do not themselves subscribe to the doctrine of total renvoi, but have either no renvoi (like Italy) or single renvoi (like France or West Germany).

The movables will devolve according to the law of Tom's last domicile, Disneyland: *Re Collens* [1986] Ch 505. Once again, total renvoi will apply: *Re O'Keefe* [1940] Ch 124. The Disneyland court would apply the law of Tom's nationality (Cartoonland) to the issue, but we do not know what the renvoi doctrine of the Disneyland courts is. If they do not subscribe to any renvoi theory, they would apply Cartoonland domestic law, and Tom would receive the whole of the property in England. If they subscribe to partial or 'single' renvoi, they would apply the legal system indicated by the Cartoonland conflicts rules, ie the law of the place of the deceased's death, England: in this case, English domestic law would be applied and the four children would take the property in equal shares.

If they subscribe to total renvoi, the Disneyland courts would behave as a Cartoonland court would do in the instant case; either (if Cartoonland has no renvoi) applying English law, or (if Cartoonland has single renvoi) applying English law including English conflicts rules, so that Disneyland law as the law of the last domicile applies and the three elder children take in equal shares, or (if Cartoonland has total renvoi), a circulus inextricabilis would arise – but the possibility of both Disneyland and Cartoonland subscribing to total renvoi is remote.

Whichever result the Disneyland court arrives at will of course be applied by the English court, which itself subscribes to total renvoi. It will be clear that if Disneyland is a total renvoi country, the English administrator would be well advised to take out a summons to obtain the guidance of the court.

Chapter 11

Recognition and Enforcement of Foreign Judgments

11.1 Introduction

11.2 Key points

11.3 Key cases and statutes

11.4 Questions and suggested solutions

11.1 Introduction

The recognition and enforcement of foreign judgments is the third main part of the conflict of laws. A plaintiff may sue in one country, hear judgment given in his favour and then discover that he has to enforce that judgment against the defendant in another country. This inevitably leads to the query as to the circumstances in which an English court will either recognise or enforce a judgment of a foreign court.

The judgments of courts in the EC were, until March 2002, governed by the Brussels Convention 1968. This has now been superseded by Council Regulation 44/2001/EC. The reasoning though remains the same; due to the detailed rules of jurisdiction that operate within the EC, the enforcement of a judgment rendered by an EC court should be very straightforward in all other EC countries. However, the judgments of courts outside the EC continue to be governed by the traditional common law rules fortified by statute.

11.2 Key points

Preliminary matters relating to the recognition and enforcement of judgments

Where a judgment is obtained against a defendant in a foreign jurisdiction, in order to enforce the judgment a successful plaintiff must apply to an English court to implement any foreign order in England. Foreign judgments are not automatically effective in English law and the courts are not bound to give effect to foreign court orders. It is a matter for the English courts to decide according to their own rules whether a foreign judgment should be recognised or enforced.

A critical distinction should be drawn between recognition and enforcement. When a foreign court judgment is recognised, this simply means that the English court will take note of the result of the case. For example, a foreign divorce decree may be recognised or acknowledged as valid by an English court when hearing a case relating to succession to property on the death of a spouse.

To be enforced, a foreign judgment must first be recognised by the English courts and then given effect by the court through a separate judgment ordering enforcement. Enforcement is therefore a two-stage process, the first stage being recognition and the second step being enforcement itself.

The distinction between judgments rendered outside the European Community and those rendered within the Community

Prior to 1982, both the issues of recognition and enforcement were primarily matters regulated by the common law. Statutory rules did exist for the reciprocal enforcement of judgments between the United Kingdom and certain foreign countries – eg the Administration of Justice Act 1920 and the Foreign Judgments (Reciprocal Enforcement) Act 1933 – but these were, on the whole, rarely applicable. Until 1982, the subject was dominated by case law and precedent.

A crucial turning point in this situation was the enactment of the Civil Jurisdiction and Judgments Act 1982 which, as we have seen earlier, gave effect to the Brussels Convention 1968. The Convention is an arrangement among the member states of the European Union to facilitate the enforcement of judgments among themselves. The basic principle is that, if a plaintiff is compelled to sue a defendant in the courts of a European Union country, he should be able to rely on the enforcement of the court order anywhere throughout the Union. However, from 1 March 2002, the Brussels Convention was, to all intents and purposes, superseded by Council Regulation 44/2001/EC. Whilst the content of the Regulation remains largely the same as the Convention, some discussion within this section will focus on the change in the numbering of the articles.

These statutory arrangements apply only to the reciprocal recognition and enforcement of judgments between the English courts and the courts of the other EU countries. The judgments of courts outside the European Union continue to be regulated by the traditional common law rules. Hence, the critical decision in selecting which rules apply depends on whether the judgment is from a Union or a non-Union country.

Finally, it should be pointed out that the 1982 Act also corrects some of the flaws and inconsistencies which had arisen in the development of this subject within the common law over the years.

The effect of an existing foreign judgment on initiating actions in the English courts

Before 1982, a plaintiff who had been successful in a foreign court had two options when bringing an action in England against the same defendant: to bring an action based on the foreign judgment or to commence litigation afresh. This situation was seen as an exception to the general principle of res judicata.

This common law rule has been abolished under s34 of the Civil Jurisdiction and Judgments Act (CJJA) 1982 which provides that:

> 'No proceedings may be brought by a person in England and Wales or Northern Ireland on a cause of action in respect of which a judgment has been given in his favour in proceedings between the same parties ... in a court of an overseas country, unless that judgment is not enforceable or entitled to recognition in England and Wales ...'

This provides a valid defence to an action brought in England for a defendant against whom a foreign judgment has been rendered: *Black* v *Yates* [1991] 3 WLR 90. The rule applies regardless of whether the court pronouncing judgment is located inside or outside the European Community: see *The Indian Grace* [1991] 1 Lloyd's Rep 124.

From the point of view of the recognition and enforcement of foreign judgments, plaintiffs with a valid foreign court judgment must proceed through the process for the recognition and enforcement of the judgments and the option of raising a new action in the English courts has been eliminated.

Judgments rendered outside the European Union

The central rule

An English court will generally enforce a judgment of a foreign court if that court was competent to exercise jurisdiction to render judgment on the facts of the case. Two important points should be noted in connection with the concept of jurisdiction in this context:

a) Whether or not a foreign court has jurisdiction is decided in terms of English law and not according to the rules applied by the foreign court to delineate its own jurisdiction: *Buchanan* v *Pucker* (1809) 9 East 192.

b) It does not necessarily follow that, because an English court would have exercised jurisdiction in similar circumstances, a foreign court is entitled to do so. This principle explains why an English court will refuse to recognise or enforce a judgment rendered after a writ has been served outside the jurisdiction of the foreign court even though the English courts can exercise a similar power: see *Re Dulles' Settlement (No 2)* [1951] Ch 842.

As a general principle, an English court will generally consider a judgment of a foreign court to be competent if jurisdiction has been exercised on the basis of the defendant's residence in the country or the defendant has submitted to the foreign court's jurisdiction.

Jurisdictional competence of foreign courts under the common law

There are, in effect, two grounds on which an English court will consider that a foreign court has exercised its jurisdiction in personam in a competent manner: (a) a period of residence by the defendant; and (b) submission by the defendant to the jurisdiction of the court.

a) Residence

> The principle that courts have competent jurisdiction over persons resident within their territory, is internationally recognised and is possibly the most fundamental principle in establishing a jurisdictional nexus between an individual and a particular court: see *Schibsby* v *Westenholtz* (1870) LR 6 QB 155.
>
> The exact period of residence required before a court can exercise jurisdiction has not been definitively established. In *Adams* v *Cape Industries plc* [1990] 2 WLR 657 Slade LJ ruled that:
>
>> 'In the absence of authority compelling a contrary conclusion, we would conclude that the voluntary presence of an individual in a foreign country, whether permanent or temporary and whether or not accompanied by residence, is sufficient to give the courts of that country territorial jurisdiction over him under our rules of private international law.'
>
> This decision suggests that the mere presence of an individual within a country is sufficient for a court to competently exercise jurisdiction over that person.
>
> The rule for the residence of companies or corporations is slightly different due to their artificial nature. Where a company carries on 'substantial business ... at some definite and more or less permanent place in the country of trial', it is considered to be residence in that country: see *Littauer Glove Corporation* v *FW Millington Ltd* (1928) 44 TLR 746.
>
> This rule was elaborated in *Adams* v *Cape Industries plc*, above, where the following principles were established in relation to the residence requirement for companies:
>
> i) A company will be considered resident in a country only if either (1) it has established and maintained a fixed place of business in that country and has, for more than a minimal period of time, carried on business from these premises; or (2) a representative of the company has, for more than a minimal period of time, carried on the business of the company in the country.
>
> ii) Whether or not a company has a representative is to be decided after considering why premises were acquired in a country, whether the representative is directly reimbursed for the costs of running the operation by the company, and the contributions made by the company to the running of the operation.

b) Submission to the jurisdiction

> If a defendant has voluntarily submitted to the jurisdiction of a foreign court, any

judgment rendered by that court will be recognised and enforced in England: *Emanuel* v *Symon* [1908] KB 302. A defendant can be considered to have submitted to the foreign jurisdiction in the following ways.

i) The defendant voluntarily appears before the foreign court and pleads to the merits of the plaintiffs case: *Guiard* v *De Clermont* [1914] 3 KB 145.

ii) The defendant has counterclaimed in the foreign court against the original plaintiff: *Schibsby* v *Westenholz* (1870) LR 6 QB 155.

iii) The defendant has entered into an express agreement to submit to the foreign court's jurisdiction: *Feyerick* v *Hubbard* (1902) 71 LJ KB 509.

iv) A defendant may impliedly submit to the jurisdiction of a foreign court through certain actions. The most common form of implied submission is through representations made in business transactions with parties resident in the country: see *Blohn* v *Desser* [1962] 2 QB 116.

In the past, if a defendant entered appearance to contest the jurisdiction of the court and failed to convince the court that it had no jurisdiction over the matter, the common law rule was that the court's judgment was valid: *Harris* v *Taylor* [1951] 2 KB 580.

This position has been changed by s33 CJJA 1982 Act which provides that a person against whom judgment has been given is not to be regarded as having submitted to the jurisdiction of the court only by reason of the fact that he appeared to contest the jurisdiction of the court. A person is not therefore deemed to submit to the jurisdiction of the court if appearance is solely for the purpose of contesting the court's jurisdiction.

Additional requirements for enforcement in common law

In addition to the need to demonstrate that the judgment has been pronounced by a court of competent jurisdiction, the judgment must also satisfy the following additional requirements.

a) The foreign judgment must be final and conclusive. All the points of law must be settled by the judgment. However, a judgment may be final and conclusive, notwithstanding the possibility of an appeal to a higher court, if no appeal is made: *Colt Industries Inc* v *Sarlie (No 2)* [1966] 1 WLR 1287.

   The principal exception to this rule is for maintenance orders which can be varied from time to time as circumstances change.

b) The judgment must be for a specific sum of money in order to be enforceable. An English court will not implement a foreign judgment for an injunction, specific implement or for delivery of goods: *Sadler* v *Robins* (1808) 1 Camp 253.

Defences to an action for recognition and enforcement

Even when a foreign court has competently exercised its jurisdiction in the proper manner and the judgment fulfils the necessary additional requirements, a defendant may rely on a number of grounds to establish a defence to the enforcement action. The following grounds are defences to an action for enforcement.

a) Fraud either by the plaintiff or by the foreign court itself

Even if the issue of fraud is not raised at the original hearing in the foreign court, a defendant may still rely on the defence in the English courts: *Syal v Heyward* [1948] 2 KB 443. But, if the issue of fraud has been raised in the foreign court, a defendant may be estopped from raising the point again when enforcement proceedings are brought in England: *House of Spring Garden v Waite* [1990] 3 WLR 347. See also *Owens Bank Ltd v Bracco and Others* [1991] 4 All ER 833.

b) The enforcement of the foreign judgment would be contrary to public policy

For example, courts will not enforce foreign court judgments imposing a penalty, although where the penalty is coupled to a compensation award, the compensation portion of the judgment may be enforced: see *Raulin v Fischer* [1911] 2 KB 93.

c) The defendant has been denied natural justice by the foreign court

A judgment is not obtained contrary to natural justice simply because it appears to be wrong. There must be a flagrant breach of natural justice such as the failure to allow the defendant to present his case or inadequate notice of the proceedings has been given to the defendant: *Jacobsen v Frachon* (1928) 138 LT 386 and *Adams v Cape Industries plc*, above.

d) Protection of Trading Interests Act 1980

This statute provides that judgments for multiple damages, such as the treble damages rule in US anti-trust law, cannot be enforced.

The courts have also given substantial consideration to situations which will not provide a valid defence to an action for recognition and enforcement. Thus, the merits of a foreign judgment cannot be reopened before an English court even if the foreign court judgment is incorrect: *Castrique v Imrie* (1870) LR 4 HL 414. This rule applies regardless of whether there has been an error of law or fact.

Where additional and new evidence is discovered after the judgment of the foreign court has been given but prior to the proceedings for enforcement, this is generally not a ground for reopening a case and is not a valid defence although there has been academic controversy on this point: see *De Cosse Brissac v Rathbone* (1861) 6 H & N 301.

Procedure for enforcement in common law

Since a foreign judgment is incapable of direct execution in England, an action must be brought against the defendant based on the foreign judgment. This procedure can be expedited by an application for summary judgment under CPR r24.

There are two statutes which allow foreign judgments to be registered in the English courts after which the foreign judgment can be treated for most purposes as a local judgment for the purposes of execution. These are the Administration of Justice Act 1920 and the Foreign Judgments (Reciprocal Enforcement) Act 1933.

Part II of the Administration of Justice Act 1920 provides for the reciprocal enforcement of judgments in the United Kingdom. and other Commonwealth countries. Hence, the statute allows for the reciprocal enforcement of judgments among England and Wales, Scotland and Northern Ireland.

Orders in Council have been used to extend the application of the statute to certain Commonwealth countries when these are considered to have granted reciprocal enforcement rights for United Kingdom court judgments. Countries within the scheme include Australia and New Zealand. The statute does not extend to either Canada or South Africa.

Where a judgment emanates from one of the countries to which Part II of the Act applies, a plaintiff can, within 12 months after the date of the judgment, apply to the High Court to register the judgment. The registration of the judgment is at the discretion of the court and by s9(2) of the Act there are six grounds on which registration will be refused.

After a judgment has been registered, the judgment has full force and effect and proceedings may be taken thereon as if the judgment had been originally obtained in an English court.

The Foreign Judgments (Reciprocal Enforcement) Act 1933 is more comprehensive in both scope and coverage than the 1920 Act. This statute authorises ministers to enact Orders in Council to extend recognition and enforcement rights to foreign states which extend similar rights to United Kingdom judgments.

Under this statute, an application for registration can be made for a foreign judgment and once registration has been granted then the registered judgment shall have the same force and effect as if the judgment had been given by the registering court. The major difference between this statute and the 1920 Act is that the court has considerably less discretion in deciding against the registration of a judgment.

The prerequisites for registration under this statute are as follows:

a) the judgment must be final and conclusive as between the judgment creditor and the judgment debtor;

b) there must be a sum payable under the judgment not being a sum payable in respect of taxes or other charges of a like nature: see *SA Consortium General Textiles* v *Sun and Sand Agencies Ltd* [1978] 1 QB 279.

Section 1(3) of the Act provides that a judgment shall be deemed final and conclusive notwithstanding that an appeal may be pending against it, or that it may still be subject to appeal, in the courts of the country of the original court.

Even after a judgment has been registered, a defendant can make an application to have the registration set aside in accordance with s4(1)–(3) of the Act. There are four grounds on which a registered judgment may be set aside:

a) the judgment was registered in contravention of the terms of the Act;

b) the foreign court did not have proper jurisdiction;

c) the judgment has been obtained by fraud or its enforcement would be contrary to public policy; and

d) the rights under the judgment are not vested in the person by whom the application for registration is made.

While the statute does not make reference to such a ground, it is also likely that a registration may be set aside in the event of a denial of natural justice, such as a failure to serve adequate notice on the defendant of the proceedings.

Also, registration may be set aside where the registering court is satisfied that the matter in dispute in the proceeding in the original court had, previously to the date of the judgment in the original court, been the subject of a final and conclusive judgment by a court having jurisdiction in the matter.

Finally, it should be pointed out that the registration procedure under the 1933 Act is the exclusive means of enforcing foreign judgments covered by the Act. In other words, where a case falls within the scope of the Act, the provisions of the Act must be used.

Judgments rendered inside the European Union

The basic principles

The CJJA1982 is designed to ensure that defendants are sued in the legal system in which they are domiciled for the purposes of the Act and the 1968 Brussels Convention. Since both the Act and the Convention ensure that a proper and genuine link is established between a legal system and an individual, it is only logical that once a judgment has been rendered in that court, the court order should be enforceable in other countries.

The new Council Regulation 44/2001/EC aims to achieve the same goal as the Brussels Convention among the member states of the European Union (though it should be noted that Denmark has opted out and as such the enforcement of Danish judgments is still governed by the Convention). Consequently, this section will make reference to the new Regulation, whilst providing the corresponding articles of the Brussels Convention in brackets as follows: art 33{26} (where art 33 is Council Regulation 44/2001/EC and 26 is the corresponding article of the Brussels Convention).

Hence, art 33{26} of the Regulation provides that a judgment given in a European Union state 'shall be recognised' in the other member states without any special procedure being required.

As regards enforcement actions, art 38{31} of the Regulation states that a judgment given in one member state and enforceable in that state shall be enforceable in another European Union state when, 'on the application of any interested party', it has been declared enforceable in the other Union state.

Judgment is defined in art 32{25} of the Regulation as 'any judgment given by a court or tribunal of a member state, whatever the judgment may be called, including a decree, order, decision or writ of execution, as well as the determination of costs or expenses by an officer of the court.' It should also be noted that proceedings for enforcement under the Convention are not limited to monetary judgments.

In addition, under the Regulation, the English courts are generally precluded from inquiring into the exercise of jurisdiction by the foreign court. Thus, art 35(3){28(3)} of the Regulation provides that, subject to one exception, the jurisdiction of the court of the state in which the judgment was given may not be reviewed: see *Interdesco SA* v *Nullifire Ltd* [1992] 1 Lloyd's Rep 180. Again this is a substantial deviation from the common law position.

Procedure for enforcement

In order to have a judgment recognised and enforced, it is necessary to apply to the court for registration of the judgment. Within England, the specified court is the High Court of Justice. The court is obliged to give its decision on registration without delay and the prospective defendant is not entitled by right to make any submissions on the application at this stage.

After a judgment has been successfully registered, according to s4(3) of the 1982 Act, the judgment, for the purposes of enforcement, shall have the same force and effect as if the judgment had been originally given by the registering court.

If enforcement is authorised, the defendant may appeal against the decision within one month of service. Where an appeal has been lodged against an enforcement order, art 47{39} provides that no measures of enforcement may be taken other than prospective measures against the property and assets of the party against whom enforcement is sought.

In addition, a court may also stay proceedings if an 'ordinary appeal' against the judgment has been lodged: art 37{30} and see *Van Dalfsen* v *Van Loon* [1992] ILPr 5. An ordinary appeal refers to an appeal against the foreign court order in that country. This rule was elaborated on by the court in *Petereit* v *Babcock International Holdings Ltd* [1990] 1 WLR 350, where three principles concerning its application were highlighted:

a) an enforcing court has a general and unfettered discretion under the Regulation to stay the enforcement proceedings if an appeal is pending in the state in which judgment was obtained;

b) a judgment obtained in a European Union state is to be regarded as prima facie enforceable and accordingly the enforcing court should not adopt a general practice of depriving a successful plaintiff of the fruits of the judgment by imposing a more or less automatic stay; and

c) the purpose of arts 37{30} and 47{39} of the Regulation is to protect the position of a defendant and to ensure that, if the appeal is successful, the defendant is not deprived of his rights.

As a final point, it should be noted that the procedures established by the Regulation, (and the Brussels Convention – as given effect by the 1982 Act), remove the possibility of relying on the common law grounds for enforcing judgments where the facts of the case indicate that the Regulation are applicable.

Grounds on which recognition or enforcement may be denied

There are a number of limited exceptions to the general rule that a judgment from a European Union court must be recognised and enforced in the English courts. These are contained in art 34{27} and are as follows:

a) where such recognition would be contrary to the public policy in the state in which recognition is sought;

b) where the foreign judgment was given in default of appearance, if the defendant was not duly served with the document instituting the proceedings in sufficient time to enable an adequate defence to be arranged (*Thierry Noirhomme* v *David Walklate* [1992] 1 Lloyd's Rep 427);

c) where the judgment is irreconcilable with a judgment in a dispute between the same parties in the state where the recognition is being sought. In other words, the recognising court does not have to give preference to the foreign judgment over its own judgment (*Hoffmann* v *Krieg* [1988] ECR 645);

d) where there is a judgment from a non-European Union state that has been given earlier and is irreconcilable with a European Union judgment, that judgment may be recognised;

e) where the judgment-granting state has decided a preliminary question concerning the status or legal capacity of natural persons, rights in property arising out of a matrimonial relationship, or will, in a manner which conflicts with the rules of private international law of the judgment-recognising state.

Provisional measures

An application may be made to the courts for such protective measures as are available under the law of that state even if, under the Regulation, the courts of other countries have jurisdiction over the substance of the matter: art 31{24}.

11.3 Key cases and statutes

- *Adams* v *Cape Industries plc* [1990] 2 WLR 657
  Presence of a corporation within a jurisdiction

- *Black* v *Yates* [1991] 3 WLR 90
  Section 34 CJJA 1982 – effect of judgment awarded by foreign court enforceable in England

- *De Wolf* v *Cox* [1976] ECR 1759
  Procedure for recognition and enforcement of a judgment granted within EC – Brussels Convention

- *Hoffmann* v *Krieg* Case 145/86 [1988] ECR 645
  Grounds on which recognition or enforcement may be refused – Brussels Convention

- *Interdesco SA* v *Nullifire Ltd* [1992] 1 Lloyd's Rep 180
  Raising the defence of fraud – Brussels Convention

- *Minalmet GmbH* v *Brandeis Ltd* [1993] ILPr 132
  Judgments issued in default cannot be enforced in another Convention state if proceedings did not come to attention of defendant in time to allow defence

- *Owens Bank Ltd* v *Bracco and Others* [1992] 2 WLR 621
  Fraud can be raised as a defence to a foreign judgment

- *Pemberton* v *Hughes* [1899] 1 Ch 781
  Lack of internal competence by the foreign court appears to be no defence

- *Showlag* v *Mansour* [1994] 2 WLR 615
  Where two competing judgments are issued by courts in different states, the judgment issued earlier in time should prevail

- *Vogel* v *R & A Kohnstamm Ltd* [1973] 1 QB 133
  Residence within jurisdiction – effect on enforcement of judgment

- Council Regulation 44/2001/EC – replaced framework for the recognition and enforcement established under the Brussels Convention 1968

11.4 Questions and suggested solutions

QUESTION ONE

Arnold and Danny are both domiciled in England. They go on a business trip to Algeria in Arnold's car. When Arnold was driving the car, Danny provoked him into driving the car at twice the speed limit in Algeria. As a result, Arnold hit a car being driven by Chuck, a resident of Algeria, causing over £5,000 worth of damage. Immediately after the accident, both Arnold and Danny returned to England.

Chuck issued a claim form out of the Algerian court claiming damages of £10,000 for the car. This was served on Arnold while he was visiting Algeria for one day to recover his car. A similar claim form, claiming £2,000 in punitive damages, was served on Danny for abetting Arnold in the commission of the accident in Algeria, but this was served on Danny in England.

Arnold did not appear before the Algerian court and Danny appeared through counsel who argued two points on his behalf – first, that the Algerian court had no jurisdiction over Danny, and second, that Algerian law did not permit an award of punitive damages.

The Algerian court dismissed both arguments and gave judgment against Arnold and Danny for the sums craved. Although both defendants were given six months to appeal, neither did so. However, it appears that the Algerian court rendering judgment had no jurisdiction in claims over £7,000.

Chuck has now started proceedings in England to enforce both judgments. Advise both Arnold and Danny of the possible defences open to them.

Question prepared by the Editor

General Comment

First of all this is testing whether the student can distinguish between instances governed by the common law and those relevant under the new Council Regulation 44/2001/EC. Some students will fail at this stage. Second, the question requires a sound application of the principles governing enforcement and jurisdiction.

Skeleton Solution

Enforcement of foreign judgment at common law – basis of jurisdiction of foreign court – excess of jurisdiction internally by foreign court.

Suggested Solution

It is to be noted that Algeria is not a party to Council Regulation 44/2001/EC (or the Brussels Convention 1968); thus, we are concerned with the enforcement of a foreign judgment at common law, and not under the Regulation (or the schemes of the Administration of Justice Act 1920 or the Foreign Judgments (Reciprocal Enforcement) Act 1933).

a) The first question is whether in the eyes of the English court, which is being asked to enforce the Algerian judgment, the Algerian court had jurisdiction over Arnold. The relevant possible grounds of jurisdiction are sometimes referred to as grounds of 'international competence', though it is stressed that they are rules of English law.

One such ground is submission, but Arnold did not appear in the Algerian court and clearly has not submitted to its jurisdiction.

The alternative ground is presence in the territory of the foreign court; the relevant time is the commencement of proceedings: *Sirdar Gurdyal Singh* v *Rajah of Faridkote* [1894] AC 670. Until recently there was considerable doubt as to whether this ground was to be stated as presence or as residence, but the Court of Appeal has now held that presence is the relevant factor (*Adams* v *Cape Industries plc* [1990] 2 WLR 657); the court explicitly assimilated the rule of international competence to the corresponding rule for the jurisdiction of the English courts, which has always required mere presence even for a very short period, cf *Maharanee of Baroda* v *Wildenstein* [1972] 2 QB 283, thus Arnold's presence in Algeria for a single day will suffice to found jurisdiction in the Algerian courts.

Given that the courts of Algeria in general could found jurisdiction, is it open to Arnold to argue that this particular court could not, ie can he raise the apparent excess of jurisdiction under Algerian internal law (in that the court is limited to claims not exceeding £7,000 – both claim and award against Arnold are for £10,000) as a bar to enforcement in England?

The general view of writers is that such breaches of domestic jurisdictional rules are, like other breaches of the foreign law, a matter for the foreign legal system (eg though an appeal there) of which English courts will not take cognisance, and this view is supported by the majority of the English cases on the point: cf *Vanquelin* v *Bouard* (1863) 15 CB (NS) 341 and *Pemberton* v *Hughes* [1899] 1 Ch 781. Cheshire takes the alternative view (*Private International Law* (1999), 13th ed at pp429–431) that a foreign court's acting in excess of its domestic jurisdiction can be an objection to enforcement of its judgment in England, provided that the error would make the foreign judgment void, and not merely voidable, in its own system. Besides the general obligation that this position requires the English court to decide what voids and what makes voidable merely in a foreign system, which may be no easy task (even assuming the foreign system has this distinction at all), both the cases which Cheshire prays in aid, *Papadopoulos* v *Papadopoulos* [1930] P 55 and *Adams* v *Adams* [1971] P 188, can be explained on other grounds.

The preferred view is therefore that Arnold will not be entitled to rely on the breach of the Algerian domestic rules, even if he can establish it. He appears to have no other grounds for objecting to the judgment; service of the claim form shows that Arnold was aware of the proceedings and could have been represented. The damage to Chuck's car was in truth £5,000, but claim and award are for £10,000. Absent further information, it would not be safe to infer fraud on Chuck's past (which, if established, would be a defence), but there is obvious reason to enquire into the nature of the evidence before the Algerian court as to quantum. The upshot is that, unless further enquiry shows that Chuck defrauded the Algerian court as to quantum, and subject to the point made below on appeals, Arnold has no prospects of a successful defence to enforcement of the Algerian judgment in England.

b) Did the Algerian court have jurisdiction over Danny? It appears that the Algerian claim form was served on him in England by leave of the Algerian court. While the English courts themselves claim and exercise such an 'exorbitant' jurisdiction to permit service abroad under CPR r6.20, they have never conceded it to foreign courts in the context of enforcement of foreign judgments, and Danny was not present in Algeria at the commencement of proceedings; his earlier presence (at the time of the accident) is jurisdictionally irrelevant: cf *Sirdar Gurdyal Singh*, cited above.

Thus, in his case the Algerian court will have had jurisdiction, in the eyes of the English court, only if Danny submitted to its jurisdiction. His appearance by counsel is certainly capable of amounting to such a submission; whether it does so amount is determined by the application of the Civil Jurisdiction and Judgments Act 1982, s33. Danny's counsel's first submission falls within s33(1)(a) and does not amount to a submission. However, by continuing through his counsel to plead on a point of Algerian internal law (the second plea), Danny has submitted to the jurisdiction of the Algerian court: Dicey and Morris, Rule 37, Third Case. Thus the Algerian court had jurisdiction.

As the claim against Danny is for £2,000, the question of internal jurisdiction of the court does not arise as regards Danny. However it may be asked whether the fact that the damages are punitive affords a defence. We must be careful to distinguish here between the issue of their legality under Algerian law, raised by Danny in the Algerian proceedings, and the issue of whether a foreign award of punitive damages will be enforced in the English courts, irrespective of its legality in the foreign country. The former issue like any other point of the foreign law is for the foreign court to decide and the English court will not be concerned with it. On the latter issue, it is well established that the English court will not enforce a foreign judgment for a fine or other penalty.

But a penalty in this same is essentially a sum payable to the public purse rather than to a private plaintiff, so that an award of punitive damages to a plaintiff is enforceable: cf *SA Consortium General Textiles* v *Sun and Sand Agencies Ltd* [1978] 1 QB 279 (per Lord Denning, admittedly obiter). Thus – subject to the next point – it appears that Danny has no defences to the enforcement of the Algerian judgment on the facts shown.

Both Arnold and Danny may however succeed in obtaining a stay of enforcement. It appears on the face of it that the judgments against them are final and conclusive judgments of the Algerian court for sums certain, and in principle they will, in the absence of available defences, be immediately enforceable by English judgment irrespective of any foreign rights of appeal: *Colt Industries* v *Sarlie (No 2)* [1966] 1 WLR 1287. But this does not prevent the English court from staying its own proceedings, as a matter of discretion, and given that the time for appeal in Algeria has not expired, it is likely that, provided Arnold/Danny undertook to lodge and prosecute an appeal in the Algerian courts, the English court would be willing to stay English enforcement pending the outcome of such appeal: *Nouvion* v *Freeman* (1889) 15 App Cas 1.

QUESTION TWO

What measures can an English plaintiff take against a foreign defendant to ensure that the latter does not dissipate his assets, remove them from the jurisdiction or otherwise deal with them so as to prevent the plaintiff executing against them?

Does it make any difference whether or not the defendant is domiciled in a Member State to Council Regulation 44/2001/EC?

Adapted from University of London LLB Examination
(for External Students) Conflict of Laws June 1993 Q8(a)

General Comment

An excellent opportunity for the student to not only demonstrate a sound knowledge of the basic principles but also the up-to-date position (ie, the Civil Procedure Rules, Council Regulation 44/2001/EC and claim forms).

Skeleton Solution

As defined by the question: freezing injunctions – how they originate and how they are served – contrasts between situations where the defendant is and is not domiciled in a contracting state.

Suggested Solution

A plaintiff with a good arguable case, who fears that the defendant may dissipate his assets, remove them from the jurisdiction or otherwise deal with them so as to prevent the plaintiff executing against them, may seek, ex parte, an interlocutory injunction under s37(3) Supreme Court Act 1981 to prevent the defendant from so acting.

Where the defendant is not domiciled within a member state to Council Regulation 44/2001/EC the traditional rules may apply, so for leave to serve a claim form out of the jurisdiction the plaintiff would need to bring his case within one of the sub-heads of CPR 6.20 excluding r6.20(2) which provides for 'an injunction [being] sought ordering the defendant to do or refrain from doing anything within the jurisdiction'. There is no power under this sub-head to order the issue of a claim form out of the jurisdiction merely because an interlocutory (freezing) injunction is sought: *The Siskina* [1979] AC 210. *The Siskina* was also authority for a freezing injunction (previously referred to as a Mareva injunction) only being granted where the English court had jurisdiction over the main action between the parties; the grant of the interlocutory (freezing) injunction had to be founded on a pre-existing cause of action against the defendant arising out of an invasion, actual or threatened, by him of a legal or equitable right of the plaintiff for the enforcement of which the defendant is amenable to the jurisdiction of the court. An interlocutory injunction did not stand on its own.

In contrast, in proceedings which have been or are to be commenced in another member state to the Council Regulation 44/2001/EC there is provision for an English court to grant 'interim relief', such as a freezing injunction, if the proceedings are or will be proceedings whose subject matter is within the scope of the Regulation. In effect, this is a statutory reversal of *The Siskina*.

Council Regulation 44/2001/EC does not apply in a non-member state unless it has been extended to that state by an Order in Council, but neither does it require the defendant to be domiciled in a contracting state: *X v Y* [1990] 1 QB 220. However, whereas leave is not required to serve a claim form on a defendant who is domiciled in a member state, the general rule is that a plaintiff must seek leave to serve a claim form on a defendant who is not so domiciled: CPR 6.20. One exception to this is provided for under CPR r6.20, which provides that 'service of a claim form out of the jurisdiction is permissible without the leave of the court' in cases which are within the Regulation (ie they are, under art 2, civil and commercial matters) but in which the defendant is outside the jurisdiction: *Republic of Haiti v Duvalier* [1990] QB 202.

There is no requirement that a freezing injunction should be confined to the assets of the defendant which are within the jurisdiction of the court. In 1989 the extent to which an injunction may issue to restrain the defendant from dealing with assets which are already outside the jurisdiction was clarified in 'a remarkable series of Court of Appeal decisions': per JD McClean in Morris, *The Conflict of Laws*, 5th edn 2000, at p475. In the first, and leading, case, *Babanaft International v Bassatne* [1990] Ch 13, when a post-judgment freezing injunction was granted, it was said that it would be

> '... improper for the court to grant, after judgment, an unqualified Mareva [freezing] injunction extending to the defendant's assets outside the jurisdiction because such an injunction would amount to an exorbitant assertion of extraterritorial jurisdiction over third parties; [accordingly] such post-judgment injunctions should be restricted so as to bind on the defendant personally and should contain a limiting provision to ensure that they did not purport to have an unintended extraterritorial operation and to make it clear that they did not affect third parties.'

In this case, Kerr LJ expressly held that, in appropriate cases, there was nothing to prevent the grant of injunctions from extending to assets outside this jurisdiction.

In *Republic of Haiti v Duvalier* it was decided that a pre-judgment freezing injunction could extend to assets outside the jurisdiction. Finally, McClean notes that 'in *Derby v Weldon (No 1)* [1990] Ch 48 the power to grant a freezing injunction in respect of assets outside England and Wales, both before and after judgments, was declared to be established law'.

QUESTION THREE

In what circumstances may an English court refuse to recognise a judgment of a French court?

University of London LLB Examination
(for External Students) Conflict of Laws June 1993 Q3(b)

General Comment

Students should be warned that it can prove far harder to achieve high marks with this type of question than the others in this chapter. Examiners will be looking for 'something more' than a basic summary.

Skeleton Solution

Articles 34 and 35 Council Regulation 44/2001/EC and case law (relating to art 27 Brussels Convention).

Suggested Solution

A brief explanation of 'judgment' in art 32 of Council Regulation 44/2001/EC is followed by art 33 providing that a 'judgment given in a member state shall be recognised in the other member states without any special procedure being required'. However, this is qualified by art 34 which provides that an application for recognition may be refused as long as it is only for one of the reasons specified in art 34, which provides four reasons why a foreign judgment may be refused, ie it provides for four potential defences.

First, art 34(1) provides that recognition may be refused where 'such recognition is contrary to public policy in the member state in which recognition is sought'. As art 34 does not have a specific provision relating to fraud, such a defence may be based on art 34(1) but only if the plaintiff has no means of redress in France. If he has, then it has been held that there is no breach of public policy in recognising and registering in England a judgment alleged to have been obtained by fraud: *Interdesco SA* v *Nullifire Ltd* [1992] 1 Lloyd's Rep 180 and *Sisro* v *Ampersand* (1993) The Times 29 July.

Article 34(2) provides for non-recognition where the French judgment was given in default of appearance if the defendant was 'not served with the document' instituting the proceedings in a French court 'in sufficient time … to enable him to arrange for his defence'. Under this provision, the concept of 'due service' must comply with the law of the judgment-granting (French) court, but that of 'sufficient time' is for the judgment-recognising (English) court: *Klomps* v *Michel* [1982] 2 CMLR 773 and *Pendy Plastic Products* v *Pluspunkt* [1983] 1 CMLR 665.

A third situation in which an English court may refuse to recognise a judgment of the French court arises (under art 34(3)) where that judgment is irreconcilable with one given in a dispute between the same parties in England, ie the English court does not need to give preference to the French judgment over one of its own.

A fourth reason for non-recognition arises where the French judgment is irreconcilable with one given in a non-member state on the same cause of action between the same parties, provided that the earlier judgment is entitled to recognition by English law: see art 34(4).

Finally, according to art 35, recognition of a French judgment may be refused if the jurisdiction assumed by that court conflicts with the provisions regarding insurance and consumer contracts or regarding exclusive jurisdiction: see sections 3, 4 and 6 of Chapter II of the Regulation.

QUESTION FOUR

Maria, an Italian domiciliary, was married to Martin, an English domiciliary. They have lived apart for several years. She obtained a maintenance order from the Italian courts but Martin refused to pay and instead sued for divorce through the English courts. After the English courts had granted the divorce Maria sought to enforce the maintenance order against Martin in England.

Will she succeed? Would your answer be the same (i) if the divorce had been obtained in Nevada but was bound under the relevant rules of English law to be recognised in England; or (ii) if the divorce had been obtained in France but was bound under the relevant rules of English law to be recognised in England?

Question prepared by the Editor

General Comment

Another relatively straightforward question. Rather than asking the students to discuss arts 33–38 of Council Regulation 44/2001/EC, the question requires application of these rules to a problem scenario. Note that students will do well only if they answer the specific questions posesd.

Skeleton Solution

Judgment within Council Regulation 44/2001/EC – art 33 – art 38 – procedure to be adopted – refusal of enforcement or recognition – arts 34 and 35 – art 34(3).

Suggested Solution

The general scheme of the Brussels Convention 1968 and now Council Regulation 44/2001/EC was a regime of strict rules regarding jurisdiction and was matched by very liberal rules in regard to the recognition and enforcement of judgments rendered by the courts of member states. Thus art 33 of Council Regulation 44/2001/EC requires that a judgment given in a member state '*shall* be recognised in the other member states without any special procedure being required'; and art 38 provides that any judgment given in one member state '*shall* be enforced in another member state when, on the application of any interested party, it has been declared enforceable there'. And art 36 spells out that 'under no circumstances may a foreign judgment be reviewed as to substance.'

Thus prima facie Maria's Italian judgment will be enforceable in England if she makes application (as set out in art 39 and Annex II). The precise procedure (as set out in art 40) need not concern us here but, broadly speaking, Maria should submit an application for the enforcement of the maintenance order to the Secretary of State (rather than a court) and he forwards the order to the appropriate magistrates' court (where the defendant is domiciled) for enforcement. An officer of the court can then register the order (which puts the order on the same footing as if it has been made by that court). However, an appeal may be lodged by the defendant (art 43(5)) within one month of service and the order cannot be enforced until that time limit has expired. (Note the enforcement procedure is different for judgments in non-maintenance cases.)

However, in limited circumstances recognition (and consequently enforcement (see art 41) may be refused. This is where the judgment falls foul of arts 34 and 35. Article 35 deals with judgment granted in consumer matters, insurance, or where jurisdiction was exercised under some head of exclusive jurisdiction, so it is not really relevant to Maria's maintenance order. Article 34 may, however, prove useful for Martin.

Article 34(1) and (2) provide defences based upon public policy (of the member state in which recognition is sought) and the failure (in default judgment cases) to give adequate notice of the case pending against him. None of the facts given suggests that Martin will be able to raise a defence under either of these.

However, with art 34(3) things stand on a different footing as it provides that the judgment shall not be recognised 'if it is irreconcilable with a judgment given in a dispute between the same parties in the member state in which recognition is sought'. And in *Hoffman* v *Krieg* [1988] ECR 645 the European Court applied art 34(3) in circumstances rather similar to ours. There a wife had obtained a maintenance order from the German courts and sought to enforce that order against her husband through the courts of the Netherlands in terms of art 38. However, the courts of the Netherlands had dissolved the marriage shortly after the maintenance order had been made. The European Court held that whether the judgments were irreconcilable depended upon whether they led to consequences that were 'mutually exclusive'. This was the case here for the foreign maintenance order 'presupposed the existence of the matrimonial bond'. This result was followed in a case with similar facts but under different although very similar statutory provisions in *Macaulay* v *Macaulay* [1991] 1 WLR 179. Thus applying this approach it follows that Martin will have a defence and will be able to resist the enforcement of the Italian decree.

If the divorce had been obtained in Nevada then once more Martin would have a defence. Article 34(4) provides that recognition shall be refused to a judgment from a member state if it is irreconcilable with a judgment given in a non-member state 'involving the same cause of action and between the same parties, provided that the earlier judgment fulfils the conditions necessary for its recognition in the member state addressed.' It is possible that the court may be persuaded that the same cause of action is not involved, so that Martin does not have a defence under art 34(4). In these circumstances Cheshire & North (*Private International Law* (1999), 13th ed at pp502–504) suggests that an extensive interpretation of art 34(3) may provide a justification.

The mention of an extensive interpretation of art 34(3) raises the final question asked: what happens if the divorce had been obtained in France but was bound under the relevant rules of English law to be recognised in England? No specific provision is made for such an eventuality in art 34 or, indeed, elsewhere in the Regulation. But such situations can surely occur and the present case is an example of one such. Cheshire & North (at p503) makes the following suggestion: the words 'judgment given' in art 34(3) should include a judgment actually given in another member state but which is entitled to recognition in the first member state. There is little warrant for this extensive interpretation of art 34(3) other than that it would not be contrary to the purposes of the Regulation and, at least, it lead to a sensible result. But it cannot provide much comfort to Maria.

QUESTION FIVE

Compare and contrast the defences open to an English domiciled defendant who wishes to challenge the enforcement in this country of judgments obtained respectively in the courts of Belgium and Brazil.

University of London LLB Examination
(for External Students) Conflict of Laws June 1995 Q5

General Comment

This question should be welcomed by better students as a question which enables good marks to be obtained via a combination of the adoption of an analytical approach and self-expression.

Skeleton Solution

Distinguish enforcement of judgments granted in member states from those granted in non-member states – compare and contrast statutory defences with those at common law.

Suggested Solution

Belgium is a member state to Council Regulation 44/2001/EC; Brazil is not. Whereas defences to the recognition and enforcement of judgments obtained within a member state, such as Belgium, are specified in the Regulation, defences to a judgment obtained in a non-member state, such as Brazil, are found at common law and are rooted in public policy. 'Public policy' is also at the basis of one of half-a-dozen defences to a judgment obtained in a member state.

A judgment that has been obtained contrary to English public policy permits the defendant to rely on that public policy as a defence to the judgment. This is established at common law (*Re Macartney* [1921] 1 Ch 522); under statute (for example s9 Administration of Justice Act 1920 and s4 Foreign Judgments (Reciprocal Enforcement) Act 1933); and by arts 34 and 45 of the Council Regulation. However, there is a considerable difference between the defences to fraud in member and non-member states.

With regard to a defence to fraud in respect of a judgment obtained in a non-member state, it is well-established law that the English courts will allow the case to be reopened on its merits. For example, in *Abouloff* v *Oppenheimer* (1882) 10 QBD 295 Lindley LJ said:

> 'If the fraud upon the foreign court consists in the fact that the plaintiff has induced that court to come to the wrong conclusion, you can reopen the whole case even although you will have in this court to go into the very facts which were investigated and which were in issue in the foreign court.'

The House of Lords' decision in *Owens Bank Ltd* v *Bracco and Others* [1992] 2 AC 443 affirmed that it was not necessary for fresh evidence to be adduced for the defence of fraud to be raised; nor is it relevant whether the issue of fraud had been raised before the foreign court.

In relation to judgments obtained in member states, first arts 34 and 45 provide that 'under no circumstances may a foreign judgment be reviewed as to its substance', which means that a judgment cannot be reviewed on its merits. Second, even if the defendant can present new evidence of fraud on the part of the plaintiff, redress lies in the courts of the member state in which the judgment was given: it is not for the English courts to decide the question of fraud. This was established in *Interdesco SA* v *Nullifire Ltd* [1992] 1 Lloyd's Rep 180 and affirmed in *Société d'Informatique Service Réalisation Organisation* v *Ampersand Software BV* [1994] ILPr 55.

With regard to other defences based on judgments being contrary to public policy and obtained in non-member states, Scarman J, in *In the Estate of Fuld (No 3)* [1968] P 675 said that 'an English court will refuse to apply a law which outrages its sense of justice and decency'. Most of the cases involving foreign laws which are repugnant to English public policy are contract cases or cases involving the 'status' of a natural person: *Dynamit AG* v *Rio Tinto Zinc* [1918] AC 260 and *Lepre* v *Lepre* [1965] P 52.

Another manifestation of English public policy which would act as a defence to a judgment obtained in a non-member state and almost certainly also to one obtained in a member state is found in s5 Protection of Trading Interests Act 1980 which was enacted to prevent the enforcement at common law or under statute of judgments for multiple damages. However, if the foreign forum is the only appropriate forum, then a claim that it would be unconscionable to permit litigation to proceed in that forum merely on the basis that multiple damages were available there is unlikely to succeed: *British Airways Board* v *Laker Airways Ltd* [1985] AC 58.

A defendant who has properly been notified of proceedings against him but who has been given inadequate time in which to prepare his defence or who has been subjected to a procedure regarded by English law as contrary to natural justice has a defence both to judgments obtained in member and non-member states. In *Pendy Plastics Products* v *Pluspunkt* [1983] 1 CMLR 665, the ECJ held that it was for the court of the state in which enforcement was sought to decide whether the defendant who had had a judgment by default granted against him had had an opportunity to receive service of the document instituting the proceedings in sufficient time to enable him to make arrangements for his defence. Whether notice of the proceedings was duly served was a matter for the judgment-granting court: *Klomps* v *Michel* [1981] ECR 1593.

The most remarkable case of breach of natural justice occurred in a judgment given in the non-member state of Texas in *Adams* v *Cape Industries plc* [1990] 2 WLR 657. Here, the trial judge had permitted counsel for the plaintiffs to determine which plaintiffs would receive a particular quantum of damages, as determined by counsel, following a judicial guideline of an average of $75,000 per claimant. Slade LJ, speaking on behalf of the Court of Appeal, held that this was contrary to the requirements of substantial justice contained in English law.

Finally, if a judgment of the foreign court is irreconcilable with that of the English court the latter will not enforce it. For example, in *Macaulay* v *Macaulay* [1991] 1 WLR 179 the English court refused to enforce an Irish maintenance order which had been succeeded by an English divorce. In that respect, the English court followed the ruling of the ECJ in *Hoffman* v *Krieg* [1988] ECR 645 where it was said that irreconcilable judgments involved mutually exclusive con-sequences and that a Dutch divorce was irreconcilable with the German maintenance order which preceded it. Where judgments are irreconcilable it would appear that it is irrelevant which is decided first and that *Vervaeke* v *Smith* [1983] AC 145 illustrates that the position is the same at common law for judgments from non-member states as it is under the Regulation.

However, where the same parties to competing foreign judgments seek recognition in the English courts, the judgment of a competent court earlier in time will prevail over the later judgment irrespective of whether the earlier judgment was given in a case involving England and a non-member state (*Showlag* v *Mansour* [1994] 2 WLR 615); or whether the case in question arises from a European judgment involving some other member state and the courts of a non-member state: art 34(4) Council Regulation 44/2001/EC.

Thus, the common law defences available to an English-domiciled defendant contain similarities and great differences from those provided for under Council Regulation 44/2001/EC.

Law Update 2004 edition – due March 2004

An annual review of the most recent developments in specific legal subject areas, useful for law students at degree and professional levels, others with law elements in their courses and also practitioners seeking a quick update.

Published around March every year, the Law Update summarises the major legal developments during the course of the previous year. In conjunction with Old Bailey Press textbooks it gives the student a significant advantage when revising for examinations.

Contents

Administrative Law • Civil and Criminal Procedure • Commercial Law • Company Law • Conflict of Laws • Constitutional Law • Contract Law • Conveyancing • Criminal Law • Criminology • Employment Law • English and European Legal Systems • Equity and Trusts • European Union Law • Evidence • Family Law • Jurisprudence • Land Law • Law of International Trade • Public International Law • Revenue Law • Succession • Tort

For further information on contents or to place an order, please contact:

Mail Order
Old Bailey Press
at Holborn College
Woolwich Road
Charlton
London
SE7 8LN

Telephone No: 020 8317 6039
Fax No: 020 8317 6004
Website: www.oldbaileypress.co.uk

ISBN 1 85836 518 X
Soft cover 246 x 175 mm
400 pages approx
£10.95
Due March 2004

Unannotated Cracknell's Statutes for use in Examinations

New Editions of Cracknell's Statutes

£11.95 due 2003

Cracknell's Statutes provide a comprehensive series of essential statutory provisions for each subject. Amendments are consolidated, avoiding the need to cross-refer to amending legislation. Unannotated, they are suitable for use in examinations, and provide the precise wording of vital Acts of Parliament for the diligent student.

Constitutional and Administrative Law
ISBN: 1 85836 511 2

Equity and Trusts
ISBN: 1 85836 508 2

Contract, Tort and Remedies
ISBN: 1 85836 507 4

Land: The Law of Real Property
ISBN: 1 85836 509 0

English Legal System
ISBN: 1 85836 510 4

Law of International Trade
ISBN: 1 85836 512 0

For further information on contents or to place an order, please contact:

Mail Order
Old Bailey Press
at Holborn College
Woolwich Road
Charlton
London
SE7 8LN

Telephone No: 020 8317 6039
Fax No: 020 8317 6004
Website: www.oldbaileypress.co.uk

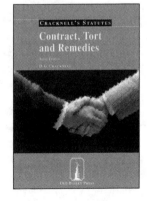

Suggested Solutions to Past Examination Questions 2001–2002

The Suggested Solutions series provides examples of full answers to the questions regularly set by examiners. Each suggested solution has been broken down into three stages: general comment, skeleton solution and suggested solution. The examination questions included within the text are taken from past examination papers set by the London University. The full opinion answers will undoubtedly assist you with your research and further your understanding and appreciation of the subject in question.

Only £6.95 due November 2003

Company Law
ISBN: 1 85836 519 8

Evidence
ISBN: 1 85836 521 X

Employment Law
ISBN: 1 85836 520 1

Family Law
ISBN: 1 85836 525 2

European Union Law
ISBN: 1 85836 524 4

For further information on contents or to place an order, please contact:

Mail Order
Old Bailey Press
at Holborn College
Woolwich Road
Charlton
London
SE7 8LN

Telephone No: 020 8317 6039
Fax No: 020 8317 6004
Website: www.oldbaileypress.co.uk

Company Law

2001–2002 LLB Examination Questions and Suggested Solutions

University of London External Examinations

Solutions by Susan Barber

Old Bailey Press

The Old Bailey Press integrated student law library is tailor-made to help you at every stage of your studies from the preliminaries of each subject through to the final examination. The series of Textbooks, Revision WorkBooks, 150 Leading Cases and Cracknell's Statutes are interrelated to provide you with a comprehensive set of study materials.

You can buy Old Bailey Press books from your University Bookshop, your local Bookshop, direct using this form, or you can order a free catalogue of our titles from the address shown overleaf.

The following subjects each have a Textbook, 150 Leading Cases/Casebook, Revision WorkBook and Cracknell's Statutes unless otherwise stated.

Administrative Law
Commercial Law
Company Law
Conflict of Laws
Constitutional Law
Conveyancing (Textbook and 150 Leading Cases)
Criminal Law
Criminology (Textbook and Sourcebook)
Employment Law (Textbook and Cracknell's Statutes)
English and European Legal Systems
Equity and Trusts
Evidence
Family Law
Jurisprudence: The Philosophy of Law (Textbook, Sourcebook and
   Revision WorkBook)
Land: The Law of Real Property
Law of International Trade
Law of the European Union
Legal Skills and System
   (Textbook)
Obligations: Contract Law
Obligations: The Law of Tort
Public International Law
Revenue Law (Textbook,
   Revision WorkBook and
   Cracknell's Statutes)
Succession

Mail order prices:	
Textbook	£15.95
150 Leading Cases	£11.95
Revision WorkBook	£9.95
Cracknell's Statutes	£11.95
Suggested Solutions 1999–2000	£6.95
Suggested Solutions 2000–2001	£6.95
Suggested Solutions 2001–2002	£6.95
Law Update 2003	£10.95
Law Update 2004	£10.95

Please note details and prices are subject to alteration.

To complete your order, please fill in the form below:

Module	Books required	Quantity	Price	Cost
		Postage		
		TOTAL		

For Europe, add 15% postage and packing (£20 maximum).
For the rest of the world, add 40% for airmail.

ORDERING

By telephone to Mail Order at 020 8317 6039, with your credit card to hand.

By fax to 020 8317 6004 (giving your credit card details).

Website: www.oldbaileypress.co.uk

By post to: Mail Order, Old Bailey Press at Holborn College, Woolwich Road, Charlton, London, SE7 8LN.

When ordering by post, please enclose full payment by cheque or banker's draft, or complete the credit card details below. You may also order a free catalogue of our complete range of titles from this address.

We aim to despatch your books within 3 working days of receiving your order.

Name

Address

Postcode   Telephone

Total value of order, including postage: £

I enclose a cheque/banker's draft for the above sum, or

charge my   ☐ Access/Mastercard   ☐ Visa   ☐ American Express
Card number

☐☐☐☐ ☐☐☐☐ ☐☐☐☐ ☐☐☐☐

Expiry date   ☐☐☐☐

Signature: ....Date: ....